DAVID HOWENSTEIN

JUMBO JUMBLE

*A Sojourn of 366 Visual
and Inspirational Delights*

A CREATION OF JAMBO INTERNATIONAL
JAMBO INTERNATIONAL PUBLISHING | KIRKWOOD, MO.

Copyright 2019 by David Howenstein

No part of this publication may be reproduced, stored in a retrieval system, or transmitted in any form or by any means, electronic, mechanical, photocopying, recording, scanning, or otherwise, except as permitted under Section 107 or 108 of the 1976 United States Copyright Act, without the prior written permission of the Publisher. Requests to the Publisher for permission should be addressed to david@jambointernational.org at JAMBO INTERNATIONAL PUBLISHING.

Print ISBN: 978-0-99946-612-4
eBook ISBN: 978-0-99946-613-1

Illustrations by Miki Howenstein: https://lovingearth.wixsite.com/miki/

JAMBO BLOGS: https://www.jambo.ngo/david-howenstein-blog

https://jambointernational.org/en/blog/

Acknowledgements

As the scope of this book spans a broad spectrum of subjects, so does my heartfelt appreciation reach out to the many who made this endeavor possible.

To those of the ancient and recent past—my ancestors and the scholars of my youth—without whom my current life would not be possible.

To the people currently gracing my life, especially my parents (Ed and Kathleen Howenstein, whose love and devotion borders on the angelic despite a few ideological differences), my brothers and sister (who continue to provide solid support throughout our history of sibling rivalries), my wife (Miki Howenstein, who continues to support our life together and the ideals embodied in this book despite the hardships they sometimes inflict), David Parmer (who helped to improve the writing and photos in this book), and to all of my students and each individual actively involved in JAMBO (all of whom provide the bread and butter for my physical and spiritual being).

To those who, from now, bravely attempt to integrate and live out the soulscapes herein, and become instrumental in the creation of a better world.

And finally to the unsung plants and animals (without which not only humanity's ingenuity but our very existence would be void of expression) and the source of life's being (whatever you wish to call it), who allows us access to her great wisdom if only we search it out.

I devote this work to all of you, in the hopes that this humble project reflects the deep gratitude for all that you have bestowed (are bestowing, or will bestow) on me.

Table Of Contents

Acknowledgements	1
Message From The Author	5
Introduction To The Second Edition	6
About Jambo's Jumbo Jumble	7
Preparing For Takeoff	10
The 24 Soulscapes – Where We're Going	12
The Journey	13
Where Do We Go From Here?	412
About The Pictures	413
Picture Bibliography	416
References	430
Bibliography	449
About Jambo	464
About The Author	467

Message From The Author

Thank you for purchasing this book. And welcome to a completely mad attempt to assemble a set of diverse notions of fundamental, deep human longings (albeit often smothered by other desires) and integrate them in a way that promotes self-development, and hopefully moves us towards the grander goal of a more enlightened society.

I was tempted to be so audacious as to assert "a completely new concept" but this is a uniquely constructed anthology of sorts with my commentaries. Therefore, such a claim would be absurd, justifying even more ridicule upon my humble first public creative endeavor.

What may be distinctive about this book is that the passages are taken from people of diverse ideologies including those with or without "religious faith"–Atheists, Agnostics, Muslims, Buddhists, Jews, Christians, Hindus, and so on. My moral psychology is simply not concerned with what a person professes to have faith in because it is much easier to perceive their belief through the way they act and treat other living beings. Therefore, this book ties together the diverse ideologies of people with different belief systems, to encourage ways of thinking and doing to create a better world for all life on our planet.

Each daily writing includes "Jambo's Remarks" (JR). JAMBO is an organization which I founded in Japan and was instrumental in setting up in the United States. The ideas in JR are my ideas (and embody my projected vision for Jambo's developmental growth), not necessarily the thinking of Jambo participants.

A word about myself. Based on the writings herein, I may appear to be a very pensive person. While I don't deny a degree of seriousness, those who know me may very well be shocked at this effort since I am known to be goofy and insistent on having fun. I myself see no contradiction between the two. Also, by no means have I personally enacted all of the inspiring words of wisdom detailed in this book. I was tempted to write on my failed attempts of implementing these, but realize that would be an endless endeavor. In other words, I have a long way to go and am calling for your help. Determined to continue living out my need for much joviality, I wish to integrate it with committing myself to working with others to create a world that is good for all.

I'm game—are you?

Sincerely Silly and Serious,
Jambo Dave

Introduction To The Second Edition

What a kick in the morning to look forward to—a new picture of nature, inspirational writings from various movers in our world, past and present, and a mental encouragement to get off my duff and do something to put these inspirations into action. Short and sweet! Something to eagerly anticipate every day—like opening the window for the new day on the advent calendar to see what gift awaits me.

The picturesque nature of this book begins with the abundant African imagery on the cover, while the pictures in the book come from Japan and the writings from all over the world. The reason for this is that, in its early days, the organization which provides the hands-on inspiration for this book (Jambo International) held its activities overwhelmingly in Japan, with the expressed purpose of supporting good organizations in (eastern and southern) Africa working towards people's betterment and wildlife protection.

Reflection and action—the two intertwining threads of this book. We are all constantly bombarded by new information, which prods us to discard some of our ideas. I also find myself questioning how true some of the material herein is and may even change my mind on some of the things I thought to be correct. Such continual questioning and seeking out further understanding encourage healthy growth. At the same time, this does not deny the underlying validity of the holistically fruitful and more uplifting way to live which is proposed in the whole process of this book, and the fundamental concepts herein which provide a bedrock for a fertile self and society.

The key to this book is that change begins with the self, and expands from there to the local environment and then further on to the world. Working at all three levels simultaneously is ideal, and local initiatives (to oneself and to one's immediate community of living beings) are of the utmost importance. It is when local people take charge and work to enrich their own society that things change for the better. And it is the responsibility of concerned outsiders to take notice when this happens, and offer much-needed support which can morph into mutually supporting networks of good. This is my main purpose, in my own life as well as Jambo International, which I started back in 1996.

Welcome to this revised edition, which has far fewer mistakes and will hopefully provide inspiration to far more people who seek to create a better world.

Lovingly Serious with more than a few grains of Fun and Laughter,

David Howenstein
June, 2019

About Jambo's Jumbo Jumble

Why the bizarre title?

Claiming to know absolutely about things which are absolutely unknowable is perhaps the greatest cause of humanity's deepest and most heart-wrenching conflicts. Yet, in all honesty, there are as many definitions of the true meaning of life (or if there is any such meaning at all), of God (or the non-existence thereof), and love (so often confused as lust) as there are people who make up this unfathomable planet.

I am forced to be humbled by my own unknowing—which is a rather sophisticated way of saying that I'm often completely clueless.

It is often attested that there is an all-loving God, but when I look at the innumerable pains, tragedies, and sufferings that people are forced to endure, I wonder how it could be so.

Some are taught in a God of Justice, yet when corrupt people are seen to be reaping (and raping) the benefits, and some extremely wealthy people revel in their riches with little regard to the poor who lie at their doors, I wonder how it could be so.

And then there are those who claim that there is no God, no Divine Source at all. But when we see, all about us, life coming into form from non-life, and all of the factors co-existing harmoniously against all odds (the correct balance of various gases, the miracle of water, and all the delicate balances that have come together) to create a living planet, I am again forced to wonder how it could be so.

In other words, my own unclarity and unabashed use of big words (such as God and Love), which I admit have very different meanings to different people, may be considered as reason enough to view the writings herein as gibberish. Several people spend their time arguing over these concepts and ideas, which often leads to more conflict and confusion than clarity. This book refuses to make such an attempt.

Concurrently, there are a few things indeed that I can be sure of.

I am clearly able to decipher the great capacity for evil among the world's people. Acts of deception, cheating, back-stabbing, and thievery are all part of the human condition. Taken to the extreme, we also commit despicable acts of mass murder (in war), torture of others, and acts of cruelty towards our fellow living companions (animals) when we raise them for our own culinary pleasures. And when a great number of people participate in such acts, we cannot help but be filled with suspicion of one another. This leads to a world of insecurity, destruction, and chaos.

At the same time, there are living examples of legendary individuals who actively demonstrate the potential for goodness within our species, choosing to live honestly, caring for others, and working to make the world a better place. These individuals integrate the concepts of forgiveness, empowerment, tolerance, and love into action. Correspondingly, with a great number of people participating in such acts, as witnessed in communities throughout history, we live in trust, deeper security, peace, and love, moving towards a paradise that is essayed as our destiny in many religions and literature.

We can choose the direction towards which we aim to move. It is the purpose of this book to choose the latter, finding words of inspiration, fostering constructive soul-searching, and encouraging the development of vision and action that help us to move in that direction.

OOPS, I simply forgot to explain the bizarre title—Jambo's Jumbo Jumble.

Jambo is the organization that attempts to put this soulscape paradigm into action.

JUMBO entails the big-hearted, all-inclusive nature of this book.

JUMBLE is self-explanatory—a fun-filled effort of mixing up all kinds of words and ideas and arduously hoping that this attempt results in a semblance of applicable significance.

More confused than ever? No worries—so am I.

Preparing For Takeoff

What's Wrong With Our World?

Be prepared for a completely unexpected answer. The most likely answers to this question are:
- Young people are addicted to their electronic games.
- Companies today care only about profits at the expense of society and the environment.
- Terrorists of all stripes plague the peace of the world.
- Fundamentalists of all kinds erode the truly spiritual nature of individuals.
- Bleeding hearts encourage laziness through their handouts.
- Greedy and selfish capitalists think singularly of themselves.

And the list is endless; however, these answers miss the mark. They indicate problems that are easy-to-see and, therefore, easy-to-blame. Thus we focus on them instead of the underlying causes from where these problems originate. It is only by digging up the roots that we have any hope of uncovering and overcoming these intractable issues. Yet, the majority of us are too busy (i.e. too lazy) to initiate a soul-searching effort to bring the conditions leading to such issues to light. And this refusal to attempt the deciphering makes all of us largely responsible for their existence.

The simple answer to the question, "What's Wrong with our World?" is YOU AND ME—the "good" people reading this book. The fact that you are reading it (and I wrote it) is evidence of our concern and heartfelt wish to make a better world. But, so far, we haven't had the courage and persistence to design it. "HMMM," you may be wondering, "this is starting to sound a lot like a guilt trip. Why should I subject myself to such misery?"

Yet, contrary to a guilt trip (which impedes any constructive progress), our journey's preparation begins with an acceptance that each of us is posited to start off at a different point. This positioning is based on a host of factors, including the environment, family life, genetics, and so on. What has happened is past, and obsessively anguishing about it only prevents us from partaking in the future grand journey that cultivates a more enlightened spirit to move the human society and the natural environment towards a more integrated entity that is universally beneficial. The other part of our preparation is to ignite the spark of hope that our personal efforts can contribute to a better world which, if seriously implemented and playfully enjoyed, would severely curtail the above-mentioned afflictions. This is because it would be so inviting that most of these "troublemakers" would be knocking at the door to join in as well.

A Challenge, A Dare, and A Lot of Fun!

Imagine living in a society based on love, compassion, fun, and constructive creation.

People feel secure because they know that they won't be left alone. People don't hesitate doing what really turns them on because they know that they'll never have to worry about being hungry or homeless. People learn how to create internal happiness, thereby eradicating the need to depend on the ever-changing surrounding circumstances for personal contentment.

Is this simply a dream? It surely is, as of now.

Just like, at one time, believing that we could fly hundreds of people through the skies was a (crazy and unattainable) dream.

Just like, at one time, believing that we could tame the unruly nature of wild animals to become our friendly companions was a dream.

Just like, at one time, having the absurd notion that we could possibly control fire's fury to be used for our benefit was a dream.

Just like, at one time, believing that the nomadic nature of the first humans could be tempered so that they would settle down to adopt agriculture and, even more ridiculously, be willing to work confined in a regular schedule was inconceivable.

These things were completely unimaginable at one time, as what is being proposed here may be seen as plain fantasy by the majority in today's world. Yet, similar to all of the previously mentioned ludicrous ideas, which have eventually come to pass, this one can as well be established. There is no question of its being possible—IT IS! It's simply a matter of if we have the will to make it come into being.

This book is to help us start putting this will into practice. No doubt, it will be challenging, with many struggles and sufferings along the way, and others will consider us quite off the wall for even considering it possible. Then, just like with any idea whose time has come, we will be seen as beacons of light—co-creators of a playful and spiritually uplifting world, which is ours for the choosing.

Fasten your seat belt and get ready to take off on the most interesting ride of your life!

We human sapiens have an obnoxious tendency to introduce the inconceivable into the realm of the possible. And now is the grandest challenge of all—to structure a society based on the high ideals that we've been taught throughout human history. These, when finally implemented, will deal with the current primary issues of poverty, crime, environmental deterioration, and more. What a concerted effort, and what a great joy, this is going to be!

Time to blast off. OOPS, something's missing. It might help to know where we're hoping to go. In so many of our lives, we make so many plans and do so many things with absolutely no idea as to where it is that we truly wish to go. We won't make the same faux pas here. Fortunately, there is a destination in mind, which is the cultivation of 24 soulscapes to prepare a solid ground for a more enlightened world.

The 24 Soulscapes – Where We're Going

The journey that you are about to embark upon will take you through a diversified mix of 24 conceptual soulscapes. These soulscapes provide the mental and spiritual nourishment to fertilize and develop an integrated balance within your own internal garden, for it to live anew and become a rich source of creation beneficial for all life forms.

The 24 soulscapes (classifications) frequently step on each other's turf and overlap, moving up from 1 to 12 (corresponding to each month, with each group including two soulscapes). The soulscapes basically go through a process of flowing from a more introspective focus to the full implementation of your deepening spirituality into the physical world. Specifically, each month focuses on two soulscapes as follows:

The Self-Cultivating Deliberations

January: Education and Reflection (Meditation)
February: Appreciation (Enchantment) and Fun
March: Love and Compassion
April: Non-Violence (Forgiveness) and Sustainability

Spurring the Inner Contemplations Outward

May: Universal Ideals and Unity (Oneness)
June: Purpose and Persistence
July: Dignity and Inclusion
August: Integration and Connection

Getting Real – The Cultivated Spirit Brought into Physical Reality

September: Spirit and Nature
October: Envisioning (New Paradigms) and Faith (Hope)
November: Action and Leadership (Proactivity)
December: Empowerment and Creating

The first page for each month explains the importance of the two soulscapes grouped for that month. The second page consists of a drawing that relates to the two concepts of the month. This is followed by one page per day of the month with picture and reflections.

You can expect the journey to be thought-provoking and jolting at times, as it forces you to question your inherent beliefs and the way forward. You may find this disconcerting in some ways, and absolutely delightful in others, but I assure you that it is a trip which promises to bring you great benefit both spiritually and practically.

The Journey

This esoteric adventure allows you to join in the expedition at any time en route, steeped in the conviction that any fellow traveler seeking ways to understand and live out the ideas presented herein should be made to feel welcomed and accommodated.

The main journey, shaping the heart of the book, consists of a series of daily reflections, each consisting of the following five parts:

1) A nature appreciation photo—Considering that humankind is one part of nature, there are also some photos including human-made structures. (See "*About The Pictures*" and "*Picture Bibliography*" for an explanation and full bibliography of the pictures.)

2) A one-liner linking the photograph to the writings

3) Writing(s) related to the soulscapes of the month (A reference for each writing is provided in "*References*" followed by a full "*Bibliography.*")

4) JR (Jambo's Remarks)—This is a commentary by the author related to the specific writings for the day, and is indicative of the JAMBO vision. (See "*About Jambo*" for an explanation of what JAMBO is and to understand its vision.)

5) PP (Personal Pondering)—This is a question or a suggested simple activity, which pertains to the day's topic, deliberately presented in a broad and open manner. Some of the important ones are repeated in different ways throughout the book for further reflection.

In short, this book provides a daily journey into the recesses of your own mind. It defines a process of discerning the things that are most important for you and ways to implement them in your life. Furthermore, for the more avid learner, the writing references provide an abundance of resources, which can help you to travel further on the path towards self-discovery and live out a life more in tune with your ideals.

JANUARY

Reflection & Education

Your journey begins with an intensive search within. It is only through better understanding of and by yourself that you can clearly see what is working for you and what isn't. A key point here is to observe yourself non-judgmentally. How do you live your life? What do you believe deep down in your heart? Is your moral philosophy reflected in the way you live? If not, perhaps you truly don't believe it. You need to keep the judgments out since neither self-condemnation nor putting yourself on a pedestal will do anything to make you see the life path clearly and, in turn, make the changes that reflect THE REAL YOU. It is good to remember that the only thing you consistently have the power to change is yourself and it is in so doing that you can affect a change in the people around you.

This kind of self-reflection is the beginning of the most significant education of your life. In coming to know yourself (understanding how your past has brought you to this point and what is beneficial for you to keep and what is best to discard), you can subsequently move towards what you wish to learn outside of yourself—specifically, the things which actually peak your interest and excite you to learn. When education becomes enjoyable, you naturally wish to continue with it progressively.

In the process of "re-educating" yourself, you come to question the truth of a meaningful education for the society at large, particularly for the youth in our schools. What kind of learning would be emphasized in order to result in a society you long to move towards? Why wait until people are adults in order to self-reflect, to generate the awareness necessary to be who they really want to be? And how best to provide education for children, which instills within them these spiritual values that can be implemented to develop a more enlightened and fun-filled society—one that fills the real world with great hope?

January 1

The darkness fades as the light returns.

Do you want to change the world? How about beginning with yourself? How about being transformed yourself first? But how do you achieve that? Through observation. Through understanding. With no interference or judgment on your part. Because what you judge you cannot understand. No judgment, no commentary, no attitude: one simply observes, one studies, one watches without the desire to change what is. Because if you desire to change what is into what you think should be, you no longer understand.

The day you attain a posture like that, you will experience a miracle. You will change—effortlessly, correctly. Change will happen, you will not have to bring it about. As the life of awareness settles on your darkness, whatever is evil will disappear. Whatever is good will be fostered. You will have to experience that for yourself.

But this calls for a disciplined mind. When there's something within you that moves in the right direction, it creates things within you that move in the right direction, it creates its own discipline. The moment you get bitten by the bug of awareness. Oh, it's so delightful.

JR: The key to beginning self-observation is to initiate it without judgment—something that is very difficult to achieve since we've all learned the difference of "good and bad." Once judgments figure into the picture, you can no longer objectively perceive what is happening because your preconceived image is distorted. As much as possible, clear out these distractions and simply observe.

PP: Think of what has brought you to this point in life. Contemplate what is working well for you and what isn't.

January 2

A mirror image, or your chosen reality?

The world is a mirror of your belief system. What do you believe? Do you believe in a world of lack and limitation? Or do you believe in prosperity and abundance? Whichever one is more dominant in your thinking will usually be reflected outwards into the world.

Inspect your mind constantly. Cleaning out old belief systems is a second by second process. Be vigilant for beliefs and thoughts that don't support your quest for the spiritual life.

Thoughts are like thieves. They enter the mind unnoticed and then start to steal all your spiritual energy. The way to get rid of them is to be constantly alert when they enter the mind. Consciousness of these thoughts instantly makes them disappear.

It is said that the light casts out all darkness. Your job, then, is to let more light in. Light is another word for being more conscious.

JR: The majority of us simply incorporate the belief systems that we have been taught since birth, without seriously questioning if we truly believe them deep down. We, therefore, end up leading convoluted lives, where our actions (often giving us pleasure accompanied by guilt) contradict our proposed beliefs. No wonder we're so often confused!

PP: What beliefs do you truly hold dear?

January 3

Beauty will reawaken your consciousness to your senses.

"Lose your mind and come to your senses."

We have become truly "senseless" in the worst sense of the word, we are blind and deaf, have lost our capacity to see and to hear and to sense and to wonder, and have drifted into a dull routine we call existence, and then complain life is not worth living. It is time we come back to our senses and rediscover the multi-colored beauty of life.

JR: *Our planet offers us unlimited opportunities to get blown away by its many ongoing miracles, large and small. It is criminal not to take the time to open up the senses to what we are blessed with and experience the wonders around us.*

PP: Take just one minute and focus on the wonder of one natural object near you, using as many of your senses as you can to experience it.

January 4

Tis much more important to introspect and look within than to stare at me!

Mullah was out in the street on his hands and knees, looking for something and a friend came up and said, "Mullah, what are you looking for?"

And Mullah said, "I lost my key."

"Oh, Mullah, that's terrible, I'll help you find it." So he got on his hands and knees, then said, "Mullah, about where did you lose it?"

Mullah said, "I lost it in my house."

"Then what are you looking out here for?"

He said, "Because there's more light here."

You know, that's hilarious, but that's what we do with our lives! We believe that everything there is to find is out there in the light where it's easy to find, when the only answers for you are in you!

JR: There have been many spiritual guides throughout human history, helping us in finding our way. However, all too often, we focus only on the guide, failing to consider who we are and what we need, to the detriment of our own development. External guides are helpful, but they are not living inside of you. Following them thoughtlessly cannot be as fruitful as seeking out and following your inner guide.

PP: What lies in the dark recesses of your soul? What "goodness" have you lost and how can you bring it back into the light?

January 5

*I know what melts me—
How about you?*

Remember those times when your eyes misted with tears of happiness and joy. Perhaps you unselfishly helped another human being. Perhaps somebody, unasked and unexpectedly, reached out to help you. Perhaps you were reading a book or watching a movie or witnessing a scene where lives were being touched by love.

Whenever your eyes well up with tears of joy, carefully stop and observe. What are you witnessing? Why does this touch you? What is missing in your life?

Now you have a strong clue about which modifications are needed to bring more joy, more happiness, more peace into your life.

JR: Finding those kinds of stories and experiences which create a wellspring of joy within yourself is a major key in self-discovery. They tell you what you treasure and can point the way to a path that brings more touching moments into your life.

PP: What are three stories (movies, books, etc.) that brought you tears of joy? What do they say about you?

January 6

Easy to find the focus point here—Now it's your turn

Meditation relaxes the body, calms the mind, and minimizes tension. After a period of practice, the racing and rushing of thoughts in the mind slow down, not only during meditation, but also in daily life. Happiness increases along the way. Tolerance, love, understanding, inner power and fearlessness increase too. The concentration ability gets sharpened and the mind becomes stronger, and under control. The ability to enjoy the present moment increases. Criticizing and blaming others ceases, or at least decreases. Practicality, strength, happiness and satisfaction increase.

All meditation techniques are means to the same final target. Most of them are ways to develop concentration, which is the ability to pay attention to one object or subject, and withholding the mind from running around. The final goal of meditation is to reach our real "I," to empty the mind from thoughts, and to be conscious of the residue, which is Pure Awareness. Along the way there are many benefits.

JR: Similar to a child experiencing a temper tantrum and disturbing everyone around him, a man with an uncontrolled mind wastes much energy lashing out aimlessly without producing beneficial results or, worse still, causing great harm to himself and the people he loves. A regular focusing of the mind and developing strong concentration introduces a consistent contentment to such an unstable life.

PP: Think of the best form of meditation (reflecting through sitting, reading, walking, etc.) for yourself and perform it regularly for at least 15 minutes each time on a daily basis.

January 7

And you think you have surrender issues!

Contemplation teaches the ways of attachment and letting go. You learn about them by clear seeing, watching the mind when it clings, watching when it doesn't. And little by little, as an act of sanity, the mind prefers to go in the direction of freedom and peace and joy, and to stay away from those things which supposedly lead to happiness—and have been strongly reinforced ever since childhood—but actually don't: accumulation, getting somewhere, being someone. You find a radically new way to look at your life.

JR: A large part of our learning about what makes us happy brings us anxiety and loneliness instead. Letting go of your attachments is very difficult initially, but as you do so, the spirit is freed. You come to realize that the very things for which you felt a need actually held you down and prevented you from soaring.

PP: What is your biggest attachment, and why do you hold it so dear? What influence is it having on the kind of life you really aspire to live?

January 8

*Bird's Paradise—
What a great place
to fly*

Since our attitudes of permanence and self-cherishing are what ruin all of us, the most fruitful meditations are on impermanence and the emptiness of inherent existence on the one hand and love and compassion on the other. This is why Buddha emphasized that the two wings of the bird flying to enlightenment are compassion and wisdom.

JR: *Everything is in a state of constant transition, and the more you try to control and hold onto something, fearing its loss, the more miserable you become when it is finally gone. Rather, one can beneficially exhibit a forthright appreciation for the good things in life, understanding that they are destined to change and rather cultivate a loving attitude towards them all.*

PP: *In words or through deeds, express your love to someone or something which is important to you, and reflect on her (its) inevitable disappearance from your life.*

January 9

Who would ever want to destroy such incredible beauty?

We have been able to wreak ecological devastation on the planet not just because we have adopted a highly partial, one-sided view of the world but also because we have succumbed to a drastically diminished view of what it means to be human.

Since many of us have been persuaded to reconceive ourselves as no more than biological computers, those aspects of human nature that were once regarded as essential—such as our ability to think morally, creatively and imaginatively—are now seen as increasingly marginal to finding solutions to the problems that we face.

JR: Our current society displays a singular focus on "getting more for me," irrespective of the resultant impact on other living beings. In the absence of a conscious prioritizing of those aspects of our human nature that make us respect others and treat them with compassion, we will surely move towards the continual destruction of the physical environment in addition to our own spiritual natures.

PP: For you, what does it mean to be human? How can you be more humane?

January 10

At times, even the scars enhance the beauty.

There once was a little boy who had a bad temper. His Father gave him a bag of nails and told him that every time he lost his temper, he must hammer a nail into the back of the fence. The first day the boy had driven 37 nails into the fence. Over the next few weeks, as he learned to control his anger, the number of nails hammered daily gradually dwindled down. He discovered it was easier to hold his temper than to drive those nails into the fence. Finally the day came when the boy didn't lose his temper at all.

He told his father about it and the father suggested that the boy now pull out one nail for each day that he was able to hold his temper. The days passed and the young boy was finally able to tell his father that all the nails were gone. The father took his son by the hand and led him to the fence.

He said, "You have done well, my son, but look at the holes in the fence. The fence will never be the same. When you say things in anger, they leave a scar just like this one. You can put a knife in a man and draw it out. It won't matter how many times you say I'm sorry, the wound is still there."

JR: When you are furious with someone, your immediate response may be to shout at her, criticize her or, in extreme cases, physically assault her. The wounds from such a response will remain forever. Is this really what you want?

PP: Think of a loved one you are angry at (and may be thinking of "attacking"). Consider a way of confronting this person without leaving a hole in the fence.

January 11

The mountains live with their shadows and so must we.

If we are unable to accept our shadow, we are likely to take a harsh view of the darker side of others. When people inveigh furiously against sexual depravity, violence, or cruelty, this can be a sign that they have failed to come to terms with their own proclivities and believe that it is only other people who are evil or disgusting.

We often attack other people for precisely those qualities that we most dislike in ourselves.

JR: A shadow lurks within us all. "Good" people too often refuse to acknowledge it, while "bad" people let the shadow define their temperament and personality. Looking at what appalls you in others can be a key to understanding the hidden disgust you harbor in yourself. This, then, is the beginning of cultivating a compassion and understanding for the scorn that previously filled you with repulsion.

PP: What do you despise in others? Can you see remnants of those attributes inside yourself?

January 12

*Only spiritual warmth
can melt a frozen soul.*

Until we have met the monsters in ourselves, we keep trying to slay them in the outer world. And we find that we cannot. For all darkness in the world stems from darkness in the heart. And it is there that we must do our work.

The mystic does not deny the darkness, in ourselves or in the world, but affirms a light that lies beyond it.

JR: Focusing on others' problems and blaming them are the most commonly adopted ways of avoiding looking at your own monsters. There is no shame in having demons within; however, there is great danger in allowing them free rein in the dark crevices of your soul. Through becoming aware of them, you can befriend them and transform their energies constructively.

PP: Be honest with yourself—what are your demons? What can you do to redirect their energies in a way beneficial to you?

January 13

The exuberance of opening up

When a negative emotion is understood, when its roots are illuminated, the energy behind the emotion diminishes and even disappears. When you feel angry, the healthy response is to learn what caused the anger, to rectify the situation if that is possible, and then to let go of the anger.

Close your eyes and take a few deep breaths. Let your walls tumble down. Examine without any judgment, criticism, or guilt what underlies the wall. What is the fear? From what are you protecting yourself? What can you do to heal this fear? How can you become whole again?

Once you truly understand your fear and its sources, the fear will dissolve. Your heart will once again open. You will feel joy.

JR: *Walls are useful in protecting you against external negative forces. Yet, they may also trap your negative emotions inside, creating a stagnant cesspool within. As you become stronger, you can become increasingly open and develop an inherent understanding of all your emotions with healthy ways to let them out and break down your walls in this growth process.*

PP: *What is one simple act you can do today to open up to others around you?*

January 14

Always felt I had a kind of hole in my soul

Scarcity consciousness arises as a result of what I call the "hole-in-the-soul syndrome." This is when we attempt to fill the gaps in our inner lives with things from the outside world. But like puzzle pieces, you can't fit something in where it does not naturally belong. No amount of external objects, affection, love, or attention can ever fill an inner void. The void can only be filled by looking within. You already have and are enough; revel in your own interior abundance and you will never need to look elsewhere.

JR: *We are constantly bombarded by advertisements for things that promise to fill our emptiness. Inevitably, these messages are selling a physical product that is intended to meet an emotional need. When you achieve the realization that it is only you yourself who can actually fill the hole, you can then start looking for ways to transition towards a life of interior abundance—a life which is no longer seduced by false promises.*

PP: *In what way do you feel empty or unfulfilled? What is one thing you can do today to start filling in that gap soulfully?*

January 15

Do you REALLY dream of going to Paradise?

All of the paradise spots in the world have this one disadvantage: the so-called civilized person quickly gets bored, not being used to the slower pace of life.

The major problem for the outsider who decides to settle in these idyllic havens, surrounded by beauty, is alcoholism. The new inhabitants drink themselves into a stupor. That was the extent of their 'new-found' life. So there is not always peace in paradise. Paradise is all in the mind.

JR: How about living in Hawaii? Or Bali? Or wherever the land of your dreams may be? It is easy to fantasize about these dream places; however, when you get there, you come to see that the baggage you bring along prevents you from "truly experiencing" that heavenly place. No paradise exists out there. It lies deep under your internal rubble and only becomes accessible if you are willing to make a conscious effort to dig through and seek to find it.

PP: Paradise is a state of mind—how can you cultivate it in your everyday life?

January 16

A good marriage between nature and humanity

The only difference between heaven and hell on this planet is the difference between running on the creative wishes of the conscious mind or running on the sabotaging, disempowering beliefs of the subconscious mind.

What if you programmed or reprogrammed your subconscious to contain the same wishes and desires from the conscious mind that created the honeymoon experience. At that point, we would all be living in heaven on Earth all the time.

JR: *Why is it that what we desire or claim to want often runs counter to the way we actually lead our lives? So many mental programs, of which we are oblivious, are running beneath the veil of awareness. If we can become cognizant of these subconscious programs and limiting beliefs, there is a dramatic increase in our potential to live out our creative wishes.*

PP: *Identify one or two "hidden beliefs" that prevent you from living out your true wishes. How can they be re-programmed to work in tandem with your conscious desires for your good?*

January 17

Enjoy splendor in the light of day

The most effective way to teach a child is not by saying "Don't do that," but "Do this." We don't reach the light through endless analysis of the dark. We reach the light by choosing the light. Light means understanding. Through understanding, we are healed.

JR: *Our lives are filled with rules, and necessarily so in a society of very different-minded individuals. However, if you choose to live your life in the light of universal values such as love and compassion, rules become increasingly unnecessary as those standards evolve into your ever-present guides.*

PP: *For you, what does it mean to live in the light? In what way, great or small, can you become a lighthouse for the important people in your life?*

January 18

The essence of the land remains the same, irrespective of its variable forms.

The notion that human nature cannot change is a convenient catch-all rationalization for apathy, passivity, helplessness, and cynicism.

Does human nature or the "inherent character, basic constitution, or essence" of a person ever change? To answer this question we can ask an analogous question: Does the essence or nature of a seed change when it grows into a flower? Not at all. The potential for becoming a flower was always resident within the seed. For the seed to grow into a flower does not constitute a change in the nature of the seed; rather, it represents a change in the degree to which the potential, always inherent in its original nature, is realized. Similarly, we can say: "human nature does not change." Yet, like the seed with the potential of becoming a flower, human nature is not a static "thing" but a spectrum of potentials. Just as a seed can grow into a flower without that process representing a change in its fundamental nature, so too can the human being grow from a "primitive" to an "enlightened" entity without that progression representing a change in basic human nature.

JR: History shows the vast potential which humanity possesses, both towards enacting great evil and great good. Reflecting on our past accords us pertinent cause to question the potential, which we wish to develop, as individuals and as a society. It is up to each and every one of us to decide which parts of our basic nature we will develop more fully and those which we choose not to adopt.

PP: Are you content with passively accepting who you now are, or do you choose to move towards further developing your potential? Where do you think your greatest potential lies?

January 19

In life and nature, challenges abound.

The heart of the problem of modern man is this. In the past, his salvation has been the hardships he had to contend with; they kept him on his toes. Now his technology has created a civilization that is becoming increasingly devoid of challenge. Vast numbers of men spend their weekdays performing some repetitive, mechanical job, and their weekends staring at the television. In such circumstances, more and more of our living is taken over by the robot. We feel vaguely, uncomfortably aware of the loss of freedom, but we have no idea what can be done about it. Buying a larger television set hardly seems to be the answer. Ascetics and mystics have always understood that the answer lies in the mind itself. All that is asked is that we shall look for a little time, in a special and undivided manner, at some simple, concrete, and external thing. This object of our contemplation may be almost anything we please: a picture, a statue, a growing plant, running water, little living things. Do not think, but as it were pour out your personality towards it; let your soul be in your eyes. Almost at once, this new method of perception will perceive about you a strange and deepening quietness, a slowing down of our feverish mental time. Next, you will become aware of a heightened significance, an intensified existence in the thing at which you look. As you, with all your consciousness, lean out towards it, an answering current will meet yours. It seems as though the barrier between its life and your own, between subject and object, has melted away.

JR: Have you become numbed by everyday living? Does everything seem routine? Challenges constantly come into your life in a myriad of ways. There are many times when you can choose to take on those specific challenges which excite you. Isn't that a lot better than having them forced on you unprepared?

PP: Think of a challenge that you would be thrilled to take on. What can you do to start on it now?

January 20

Step back and soak it in

1) When you've reached the brink of an abyss, the only progressive move you can make is to step backward.

2) Between the conception of the machine and its utilization, a necessary psychological and social process was skipped: the stage of evaluation.

JR: New products and new ideas come into our lives without our ever questioning their effect on us in the long run. Our technologies continue to grow exponentially, while our spiritual development lags far behind, thereby creating an increasingly dangerous world. One of our primary tasks, as a species, is to flip this tendency.

PP: Look at three important technological devices in your life, and evaluate them? What good and what bad are they bringing to you? Are these devices worth keeping?

January 21

How important it is to question the true existence of things

Within the confines of Auschwitz, the doctors did everything they could, except for the most important thing of all: they never questioned the existence of Auschwitz itself.

We as environmentalists do the same. We work hard as we can to protect the places we love, using the tools of the system the best we can. Yet we do not do the most important thing of all: we do not question the existence of this current death culture. We do not question the existence of an economic and social system that is working the world to death, that is starving it to death, that is imprisoning it, that is torturing it. We never question a culture that leads to these atrocities. We never question the logic that leads inevitably to clearcuts, murdered oceans, loss of topsoil. dammed rivers, poisoned aquifers, global warming. And we certainly don't act to bring it down.

JR: As individuals and as a society, we commit many atrocious acts that would shock us if we became truly conscious of them. Guilt trips are futile and offer no help. Rather, we should try to understand why we allow these acts to take place at all and discover what we can do to create a world that no longer accepts them as a part of our lives.

PP: Seek out one atrocity which is able to be perpetuated due to your lifestyle (human slavery, animal cruelty, environmental destruction, or something else) and think of a way to lessen your harmful complicity.

January 22

Priceless means having no price.

Money can buy almost anything we want—the problem being that we tend to want only the things that money can buy. Money can be a reconciling influence, harmonizing conflicting forces—but from the outside, rather than from within the individual. To depend on money is to depend mainly on a force that comes from outside the initiative and inner depth of the individual.

The wrong dependence on money to get through difficulties puts something external in the place of an internal, psychological force that needs to be developed and exercised in every normal adult man or woman.

JR: Money has become the focal point not just of our economy but also of our lives. How much does something cost? Financially, how much are you worth? Money serves an important role in our society, but when you ignore those aspects of your life which are priceless—love, compassion, friendship—you are left with a void which no amount of money can possibly fill.

PP: What is the role of money in your life? Is it in good balance with the precious gifts which money can't buy?

January 23

And you think it's taking a long time to learn? OH, but what a joy!

Learning is a pleasurable and fulfilling activity that is developed rather than diminished by sharing.

Enjoyment in creating and appreciating literature, music, and art similarly are not diminished if shared and should be emphasized in a sustainable society. Instead of life being bleak and cold when we are forced to slow down, it could be a flourishing period of creativity and learning.

If we can understand how our possessions have failed us, we can more readily decrease our thralldom. Turning instead to a focus on the quality of our relations to others, on the clarity and intensity of our experiences, on intimacy, sensuality, aesthetic sensibility, and emotional freedom we can see how a more ecologically sound society can be a more exciting and enjoyable one as well.

JR: Herein lies the key to developing a sustainable society—one that de-emphasizes development on the physical and places more importance on the non-tangible joys of life. Contrary to popular opinion, slowing down your frenzy for more money and material goods can bring much more joy to your life when you strive towards learning and teaching those things that most energize you.

PP: In your childhood, what was something that you loved to learn? How about taking it up again or, if you have learned it well, enthrall others by teaching it?

January 24

When I change, everything around me changes.

The easiest way to initiate change in the people around you is to change yourself. If you are in a relationship that is suffering from constant arguments and you stop responding to negativity from your partner, he or she, too, will have to change and either find a new way of exasperating you or give up arguing completely.

JR: We spend so much of our time trying to change other people, usually resulting in their increased resistance to change. Think of when someone tries to change you—don't you dig in your heels and insist on your "right" to stay as you are? But when you yourself decide to change, your relationships with others necessarily change because the old ways simply no longer work.

PP: What is one change you seek in others? How about changing that in yourself first?

January 25

Identity Search Center

Only to the extent that we decrease the mode of having, that is on nonbeing—stop finding security and identity by clinging to what we have, by 'sitting on it' by holding onto our ego and our possessions—can the mode of being emerge. 'To be' requires giving up one's egocentricity and selfishness, or in words often used by the mystics, by making oneself 'empty' and 'poor'.

But most people find giving up their "having" orientation too difficult; any attempt to do so arouses their intense anxiety and feels like giving up all security, like being thrown into the ocean when one does not know how to swim. They do not know that when they have given up the crutch of property, they can begin to use their own proper forces and walk by themselves. What holds them back is the illusion that they could not walk by themselves, that they would collapse if they were not supported by the things they have.

JR: This is a toughie since it can justifiably be said that you need to develop your ego to develop a healthy identity. This passage speaks to those of us who have been fortunate enough to have developed a healthy identity and seek to "grow it" more. The major world spiritual paths claim that our fundamental identity lies in our spiritual essence, our "true being," and that in further developing that, you will attain much greater fulfillment.

PP: Go to your personal Identity Search Center and ponder on "How can I more BE the real ME?"

January 26

A contradiction that co-exists is rare, like green plants amidst freezing snow.

The contradiction between wanting rapid economic growth and dynamic economic change and at the same time wanting family values, community values, and stability is a contradiction so huge that it can only last because of an aggressive refusal to think about it.

JR: There's no way around it—relentless economic growth and building strong community values cannot co-exist. At the personal level, when you choose to work more to make more money, you must sacrifice time with family and friends. If making more money becomes your primary goal, you become willing to cut corners (chop down a forest, pollute, pay low wages, and so on). It is the responsibility of each society and each person to find a good balance between the two.

PP: Is your work interfering with those values and relationships most important to you? If so, how can you change the situation?

January 27

Would someone please point out the way to wisdom?

If human vices such as greed and envy are systematically cultivated, the inevitable result is nothing less than a collapse of intelligence. A man driven by greed or envy loses the power of seeing things as they already are, of seeing things in their roundness and wholeness, and his very successes become failures. If whole societies become infected by these vices, they may indeed achieve astonishing things but they become increasingly incapable of solving the most elementary problems of everyday existence.

The foundations of peace cannot be laid by universal prosperity, in the modern sense, because such prosperity, if attainable at all, is attainable only by cultivating such drives of human nature as greed and envy, which destroy intelligence, happiness, serenity, and thereby the peacefulness of man.

No one is really working for peace unless he is working primarily for the restoration of wisdom.

JR: In today's world, we see technological marvels and super-human feats happening at a frantic pace. Yet, the most important issues confronting humanity (like poverty, environmental destruction, war and so on) are also worsening on many fronts. Humans have become very smart in a wide range of fields, but our lack of wisdom largely fails to apply our great progress to the disadvantaged and other life forms on the planet.

PP: In your eyes, who is wise? Learn more about this person or find a way to support her.

January 28

Proper alignment adds to the beauty.

A course of study in all American schools that would focus on self-development is needed. This course, which would run for all 12 years of one's schooling, would expand one's self-awareness; nurture and maintain one's self-esteem; teach personal and social responsibility; enhance communication skills; teach nonviolent conflict resolution methods; provide practice with problem-solving methods; provide relaxation and centering skills; foster the discovery of an alignment with one's life purpose; teach the fundamentals of goal setting, achievement motivation, and management; provide instruction in character, ethics, and values; teach emotional literacy and encourage the expression of one's feelings; provide instruction in accessing one's creativity; and promote the value of service to others.

JR: If we are serious about moving towards a sustainable world based on basic universal values, this must be reflected in the education that we provide for the young. Memorizing facts has little value in later years, but learning how to deal with conflict constructively, finding a life purpose and aligning one's learning and work with it would be precious gifts that can be used throughout life.

PP: Think of one thing you can do now to further implement what you truly value into your life.

January 29

Will we ever know the real truth of who we really are?

1) Until we can understand the assumptions in which we are drenched, we cannot know ourselves.

2) Human history becomes more and more a race between education and catastrophe.

JR: We all carry conscious and unconscious assumptions. The unconscious ones are more dangerous since it is difficult to discover them and expose their invalidity. Without being able to do so, these beliefs steer us towards treating others unfairly and potentially leading us to act treacherously, as we have seen happening again and again throughout history. To lessen the harmful results of our ignorance, education (of the self and in the society) must expose these assumptions and move us onto a more enlightened path.

PP: What is one assumption that you hold? Where did it come from? Look at an example that contradicts this belief and open yourself to another way of seeing.

January 30

The heat of fire will release pent-up potential.

1) "Education is not the filling of a bucket, but the lighting of a fire."

2) "Most people are mirrors, reflecting the moods and emotions of the times. Some people are windows, bringing light to bear on the dark corners where troubles fester. The whole purpose of education is to turn mirrors into windows."

JR: In most of the schools throughout the world, education centers on teaching subjects. This has limited merit since most of this knowledge will be forgotten or unused in adulthood. Rather, developing the students' eagerness for their own discoveries and making them passionate about learning to build character lets them become their own teachers. Then, when they feel stimulated by their own self-education in the things they are interested in, their enthusiasm will shine a light upon the world around them.

PP: Ask a child you know what she loves to do and learn. Help her to find a way to pursue this passion on her own.

January 31

The best things in life are free.

It is truly unfortunate that spirituality and religion have come to have negative connotations for so many. There's no question that there are people who misuse them for their own purposes. And yet, their deeper significance is meant to provide a strong foundation to uplift the human spirit, and to develop a grander perspective of our existence.

In more simplistic terms, they force us to re-learn—to see the natural world around us with the eyes of a child, filled with awe and wonder. They also encourage us to cultivate appreciation for the many splendid, FREE gifts which come with this life—the air and water we depend on, and the plants and animals which join us in this worldly adventure. When we are able to develop these capabilities, there is less need to make more money or get more things, since we are able to more fully enjoy the deeper pleasures which make life more meaningful.

JR: *All around you, there are ample opportunities to learn new things of interest to you and, in turn, create a deepening delight and gratitude in your life. The only thing preventing you from doing so is your inability to look and really "see."*

PP: *Take a few minutes to fully appreciate something today, letting your spirit feed you some positive energy in the process.*

FEBRUARY

Appreciation & Fun

There are times when you feel grateful for all you are and the good things surrounding you. Hopefully, a fuller awareness of your true self will help to cultivate such a feeling. Yet, there will still be times when it is difficult to appreciate anything. For example, everything may be going wrong or you may be simply getting into one of those ornery moods. Like any worthwhile spiritual gift, a spirit of gratitude requires a discipline of consciously incorporating it into your life. Just like meditation, expressing appreciation is most beneficial when done regularly, even when (or rather, especially when) you don't feel like it. And living in a spirit of gratitude enriches both the one bestowing it as well as the one receiving it. Grounding yourself in a spirit of appreciation fills you with a firmly planted contentment.

Being more consciously aware of the good things around you, and the countless miracles of this mystery called life, can only make you feel mesmerized with this magical place called Earth. Many will question the concept of "fun" as being a spiritual precept, but feeling enchanted, developing a curiosity for life's wonders, and affirming life through joyful play can be considered the most blessed activity anyone can undertake. It fills the doer with joy and is seductively infectious to those fortunate enough to be nearby. Too often, spirituality is seen as a solemn endeavor. Such an idea is the primary reason why many have no interest in it. When spirituality is made to be instilled with fun, with things that uplift you while also making others' lives more joyful, how can people not be attracted to it, and to all of the good that it can bring to the world? The active implementation of spirituality into your life becomes much more enjoyable and appealing when infused with an element of play and having fun.

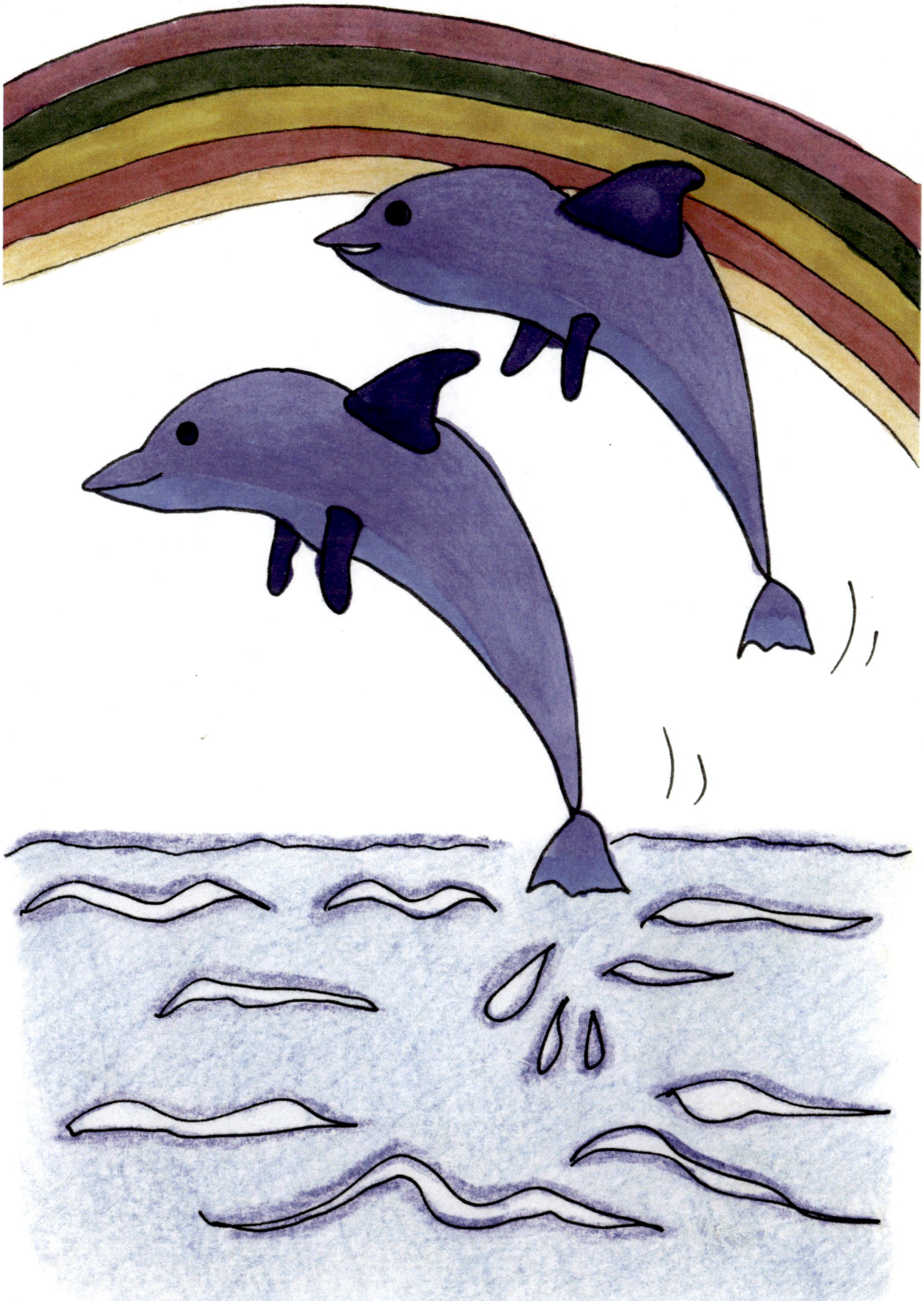

February 1

It's all so alive, even in the midst of winter.

1) The truly experienced person delights in the ordinary.

2) If you have no prejudice, no bias, if you are open, then everything around you becomes extraordinarily interesting, tremendously alive.

JR: When we can again see our world and our existence with the eyes of a child, full of curiosity about everything around us, we come to realize that we live in a world of mystery and miracles. Such wonderment can't help but to make us ask what life is and marvel at the myriad of forms it takes.

PP: Focus on any plant, even if it is "shut down" for winter, and ponder on the life force that is flowing through it.

February 2

Just imagine no such beauty—and be forever grateful

The Sages taught another exercise for having gratitude. And, that is to, first, imagine yourself not having something. For example, imagine you lost your eyesight, your hearing, your ability to speak, to feel with your hands, to smell or taste food. Imagine you lost your home, etc. Now, one by one, imagine yourself getting all of these back, and just consider how grateful you would be for each and every one. Try this; it's quite powerful. This exercise brings with it a new appreciation for those things that we tend to naturally take for granted!

JR: How conditioned we have become, living on auto–pilot and taking most of our incredible existence for granted. This exercise can be so insightful in helping you to regain a sense of appreciation for the many gifts that bless your life. Doing it regularly instills your spirit with a soothing sense of gratitude.

PP: Picture not having your most important faculty (eyesight or hearing, for example) for one week, and then have it suddenly return to you.

February 3

Miracle built upon miracles—How can you miss it?

My question for you is "How can you not believe in miracles when nature is pulling off one after another endlessly?" Look at the lowly crab, who grows out of its home (shell) only to construct one by itself again. Or the often despised spider, who spins a web, the threads which are stronger than steel (weight for weight). Bees that can navigate without maps. Termite towers (of mud) which keep a steady temperature. Those ugly, furry worms (caterpillars), which build a cocoon to emerge as beautiful butterflies. And, most mysterious of all, green immobile life (plants) which grows from "non-life" (water and soil), and makes food from "non-matter" (sunlight). I myself don't believe anyone could write a fictional book with more surprises.

JR: *Amazing things are happening around us all of the time, many beyond our perception. The wonders mentioned in this passage can be seen and, when paid attention to, greatly appreciated. But how about the millions of microorganisms in the soil that make it alive? Or the electric waves which power modern society? How mind-boggling when you take the time to think about it!*

PP: *Breath is sometimes equated with spirit. Hold your breath and imagine no longer being able to breathe. Then, take a few deep breaths and feel the spirit surging through you. Yet another miracle, which we usually take for granted.*

February 4

You never know when it will disappear— treasure it while you can.

Remember the day I borrowed your brand new car and I dented it?
I thought you'd kill me, but you didn't.

And remember the time I dragged you to the beach,
and you said it would rain, and it did?
I thought you'd say, "I told you so." But you didn't.

Do you remember the time I flirted with all the guys
to make you jealous, and you were?
I thought you'd leave me, but you didn't.

Do you remember the time I spilled strawberry pie all over your car rug?
I thought you'd hit me, but you didn't.

Yes, there were lots of things you didn't do.
But you put up with me, and you loved me, and you protected me.

There were lots of things I wanted to make up to you
when you returned from Vietnam.
But you didn't.

JR: Various people have influenced your life and are a part of what you have become today. And there are those who are in your life now who continue to mold you into ever-newer forms. Some you may treasure, while others you may despise—but all of them affect this unique being called ME.

PP: Think of one person who is very important in your life right now. Imagine that he dies suddenly in an accident. How would you feel? Let this exercise become a deepening of your appreciation for him.

February 5

Just get a grip on reality, would ya?

If we were truly moved by the beauty of the world around us, we would honor the earth in a profound way. We would understand immediately and turn away with a certain horror from all those activities that violate the integrity of the planet. That we have not done so reveals that a disturbance exists at a more basic level of consciousness and on a greater order of magnitude than we dare admit to ourselves or even think about. This unprecedented pathology is not merely in those more immediate forms of economic activity that have done such damage; it is even more deeply imbedded in our cultural traditions, in our religious traditions, in our very language, in our entire value system.

JR: We so often point our finger at others—the non-religious Japanese, the greedy Jew, the hypocritical Christian, the Islamic terrorist—and feel relieved that we are "good." While the majority of the world's people may have good intentions, all of us are also complicit, whether we're aware of it or not, in the harm done to the world surrounding us. Through generating an awareness of the damage you are inflicting on other people, other creatures, and the planet, you understand the pain of the whole process. However, when it leads to taking action that heals both inside and out, you will feel empowered and live more lightly (meaning both in the light and more simply) and joyfully.

PP: What do you do (or consume) that hurts others (either consciously or not)? How can you change your ways to avoid inflicting harm?

February 6

Be fully present and bathe in the sunlight

Try smelling the fragrance of a flower as if you are experiencing it for the very first time. Try eating just one mouthful of your next meal in full presence. Try walking through your garden, being fully present with each flower and each tree. Try being fully present with your children or your friends even if it is just for a few moments.

You will begin to feel the difference between life lived in the mind and life lived in the joyful reality of the present moment.

I know that you cannot live in the world like this all of the time. But to spend some of your time each day in a state of innocence and presence will open you up to a heightened awareness of the sacredness of all life. This in turn will transform you. You will begin to remember who you are. You will begin to have a taste of Heaven on Earth.

JR: We are so bombarded by a variety of stimuli that we get lost in the orgy of sensations that leads to either a numbing of feeling or getting overwhelmed by all the excitement. Becoming fully present to a singular experience, imagining that you are being exposed to it for the first time, and treasuring the resultant sensations, bestows on you a small taste of paradise.

PP: Choose one thing (person, object, experience) to focus on for five minutes today, devoting all of your attention (and senses) only to that, and perceive how it feels.

February 7

A luscious Earth mat

The Moghul Emperor, Akbar, was out hunting in the forest. When it was time for evening prayer, he dismounted, spread his mat, and knelt to pray in the manner of a devout Muslim.

Just then, a peasant woman, perturbed because her husband had left home that morning and hadn't returned, went rushing by, anxiously searching for him. Preoccupied, she did not notice the Emperor and tripped over him, then got up and rushed farther into the forest. Akbar was annoyed, but being a good Muslim, he observed the rule of speaking to no one during prayer.

When his prayer was about over, the woman returned with her husband, whom she had found. She was surprised to see the Emperor and his entourage there. Akbar gave vent to his anger against her and shouted, "Explain your disrespectful behavior or you will be punished."

The woman suddenly turned fearless. "Your Majesty, I was so absorbed in the thought of my husband that I did not even see you here, not even when I stumbled over you. Now while you were at namaaz, you were absorbed in One who is infinitely more precious than my husband. And how is it you noticed me?"

The Emperor was shamed into silence and later confided to his friends that a peasant woman, who was neither a scholar nor a Mullah, had taught him the meaning of prayer.

JR: Some of us love to make a show of our faith and devoutness, while others constantly focus on how terrible they are. In all probability, neither attitude will bear much fruit. However, determining what is truly most important in your life and praying for how to live that out would most likely move you in the right direction.

PP: When you pray, do you earnestly believe in what you are praying for, or who you are praying to? If so, good for you. If not, consider how to make prayer more significant to you.

February 8

*Permanently coated—
for the time being*

I've begun to understand why those realized teachers don't need to go out to have fun. It's not that they are antisocial or afraid of the world. They already have what everybody else wants and is looking for—contentment and joy. However, theirs are of a more permanent variety. Satisfaction and joy arise from exerting ourselves towards a meaningful life, developing confidence in basic goodness, and expressing it with wisdom and compassion. Exerting ourselves toward virtue creates stability in our lives—happiness that we can depend on.

JR: The enlightened masters throughout history have found a solid contentment and joy in their lives. Most of us other simpletons find this kind of illumination periodically through our lives, as it is transient based on our outer circumstances and internal weathering. How does the temporary ecstasy lead to a more lasting gratification?

PP: When do/did you feel "high on life?" How can you bring this feeling more into your life?

February 9

The question is how to unlock the many treasures trapped underneath.

The key is the heart. Until we understand people's hearts, not just their minds and ideologies, nothing can happen. That's why it's absolutely essential to create opportunities for people to listen to each other with the heart, mind, and spirit. Only then can people move past the old destructive ways to "the better thing."

JR: Each of us has a treasure lying within our core. Unfortunately, it too often remains unseen, even by the person who harbors it. In order to bring out people's gifts, your own as well as those of others, you must learn to listen with an open heart. Even with your enemies, understanding has the potential to move you towards a more compatible course of action.

PP: Who is someone that you have not really been listening to (it could be your own inner spirit as well)? Take some time to listen and try to truly understand what she is trying to tell you.

February 10

Nature—forever shedding her radiance, expecting nothing in return

We are likely to experience joy and fulfillment not by trying endlessly to satisfy our own interests but, rather, by serving others in greatest need. It is also the case that one of the pathways to change in our own lives occurs through the actions we take on behalf of others. It isn't that happier people are significantly more generous than others, but that generous people tend to be happier.

JR: It feels good when you buy something for yourself or treat yourself to a good time, and you deserve to do so. At the same time, the joy is often short-lived and limited to yourself. When you give to others, the pleasure is multiplied and transformed into a longer lasting good feeling, having a good effect on others as well as yourself.

PP: Start today to make it a daily habit of giving something (either material, in an act, or with words of kindness) to another living being.

February 11

One of the many wonders of the world

A group of students were asked to list what they thought were the present "Seven Wonders of the World." The following received the most votes:

1. Egypt's Great Pyramids
2. Taj Mahal
3. Grand Canyon
4. Panama Canal
5. Empire State Building
6. St. Peter's Basilica
7. China's Great Wall

While gathering the votes, the teacher noted that one student had not finished her paper yet. The girl said, "I couldn't quite make up my mind because there were so many."

The teacher said, "Well, tell us what you have, and maybe we can help." The girl hesitated, then read, "I think the 'Seven Wonders of the World' are:

1. to see
2. to hear
3. to touch
4. to taste
5. to feel
6. to laugh and
7. to love."

The things we overlook as simple and ordinary and that we take for granted are truly wondrous! A gentle reminder—that the most precious things in life cannot be built by hand or bought by man.

JR: Focusing only upon those things which can be bought with money or the things which you don't have undermines your capacity to be contented with the most precious things in life (as seen in the numerous examples in this passage). Focusing on these things, which are essentially "gifts from God," moves you towards living your life in more steady wonderment.

PP: Having already pondered upon your senses, try out laughter today. Catch yourself when you laugh today, or find something to make you laugh, and feel the sensation it gives to you.

February 12

A treasure of incredible beauty— offered freely

What if you had access to an infinite treasure of amazing beauty? Something of great value that you don't have to pay for. A place of peace and tranquility that doesn't take a journey to get to. A time of joy that you don't have to wait for. A nonprescription medicine that will put a lasting smile on your face. What would you do to find it? What would you do to keep it from being disturbed?

Think of sunsets. No two are ever the same. Some people say they can hear music when the sky changes color. You don't need to buy a ticket or pay a subscription fee to see a sunset. It's just there for you and for everyone and all you have to do is attend. Think of the elegance of flowers and majesty of trees, the infinite dance of animals, insects, fish—eating and being eaten, coupling, growing, sleeping and dying. It's all happening now. Think of that tiny droplet of water on the budding leaf. A minute ago it was a unique snowflake. In a minute, it will be gone, as will be this very moment.

All you have to do is slow down, open your senses, and pay attention. Enjoy Life!

JR: The majority of our fairy tales and mythologies are filled with stories of hidden treasures and supernatural beings. They help us to contemplate other worlds and decipher the meaning of our existence. At the same time, we need to be reminded that this real world, which we inhabit, has verily visible gems all around us. However, we have become blind to many of them because we are too occupied or have dulled our senses to the point of being unable to appreciate them.

PP: Choose any one of the examples in the passage (or find one of your own) to bring a moment of delight to your day.

February 13

*How fortunate you are—
oh, young one*

Reawaken Your Curiosity

1) "What a distressing contrast there is between the radiant intelligence of the child and the feeble mentality of the average adult."

2) Young children possess what Zen calls 'beginner's mind.' They are awed and fascinated with the wonder of the world. Anything is possible. Life is a great adventure. For most of us, the systems that 'educate' us to be adults stifle our natural curiosity. We lose touch with our innate appreciation of life. We forget how to dream. The blessing is that with attention, patience and love, we can reawaken our sense of wonder. We can again dance with life.

3) "We're so engaged in doing things to achieve purposes of outer value that we forget that the inner value, the rapture that is associated with being alive, is what it's all about."

JR: It is a travesty that our society and our education systems kill those things that make us feel so alive, namely, curiosity and dreams. We must work to earn a living. We must put up with drudgery so that we can support our families. Inherent in these messages is that the desire to seek new discoveries and attempt to live out our dreams are dangers that may lead us to ruin. What have we done? And how can we make it right to transit towards a society where we train people to enjoy the thrill of discovery, live out their dreams, and feel securely cuddled in the arms of society?

PP: What is a dream that you have for yourself, or one that you had before? What is one step you can take towards making (part of) it a reality?

February 14

Contribute to this miracle of life

An important form of self-compassion is to make choices motivated purely by our desire to contribute to life rather than out of fear, guilt, shame, duty, or obligation. When we are conscious of the life-enriching purpose behind an action we take, when the sole energy that motivates us is simply to make life wonderful for others and ourselves, then even hard work has an element of play in it. Correspondingly, an otherwise joyful activity performed out of obligation, duty, fear, guilt or shame will lose its joy and eventually engender resistance.

JR: So much of what we do, and what we are taught to do, is grounded in fear, and this results in our feeling weighted down and constricted. On the other hand, when we do things out of love and to contribute to life, our spirits soar and we feel unpolluted and unrestricted delight in the activities that we take on. Play becomes a part of everything we do, and experiencing the fun of a child returns.

PP: What is something that you do because it enriches your and others' lives? How can you add an element of fun and play into it, so that it adds delight to the experience?

February 15

What a magical wonderland!

Science is mostly about the details of how things work, but continues to be blind to the truth that our world is sacred. If anything will turn the tide, it will be the switch from studying the world to loving it. A spiritual awakening, one that returns us humbly to our magical place within the web of life will be the start of a chain reaction that allows us to implement change with the conviction and force of a united front.

JR: *Something that every healthy individual seeks is the experience of love. And yet, it is not something that we attempt to teach or strive to better understand, perhaps because it is so difficult to define and quantify. So we spend much of our time teaching and learning (especially in our schools) those restrictive things that have little benefit in our later lives. How can we cultivate feelings of love and compassion, for other people and for our respective community of living beings? When we can increasingly enhance these qualities within, we naturally will want to do what is good for others, for nature, and for us.*

PP: *What is one thing you love in nature? Why do you feel that way towards it? Is there any way you can expand that feeling of love to be more inclusive of all of nature?*

February 16

No use fighting against the elements—might as well enjoy whatever you can

What is essential is to live life in wonder. All this magic that's around us, but we let it go by! In Asia, they say life is a great river, and it will flow, no matter what you do or don't do. We can decide to flow with the river, and live in peace and joy and love, or we can decide to battle it, and live in agony and despair. But the river doesn't care. Life doesn't care. In either case, all of our streams run into the same sea. It's up to you.

JR: It is very important to be able to discern what can be changed and what can't. Then, for those things that you cannot alter, you are only in control of your reaction to them. For instance, the cold weather may be uncomfortable, so you may rant against it, making yourself miserable in the process. Or you can focus on the beautiful contrast between the pink flowers and the white snow and, even in the discomfort, fill yourself with a feeling of amazement on this miracle.

PP: What is something you often rail against in your life at this time and which is beyond your capability to change? Can you find something good in it so that you feel less irritated the next time you experience it?

February 17

Bring the peaks home within you

The more people discussed peak experiences, the more they began to have. Merely thinking about them, talking about them, was enough to make them happen. The crucial element was an attitude of optimism. The conscious knowledge that such powers exist is the most important step towards developing them. All human beings share a desire to expand their powers, to experience greater freedom and vitality, to have life more abundantly. What deters them from making an effort is a lack of any idea of where to begin. All that is necessary is to know that these powers are associated with the hidden part of the mind, and that they can be called upon by conscious effort. We simply need to be convinced that they exist. And this conviction can be gained by studying the evidence until dawning understanding turns into insight. No 'belief' is required, and no mystical disciplines are necessary. With study, it is almost impossible to avoid the conclusion that the human mind is a vaster and stranger realm than we ever supposed. Moreover, the greatest step towards exploring its latent powers is simply to recognize clearly that they exist.

JR: What a wonderful way to empower yourself, and this is something which is possible for anyone! Doing this exercise, remembering and talking about your peak experiences, past and present, brings more of them into your life. This can be simply a first step towards further training your mind to bring increasingly more beneficial experiences into your life.

PP: Think of one peak experience you've had and talk about it with someone. Encourage her to do the same with you. Make it a regular practice, bringing more peak experiences into your life in the process.

February 18

Life—overpowering the elements

1) The Dalai Lama was once asked, "What is the most important quality in a spiritual teacher?" His answer: "Cheerfulness." That cheerfulness is a kind of invitation that says, "It feels good to be here. Wouldn't you like to come too?"

2) Morality should be joyous, an affirmation of life rather than a denial.

JR: *Living morally is often seen as a burden because of the mistaken idea of what morality is. Ethical values give you a grounding in which you can integrate your life and become whole. And, as you come to feel "holy," the joy of living fills your being, and your life becomes a conduit nourishing all forms of other life which you have contact with.*

PP: *How do you view morality? As a burden, or as a pleasure? How can you make it feel more life-engendering so that you long to make morality more a part of your life?*

February 19

Transforming the way we live

1) The way to transcend a corrupt system is through generosity—giving, not holding back. Active, creative, transforming ways of the kingdom of God—overcoming violence not with violence but with creativity and generosity.

2) "I cried because I had no shoes until I saw a man who had no feet."

JR: It's easy to feel cynical and despair at the corruption all around us. Many simply give up any hope of combating it, while others fight to change it. With any luck, the corrupt act is terminated, but the spirit of the perpetrator remains unchanged, simply awaiting another chance to commit another fraud. It is only by our living with love and generosity that the hard hearts of the wicked will change and come to see the possibility of a deeper, more gratifying life.

PP: When do you hold back, feeling like you cannot be generous for fear of being taken advantage of? How can you become more giving in this situation in accordance with what you believe?

February 20

Thinking small cripples humanity.

If the thought of lack—whether it be money, recognition, or love—has become part of who you think you are, you will always experience lack. Rather than acknowledge the good that is already in your life, all you see is lack. Acknowledging the good that is already in your life is the foundation for all abundance. The fact is: Whatever you think the world is withholding from you, you are withholding from the world. You are withholding it because deep down you think you are small and that you have nothing to give.

Try this for a couple of weeks and see how it changes your reality: Whatever you think people are withholding from you—praise, appreciation, assistance, loving care, and so on—give it to them. You don't have it? Just act as if you had it, and it will come. Then soon after you start giving, you will start receiving. You cannot receive what you don't give.

JR: It is easy for those brought up in abundance or with a positive disposition to ask others to think positively. Yet, this advice is about as helpful as telling a horny teenager, "Just don't do it." This passage provides a good alternative—even if you don't have it, act like you do. Give someone praise and appreciation (even if you get none). Doing so repeatedly, even though you may not be keen at first, will eventually bring it to heart, and what you give will come back to you.

PP: What is some intangible good that you don't have enough of? Start giving that to others regularly and see how it then comes into your life.

February 21

Enhance your life with positive energy

"I think there is nothing, not even crime, more opposed to poetry, to philosophy, say, to life itself than this incessant business. If a man should walk in the woods for love of them half of each day, he is in danger of being regarded as a loafer, but if he spends his whole day as a speculator, shearing off those woods and making earth bald before her time, he is esteemed an industrious and enterprising citizen."

JR: "I'm too busy." This is a great excuse to avoid difficult situations, which prevents you from contemplating the negative effect of your life on others, or helps you weasel out of a previously-made commitment. When you bring this busy-ness into your business, you tend to overlook the acts against humanity, nature, and life. The statement of "That's nothing but business" does not justify the horrendous destruction you are inflicting on the world. If anything, it demonstrates the need to find a different way, where your business and life's business develop in harmony.

PP: What is one beneficial and one detrimental result of the business you are in (or the life you are leading)? How can you build on the positive and diminish the negative?

February 22

HA! And you thought your species had a monopoly on looking sexy.

1) Forfeit your sense of awe, let your conceit diminish your ability to revere, and the world becomes a market place for you. The loss of awe is the avoidance of insight. A return to reverence is the first prerequisite for a revival of wisdom.

2) Retirement is when you stop living at work and begin work at living.

JR: As a species, we have become so human-centered that we fail to closely observe, attempt to understand, or honor the commonalities that we share with other life forms. We have become conceited and drugged by our technological prowess, to such a degree that we forget about our dependence on the natural environment. Look at the beautiful body of this deer, and contemplate that it, similar to us, has blood flowing through its veins and is breathing the same air as we are. Cherish it for being of the same life force as you are.

PP: In nature, what animal or plant do you treasure? What is it that you revere about this living thing?

February 23

The distinction between true spirit and nature is but an illusion.

1) "We can't survive without enchantment—the loss of it is killing us."

2) "There is one thing that all true spirituality has in common, whether that spirituality is derived from faith, from science, from nature or from the arts—a sense of wonder."

3) "There are only two ways to live your life: One is as though nothing is a miracle. The other is as though everything is a miracle. I believe in the latter."

JR: What is spirit? What is breath? What is nature? These concepts are intertwined and inseparable. And an acute awareness of this can only make us feel enchanted by this perplexing existence of ours. While you may feel independent, you are completely dependent on the plants for oxygen, clean air for breathing, and the water that sustains you. There are still so many mysteries in the myriad of living beings around us which we have yet to fathom, waiting to be discovered so as to mesmerize us still the more.

PP: Think of one aspect of nature which fascinates you and find out more about it.

February 24

A gem radiates her light on all around her.

The first day of school, I found a little old lady beaming up at me with a smile that lit up her entire being. She said, "Hi handsome. My name is Rose. I'm eighty-seven. Can I hug you?"

"Of course you may!" We became instant friends.

Rose was invited to speak at our football banquet. Dropping her cards, she said, "I'm sorry I'm so jittery. I gave up beer for Lent and this whiskey is killing me!" Then, she began.

"We do not stop playing because we are old; we grow old because we stop playing. There are only four secrets to staying young, being happy, and achieving success. You have to laugh and find humor every day. You've got to have a dream. When you lose your dreams, you die. We have so many people walking around who are dead and don't even know it! There is a huge difference between growing older and growing up. Anybody can grow older. That doesn't take any ability. The idea is to grow up by always finding opportunity in change. Have no regrets. The elderly usually don't have regrets for what we did, but rather for things we did not do. The only people who fear death are those with regrets."

REMEMBER, GROWING OLDER IS MANDATORY. GROWING UP IS OPTIONAL. We make a Living by what we get, we make a Life by what we give.

JR: What a fantastic example of the importance of play in keeping an individual youthful and energetic, and it is to the benefit of all she comes into contact with! Laughing and playing for the sake of having fun—what could be more spiritually uplifting to the doer and those around her? In the absence of introducing these elements into our spirituality, it lacks vigor and appeal.

PP: Do something fun today—an act of playing that you usually don't do but know you'd enjoy. See how it elevates your spirit.

February 25

*Owning nothing,
and still enjoying a
wonderful life*

The never-ending desire for more is in reality the urge for more life, more experience, more growth in understanding and consciousness. This evolutionary drive is the source of our divinely inspired dissatisfaction with whatever has been achieved. However, a basic misunderstanding of this drive focuses it exclusively in the material realm. But, rightly understood, it can move human attention from the quantity of goods to the quality of life.

JR: With the understanding that your desire for more has a spiritual and life-giving source, you can subsequently influence your life towards seeking more learning, more giving, and more of that which gives you intrinsic satisfaction. And, in turn, you realize that acquiring more and more material goods often runs counter to "growing" your true vitality.

PP: What is it that really makes you feel alive—filling you with energy? How can you bring more of this into your life?

February 26

*Restorative therapy
at its best*

There's a critical difference between passive relaxation and restorative relaxation. We all need time to unwind, and we are usually refreshed by the beauty of nature on a hike, a depth of calmness when we meditate, or the sense of gratitude and delight we get from playing with our kids or the dog. I think of these activities as restorative and creative relaxation. But when we are simply under the spell of commercial stimuli on the tube or at the mall, we aren't creating ourselves but rather allowing ourselves to be created. We aren't aligning our actions with our values, but aligning our inactions with someone else's values.

JR: Relaxation can sometimes be exhausting. Pretty strange, huh? Yet, like a sugar high, it exhilarates you for a short time, followed by a crash or disappointment. The buzz doesn't last long. Then, there are other forms of relaxation which delight body, mind, and soul, like those in the passage, and provide you with a calming sensation for a much longer time.

PP: What form of relaxation do you find to have positive, long-term effects? In other words, when you do it regularly, the good feeling lasts longer and isn't followed by a letdown.

February 27

Explore a winter wonderland—one way to be good to yourself

Many of us in today's world have either become so busy, or so bored with our lives, that we have forgotten how to have fun. For others, having fun seems like "a waste of time," preventing us from doing more "important" things. Yet, this is exactly what we need in order to enjoy life, rather than feel burdened by it. By having something to look forward to (every day), our lives become touched with joy and excitement.

Having fun is good for our health, in that it makes us forget our worries. Also, during that time, the mind is relaxed and able to gain a new perspective, which may give us insights that make our lives more fulfilling. Most importantly, having fun means that you value yourself enough to treat yourself well. The best thing you can do for others, for your work, for your life is to be good to yourself.

JR: Religion and spirituality often emphasize doing good to others. While this is surely important in order to bring a deeper joy and contentment into your life, it is impossible to do so without first doing good to yourself. Unfortunately, this is difficult for some people because of their sense of guilt or having been told that they are unworthy. Being good to yourself is not selfish, but rather is a first step in being able to be good to others.

PP: Decide on something that you will do later today that you can look forward to. See how it makes you feel better throughout the day.

February 28

Completely organic—and looking good

Instead of buying entertainment, it's better to create it. For example, organic gardening has many intrinsic rewards. I burn calories digging soil, turning the compost, and gathering organic materials to grow high-quality food; in turn, the food gives me more energy. It just makes sense. In the neighborhood garden, I work with friends to devise strategies to beat the heat or outwit invasions of villainous insects. "The challenge is similar to a video game, only real; and the solutions use martial arts approaches rather than handheld missile launchers." In the garden, we constantly use all our senses—including the climactic experience of tasting a fresh peach or a salad of juicy tomatoes and basil—all within prescribed rules that avoid the use of hazardous chemicals. It's a game you can eat. Skillful gardening is as challenging as golf or downhill skiing but instead of costing $50–$100 a day, it yields an ongoing income.

JR: What a wonderful example of creating your own entertainment with physical, environmental, and economic benefits! Wherever you live, there are many unmet needs waiting to be addressed. Creating your own excitement and entertainment requires effort and, because of this, it ends up becoming rewarding as well, a component that is usually missing when being entertained by someone else's efforts.

PP: Think of a way to create your own entertainment, one that has added side benefits (to people or other living things).

February 29

*Creativity unleashed
can give rise to
magical places.*

Play returns us to a state in which we can see what's possible—not what's so. When we look (at a trashed up vacant city lot) through the eyes of play, we see a children's garden; when we look through the eyes of power, we see only trash.

Creativity is in everyone, play unleashes that creativity, and if we want to create a healthy and resilient community, we need to invite the members of that community to play together. When we play, everything once again becomes possible.

JR: As adults, we've been schooled and trained to do things in a certain way, based on our culture, biases, and education. Children are perceptive and observe the same thing. Since the children have not yet been "contaminated," they are able to perceive the possibilities. In addition, they innovate on ways to have fun with it, since play comes naturally to them. How much we adults have to learn from such a liberating attitude towards life!

PP: Look at a run–down place in your area, or someplace nearby that has gone to pot. Look at it with the innocent and unsullied eyes of a child and see how it can be reformed into a "playground."

MARCH

Love & Compassion

Love is one of the most puzzling words in the English language. It carries diverse meanings ranging from a raging passion (often to the exclusion of anything else) to an all-encompassing attitude towards all life, with a beckoning spirit to let it all in. These reflections are based on the latter description and, in turn, justifiably criticized as being unattainable. Yet, the purpose underpinning these ponderings, and towards cultivating a loving spirit, is not to express an abstinence from unpleasant feelings towards others or existing personal barriers preventing us from fully loving others. Rather, the idea is to search for and understand these obstacles to love and find ways of diminishing or overcoming them.

The art of true love necessitates cultivating compassion, with an often forgotten (or ignored) aspect of compassion for yourself. In the absence of self-compassion, it is impossible to be compassionate towards others. Learning to come to love even your weak points while concurrently working on bettering your strong points can help you to become a person more accepting of others' weaknesses. Repressing your own sorrow will only harden you; however, facing your sorrows and weaknesses without judgement can melt your hardened heart and fill it with compassionate understanding. In turn, your judgements of others and the futile efforts to change them will start to dissipate as the compassion you have come to feel for yourself also flows out to them.

These reflections help in developing more sensitivity to yourself and others, realizing that all of us are doing what makes sense to us, based on our unique pasts and personalities. And in becoming so, you discover the true enrichment of your own spirit and the world around you by the power of love.

81

March 1

Decide to be you yourself—unique and beautiful

Love is not a response, it's a DECISION!

The most important single ingredient in successful long-term relationships: friendship. And right next to that: tolerance—which, of course, is what true friendship produces, and, in turn, what produces true friendship.

A relationship is "right" because you decide to make it right. And what could cause you to decide that? Your decision about what is important to you. Your decision about Who You Are, and who you Choose To Be.

Don't search for "someone right," choose to BE "someone right."

JR: What a powerful message! When you choose to be "someone right," you attract desirable people into your life. Instead of searching for the right people and depending on external forces, you take control of the reins by deciding on who you want to be and moving towards that personality. While "falling in love" is largely beyond your control, "being in love" is a matter of cultivating a loving feeling within you and bringing it into your relationships.

PP: How would you like your relationship with your partner to be: fun, giving, considerate? Make a commitment today to be one of these and see how it feels. Why not keep continuing with it?

March 2

My existence transforms my world for the better—how about doing the same?

1) Love will arise in your heart when you have no barrier between yourself and another, when you meet and observe people without judging them.

2) The moment you have in your heart this extraordinary thing called love and feel the depth, the delight, the ecstasy of it, you will discover that for you the world is transformed.

JR: Love transforms not only others who are its recipients, but also the lover himself. His whole world becomes lighter and his spirit soars. Love, in this sense, is not the enthralling passion of two newfound lovers who experience the cycles of ecstasy, despair and move back & forth, but rather the deep, steady feeling of delight firmly grounded in an awareness and appreciation for this miraculous gift of life.

PP: Who do you judge as very good or very bad? Try to strip away the judgement and look at him objectively. Can you do it?

March 3

Unquestionable commitment to spreading this gift called life

1) There is so much love in the human heart, yet hatred threatens our planet. And why? Because hatred is currently more committed than love.

2) "When I give food to the poor they call me a saint. When I ask why the poor have no food, they call me a communist."

JR: The news and politics of today are moving us towards increased fears and hatreds while simultaneously smothering our great capacity to love. As we become more filled with hate and fear, we find more ways of fighting "them" and building walls to keep "them" out. At the same time, those who seek out ways to love and help "them" are often considered lunatics or dangerous to society. Indeed, this is the way we create a hell on earth.

PP: What is one hatred that you harbor? How can you diminish it and make more of a commitment towards love and life?

March 4

Being bugged can be a blessing.

With other people's problems, we are called not to fix things but to bind up wounds through the power of love, realizing that the human person is strengthened when love triumphs over fear.

A Yiddish tale tells of an old wise woman who was asked, "What is the greatest burden in life? Is it helping the sick, feeding the poor or putting up with your neighbor?" She responded by saying, "It is none of these. The greatest burden in life is to have nothing to carry." Sometimes the very struggles we try to avoid are the very blessings of our lives.

JR: *Just like the flower in the picture which is benefiting from the ladybug's presence, there are times when someone bugging you can be transformed into something of value. Study after study evidence the health benefits resulting from caring for and helping others. While often perceived as a burden, showing concern for those who are hurt can serve as an ideal way to heal your own inner wounds.*

PP: *Who is "causing" a problem in your life? Try to find some value that arises from this issue (for example, increasing your patience). How much are you contributing to the problem, simply because of your attitude?*

March 5

Don't hate things just because they're different

"The ultimate weakness of violence is that it is a descending spiral, begetting the very thing it seeks to destroy. Instead of diminishing the evil, it multiplies it. Through violence you may murder the hater, but you do not murder hate. In fact, violence merely increases hate. Returning violence for violence multiplies violence, adding deeper darkness to a night already devoid of stars. Darkness cannot drive out hate; only love can do that."

JR: The physical manifestation of hell results from a never-ending fall into negativity, violence and destruction. Its opposite occurs with an ongoing renewal of constructive creativity, love, and honoring life. Instead of being used as a last resort, violence is often used as the primary means to solve problems, which simply become more intractable because subsequent seething hatreds fester and ooze out in a myriad of ways later on.

PP: When have you used violence? While possibly temporarily dealing with the issue, what negative remnants remain because of it? Is there any way you can get rid of them?

March 6

Share and spread your goodness to all

Help us to remember that the jerk who cut us off in traffic last night is a single mother who worked nine hours that day, that she is rushing home to cook dinner and help with homework, to do the laundry and spend a few precious moments with her children.

Help us to remember that the pierced, tattooed, disinterested young man who takes forever at the checkout stand, is a worried 19-year-old college student, who is balancing his apprehension over final exams with his fear of not getting his loans for next semester.

Remind us that the scary looking bum, begging for money in the same spot every day (who really ought to get a job!) is a slave to addictions that we can only imagine in our worst nightmares.

Help us to remember that the old couple walking annoyingly slow through the store aisles and blocking our shopping progress are savoring this moment, knowing that, based on the biopsy report she got back last week, this will be the last year that they go shopping together.

Let us be slow to judge and quick to forgive.
Let us show patience, empathy and love.
Open our hearts not to just those who are close to us, but to all humanity.

JR: This exercise is of more value to the giver than to the receiver since, in such scenarios, the people who are the objects of compassion are, most likely, not able to feel it. When we get irritated and angry at others for the way they are or what they are doing, we create stress in ourselves. By cultivating a "compassionate imagination," we create a healing serenity within.

PP: Throughout the day, whenever you get upset with someone, imagine possible, merciful reasons why she is doing that and experience the resultant calming effect it has on you.

March 7

So much variety to choose from

People increase their earth bonding by a variety of experiences, including deepening their awareness of the wonders of the natural world, learning to enjoy experiencing their spirituality being enriched by nature, and investing themselves in helping to care for nature more lovingly. Earth bonding also may be strengthened by deepening awareness of how we are a part of the marvellous, eon-spanning evolutionary process by which the entire biosphere, including ourselves, came into being and continues to change and grow.

JR: When we experience the earth in different, beautiful ways of our choosing, we cultivate a feeling of love and concern towards it and our everyday lives benefit as this affection is extended to those around us. While experiencing nature through the media can be beneficial, having direct multi-sensory contact with nature bestows a much stronger bond.

PP: Try to spend some time in a natural environment today and take it in with all of your senses. Or, "fully sense" one object of nature (a plant or animal) nearby.

March 8

It's sometimes difficult not to be attached.

Love is not a relationship to a specific person: it is an attitude, an orientation of character which determines the relatedness of a person to the world as a whole, not toward one "object" of love. If a person loves only one other person and is indifferent to the rest of his fellow men, his love is not love but a symbiotic attachment, or an enlarged egotism. Yet, most people believe that love is constituted by an object, not by faculty. In fact, they even believe that it is a proof of the intensity of their love when they do not love anybody except the "loved" person. This is the same fallacy as the one mentioned above. If I truly love one person, I love all persons, I love the world, I love life. If I can say to somebody else, "I love you," I must be able to say, "I love in you everybody, I love through you the world, I love in you also myself."

JR: Love, as sourced here, is not only different from but in direct opposition to the romantic love typically portrayed in our love stories. In romantic love, you become singularly focused on, and often obsessed with, the object of your love, often to the absolute exclusion of all else. Your heart throbs easily at the simple thought of your lover and aches when you are separated from her. Alternatively, the "spiritual love" of this passage is ever-expansive and inclusive of all, because it's a sensation which floods your whole being and affects your relations to every being you come into contact with.

PP: Would you qualify the way you "love" others as expansive or constrictive? Does it fit your needs and the way you wish to relate with others?

March 9

Nothing like living with passion

When we live mostly in fear, trying to avoid those things which create discomfort, pain and worry, we end up closing ourselves down. We become afraid to go out or try something new, and our energy gets trapped inside, feeding on our anxiety. And we, consciously or unconsciously, use much of our energy running away from our fears, towards nothing.

But when we come to know what we love and move towards that, our lives are energized and we live with passion rather than out of fear. The main problem for most of us is that we don't know what we truly love. For example, perhaps you think it is money. However, money is only paper or metal. It isn't the money you love, but its significance—the opportunity, the experiences and things you can get with it—that you treasure. If you dig farther and farther in this way, you can find your TRUE LOVE. This, indeed, is your greatest challenge, because once it is found and you focus on moving towards that, then and only then will fear lose its power over you, and the passion of love become the source of your existence.

JR: *FIND WHAT YOU TRULY TREASURE! It sounds so simple, but this is one of the greatest challenges faced by each one of us. You think you love your car but it's the cool image which owning it gives to you that you really esteem. Why do you value this image? Because it gives you a sense of worth. And you can keep unearthing and uncovering until you find that gem called true love. Then, you become instilled with a passion to do all you can for this love, and your life is filled with purpose.*

PP: *What is something (or somebody) that you love? Why do you love it (her)? For each answer ask "WHY," and keep the question alive until you find the wellspring of your love.*

March 10

AFRAID—you better believe it, not knowing what this knucklehead has in store for me

What we think of as people's guilt is their fear. All negativity derives from fear. When someone is angry, they are afraid. When someone is rude, they are afraid. When someone is manipulative, they are afraid. When someone is cruel, they are afraid. There is no fear that love does not dissolve. There is no negativity that forgiveness does not transform.

JR: Realizing that all of our negativity is caused from being afraid can completely change the way we perceive the negative behaviours of others and ourselves. For example, when your boss shouts at you for bad work, she may be actually afraid of losing business. When you harshly criticize your son for being a dreamer, you are really worried he won't be able to make it in the real world. Achieving an understanding of the underlying fears helps you to become more compassionate and forgiving.

PP: Think of a time recently when you behaved badly. Did it arise, in reality, from the underlying fear that caused it? Understand it, learn from it, and forgive yourself.

March 11

*Moving towards,
not against*

Q: How can I handle unpleasant emotions from others?

A: Understand them. If someone is furious, see it as an outburst of his false self. A furious man acts out a false role, having no relation to reality. He has unhealthy notions that life should conform to his demands. Understand the furious man, but never coddle, for that only worsens him.

Your task is not to seek for love, but merely to seek and find all of the barriers within yourself that you have built against it. It is not necessary to seek for what is true but it is necessary to seek for what is false.

JR: It can be rather scary to love another, when you let down your defenses, become vulnerable and truly open up. But it compels a lot of energy to keep those barriers up, which eventually deadens the wall-builder since the walls prevent any fresh energy from coming in or going out. And just like the wealthy man who barricades himself from the outside world for fear of being burglarized, the life source is smothered in the mildew of his self-imposed prison.

PP: Contemplate one barrier that you have erected which prevents you from loving or being loved. How can you start to dismantle it?

March 12

Accord me your time, and I'll grant you serenity.

SON: 'Daddy, how much do you make an hour?'

DAD: 'If you must know, I make $50 an hour.'

SON: 'Oh,' the little boy replied. 'Daddy, may I borrow $25?'

The father was furious, 'You march yourself straight to your room and think about why you are being so selfish.' After about an hour or so, the man went to the little boy's room. 'I've been thinking, maybe I was too hard on you earlier' said the father. 'It's been a long day and I took out my aggravation on you. Here's the $25 you asked for.'

'Oh, thank you daddy!' he yelled. Under his pillow, he then pulled out some crumpled up bills.

'Why do you want more money if you already have some?' the father grumbled.

'Because I didn't have enough, but now I do,' the little boy replied.

'Daddy, I have $50 now. Can I buy an hour of your time? Please come home early tomorrow. I would like to have dinner with you.'

The father was crushed. He hugged his little son, and he begged for his forgiveness.

JR: What is the worth of working hard and making a lot of money if you ignore the lives most important to you? We've come to treasure being occupied with work over spending time with loved ones. When you get old, you are much more likely to savor and remember the precious times spent with family and friends than the time spent working. Sharing time and experiences with the people you really care for brings both immediate gratification and remains as a fortune which can be dug up for recollection time and again in the future.

PP: Give your undivided attention to someone close to you for 15 minutes. Your completely BEING THERE for her is much more important than the amount of time spent. Create a comforting and intimate atmosphere enabling both of you to share deeply.

March 13

The flower's lure can be healing.

To love is to be about the task of healing. The lover's vocation is to lure others (and that part of the self that nurses old injuries and fears, takes pride in autonomy, and harbors the illusion of self-sufficiency) into re-cognition of their true being and their true allegiance. It is to practice the art of forgiveness and to expand the circle of care. Love's way is always vulnerable because it abandons the rules of power-politics and the paranoid game upon which the social consensus is based.

In the passionate life, one is always in the process of forgetting one's self and becoming self-transcending spirit.

JR: True love and grooming a big ego are mutually incompatible. When you are only seeking to fulfill the ego, in terms of acquiring more power or being proud of success, it becomes impossible to recognize your deeper self, which transcends even beyond. Living egoistically implies living in separation from others while living in love means living in unity and realizing our oneness as humanity. Ego-development may be important to develop a healthy sense of self, but continually feeding it is as unhealthy as continuing to eat like you did when your body was rapidly growing at the time of adolescence.

PP: Do you continue feeding your ego? How does it affect your "love" life?

March 14

A healthy interdependent sustenance means a lot of work—but is so rewarding.

Developing a living relationship, biology informs us, runs quite contrary to the quick-fix orientation of our culture. It is time we shift our personal and societal focus from "falling in love" to "being in love." Sustaining a relationship demands care, attention and sensory inputs that are visceral, vivid and frequent.

We have the ability to emotionally change and expand the people we love. Who we are and who we become is dependent in large part on whom we love. As Dr. Martin Luther King Jr. put it: "Along the way of life, someone must have sense enough and morality enough to cut off the chain of hate. This can only be done by projecting the ethic of love to the center of our lives," since "love is mankind's most potent weapon for personal and social transformation."

JR: Contemplate the time and energy you invest in someone who you have fallen in love with. In time, hopefully, this infatuation transforms you into a loving being offering a deeper love and devotion to your loved one. Some may ask "Why trouble myself with such a burden?" Because the wellspring of love carried in the acts of compassion and caring embodies a deeper, more firmly grounded spiritual contentment compared to any short-term infatuation, with its inevitable longings and battering, ever could.

PP: Make an "act of attention" today to your love and feel the comfort that it brings to yourself and your beloved.

March 15

Go ahead and make the jump

We yield the potential to move towards creating a better environment. However, we won't do so until we "fall in love" with it. We can "grow that LOVE" by going into nature and fully experiencing it with our 5 senses—feeling the soft moss, smelling the flower's fragrance, listening to the chirping cicadas, tasting the spring-fed waters, and seeing the many plants and animals which share our lives here on earth. It is a truly miraculous existence and completely absorbing yourself in nature is the first step towards falling in love with her and committing yourself to her care as you would your own child. Could there be any more incredible feeling?

JR: Taking a big leap into the unknown can be very scary, but refusing to change our ways can be even scarier. Perceiving ourselves as separate from the natural world has allowed us to perpetrate colossal damage upon it. Only by bouncing back into this world through an integral experience and realization of our oneness with it can we again devote our efforts to the betterment of all life.

PP: Connect with any one of nature's blessings, and concentrate on it wherever you are, anything from the subtle gift of breath to a mountain's majesty.

March 16

Nature's expansive beauty is offered to all.

While the lover's identity is rooted in a transnational loyalty, there is no world community; therefore the lover, like the bodhisattva or the prodigal son, returns home to work among kinfolk, encouraging them to be more just, to open their hearts to aliens, to love their enemies.

The lover is always a prophet, standing with one foot in and one foot out of the local community. The majority will interpret the lover's criticism as an act of disloyalty, atheism, heresy against the official cult. Lovers bear the burden of being misunderstood because compassion obliges them to look upon the ideology, theology, and mythology of their own people as propaganda, which limits rather than expands consciousness.

JR: *Those who have left the greatest marks on human history are the individuals who have expanded their love beyond their own families, countries, or religions. This is because the truly spiritual person sees the same spirit in everyone around her. In doing so, her love is extended to all, and such behavior incites the criticism of many whose loyalties are still confined to a limited group.*

PP: *Becoming a "transnational lover" may be difficult for many, but extending your support to those who are is also pertinent. How can you best support someone who you think is living out this kind of expansive vision of love?*

March 17

Colorful integration adds to the whole.

We must help people develop compassion for themselves and their own lives. Part of this process involves understanding how the pain in their lives does not reflect their own personal inadequacies, but results from living in a society whose basic human relationships have been deformed by the market-driven ethos of selfishness and materialism.

JR: When a society is filled with compassion, it provides a guiding light for those who stray wayward as well as becomes a benevolent partner of the natural environment. However, to produce and structure such a society, we must first exhibit compassion for ourselves, understanding and either changing or integrating those parts of ourselves that we previously condemned. Then, and only then, can we extend a kindhearted openness to others.

PP: What part of yourself do you condemn? Try to understand why it is there and come to accept it or, if you feel the need, transform it in a way beneficial to you and to the world.

March 18

Scary to see the outcome when the foundation erodes

A tension has always existed between the capitalist imperative to maximize efficiency at any cost and the moral imperatives of culture, which historically have served as a counterweight to the moral blindness of the market. This is another example of the cultural contradictions of capitalism—the tendency over time for the economic impulse to erode the moral underpinnings of society. Mercy toward the animals in our care is one such casualty.

The industrial animal factory offers a nightmarish glimpse of what capitalism is capable of in the absence of any moral or regulatory constraint whatsoever.

JR: *An economic system is generally as good as the people who structure it, and so it is with capitalism. Problems arise when we think that capitalism can function well without any ethical base. When the instrumentalists in the capitalist system disregard morality, it becomes a system which allows the rich and powerful to destroy and crush the others. In the absence of a strong ethical foundation, no system can stand firm.*

PP: *What act of mercy can you do today towards a "weaker" being (a kind act to an animal, helping someone who is depressed or downhearted, or whatever else you can think of) as a way to introduce the light of compassion into an often disheartened, neglectful society?*

March 19

Forever becoming

Remember these two important teachings:
- No one acts inappropriately, given their model of the world.
- All attack is a call for help.

People hurt each other because they want something they think they can't have, or have something they don't want. They think that the only method of getting their way, having their desires met, etc., is to hurt another. They do not understand how to "have what they want," or "not have what they don't want," without hurting another. The problem is education, not intent.

Greet each instance of hurt with compassion and love. Compassion for others' lack of understanding (we have all been there), love for others' humanness, and their attempts—however misguided—to solve their dilemmas and keep on trying to make their lives work.

We are engaged here in a process of becoming. Of creating. Of being. Some of us are "being" more than others. That's what I call "Isness." It's just what's true.

Understand deeply that no one wants to hurt you. They simply do it inadvertently, or perhaps, indeed, on purpose, because they know no other way to have the experience they desire.

JR: What an insightful passage on the deeper reason why people usually hurt each other! When you understand that a person's attack is a result of confusion (not knowing how else to get what he wants/needs) and his conditioning, you can condition your response appropriately. You may still need to protect yourself and/or state your own needs, but you are able to do so within the framework of understanding and compassion.

PP: Who is someone who has hurt you? Look for the deeper intent driving him to cause the inadvertent hurt.

March 20

Here to heal

1) There is one question that no one will ask of those who use violence to make their point: What hurts you so bad that you feel you have to hurt me in order to heal it?

This does not condone violence, but it can help us to understand it —and to understand how to stop it. CwG (Conversations with God) says, "No one does anything inappropriate, given their model of the world." Embracing the wisdom in those eleven words could change the course of human history.

2) The next time someone hurts you, ignore the hurt and ask this question (in passage 1 above) silently, in your heart, or, if you have a particularly open and honest relationship with the other person, you can actually address the question verbally.

Try it sometime. It is a terrific argument stopper. It is a terrific abuse ender.

JR: Building from yesterday's reflection, this one digs deeper, seeking to comprehend another's pain and the underlying cause of that pain. Through grasping the deeper source of the other's distress, you can be more understanding of the real reason behind her lashing out. And perhaps even more importantly, by realizing the root of your own emotional malaise, you can search for ways to heal the wound without inflicting injury on others.

PP: Who are you hurting now, in actions or in words? What is the cause of your hurt that is making you do this, and in what way can you better deal with it, moving towards healing?

March 21

It can feel lonely being different.

When you face differences with people of other faiths that present challenges to both of you, and your emotions intensify, remember to ask yourself this key question: "What does it feel like to be the other?"

JR: When you get caught up in feelings of intense frustration or anger, it becomes impossible to see the perceived cause of this feeling objectively. To step back and try to view the situation from the other's perspective may be the most difficult, but most rewarding, thing you can do. This is because, when you do so, your rage is subdued and you can relate to him as a feeling human being rather than as an evil enemy.

PP: Who do you most despise? Put yourself in his shoes and try to understand why he acts and talks as he does.

March 22

Talk about feeling distraught—It's so lonely up here

The pattern laid down by the ancients for calming distraught or inconsolable people was: First of all you identify with, rather than blame them. ("You're in pain. I'm sorry.") Then you give them some detachment by reminding them of the first thing we all lose sight of when we're in such a state—that what they're going through is a universal human experience. '"Everybody has pain in their life." Remember Hamlet's uncle: "You must know your father lost a father. That father lost his..."') You can also remind him or her that the unbearable moment they are experiencing has got to pass, and finally exhort them to snap out of it. ("We can work it out.")

JR: At times, when you fall into despair, it seems like it will never end. It's a miserable feeling of being separated from others and isolated. Therefore, when a friend comes and connects with you, highlighting that you are not alone, the healing begins. Slowly, by realizing that this type of distress affects everyone to some degree, you feel re-connected and become aware that, similar to others, you too will break out of it and the light will return.

PP: Who is someone you care for who is feeling down? Try this three step process with her to start the healing process.

March 23

*Get closer and
truly experience*

1) There's only one way to come to understand the other person's story, and that's by being curious. Certainty locks us out of their story; curiosity lets us in.

2) Anytime you think a conversation might be difficult, keep the following 3 purposes front and center in your consciousness:

- Learning their story
- Expressing your views and feelings
- Problem-solving together

JR: Being curious about another, listening to her story to understand where she's coming from and how she came to be who she now is, is a wonderful way to connect with her and encourage her to do the same for you. Unfortunately, many religious teachings insist that they are the one and only correct path and, in effect, they close off any possibility of objective seeking and understanding, since the believer of such a faith is certain she is right (so the other is wrong). Opening yourself to the possibility of other correct paths and trying to learn from them can help you connect with all kinds of people who were "inaccessible" before.

PP: Find someone who is very different from you and invite him to tell his story. How did he come to be as he is? Listen as objectively as you can.

March 24

Discover your kin all around

When someone asked the Vietnamese Zen poet Thich Nhat Hanh, "What do we need to do to save our world?" his questioner expected him to identify strategies for social and environmental action. But he answered: "What we most need to do is to hear within us the sound of the Earth crying." When the Canadian geneticist David Suzuki met E.O. Wilson, he had one big question for the eminent biologist: "What can we do to stop the catastrophic level of extinction that's going on around the world?" Wilson surprised the younger man with his reply. "We have to discover our kin," he said simply. "We have to discover our relatives, the other plants and animals who are related to us through our DNA. Because to know our kin is to come to love and cherish them."

Conditions are right for a sharp turn in the direction that elders like Wilson and Thich Nhat Hanh recommend. Most of humanity want to know how to make the change.

It's not a matter of having better information, nor of having the right politics. It's a matter of moral imagination, a wisdom of the heart.

JR: Families can be so irritating, partly because they know you well and know how to push your buttons. But healthy families also encourage each other to grow and develop their own unique capabilities. The loving feeling of the nuclear family is so important for the healthy development of the children. And the very same feeling of love for the world family of living beings must be cultivated in order to grow and maintain a healthy environment for the planet. Presently, we are sorely lacking in the embellishment of this feeling of kinship.

PP: Truly feel all of life as being one family, since we all have the "breath of life." How does this perception make you want to treat other living beings?

March 25

Please resist the urge to pluck however tempting it may be

Being sensitive means, surely, to have a tender feeling for things: to see an animal suffering and do something about it, to remove a stone from the path because so many bare feet walk there, to pick up a nail on the road because somebody's car might get a puncture. To be sensitive is to feel for people, for birds, for flowers, for trees—not because they are yours, but just because you are awake to the extraordinary beauty of things. And how is this sensitivity to be brought about?

The moment you are deeply sensitive, you naturally do not pluck the flowers; there is a spontaneous desire not to destroy things, not to hurt people, which means having real respect, love. To love is the most important thing in life. But what do we mean by love? When you love someone because that person loves you in return, surely that is not love. To love is to have that extraordinary feeling of affection without asking anything in return.

JR: Even good-hearted people cause a great deal of harm to life, most often unconsciously, through killing insects, picking a flower and giving it to your love, eating meat, and other analogous actions. Our society doesn't teach us to be sensitive to other life forms, or to fully appreciate the uniqueness and the beauty of a blooming flower, a flowing stream, or a meadow teeming with life. So it is up to each of us to bring such sensitivity into our own lives and, better yet, discover ways of teaching it to others.

PP: Look for a way you can commit a sensitively caring act to a plant or an animal today.

March 26

Only you can free yourself.

"Our task must be to free ourselves from this prison by widening our circle of compassion to embrace all living creatures and the whole of nature in its beauty."

JR: The majority of our preset ideas of love and compassion have trapped us into an exclusivity mindset where I love those close to me while remaining indifferent (or worse, hateful) towards those outside of my intimate circle of relationships. In a spiritual sense though, your love is meant to become ever more expansive and inclusive, thereby freeing your spirit to be compassionate to all.

PP: How far does your love and compassion reach out? What is one way in which you can stretch it a bit farther?

March 27

Problems wither when the spiritual and the physical are fully integrated.

We must remember that the world's current problems are fundamentally a spiritual crisis, created by the limited vision of human beings—a loss of a sense of connection to one another, a loss of community, and most deeply a loss of connection to our spiritual values.

Political and economic change have never been sufficient in themselves to alleviate suffering when the underlying causes are not also addressed. The worst problems on this earth—warfare, poverty, ecological destruction, and so forth—are created from greed, hatred, prejudice, delusion, and fear in the human mind. To expand the circle of our practice and to face the sorrow in the world around us, we must face these forces in ourselves. Einstein called us nuclear giants and ethical infants. Only when we have found a compassion, a goodness and understanding, that transcends our own greed, hatred, and delusion, can we bring freedom alive in the world around us.

JR: We must face the sadness in ourselves in order to truly experience the sorrow in the world—and then move towards a combined healing. We often hide or suppress our feelings of sadness and woe in order to appear happy to those around us. This results in the covert hijacking of other feelings since they aren't appropriately released. Find the sadness and allow it to be expressed.

PP: What sorrow do you feel right now? What is the cause of it and how can you move towards healing?

March 28

*A sense of community—
so comforting*

Community can only be built when empathy for each person is part of framing the problem. The major issues in our country will continue to prompt the politics of personal destruction if we do not strive to understand life from the other person's point of view. We do not need to agree with each other, but we need to listen and love and admit they have reason to believe what they do.

The struggle for a country dedicated to the common good does not demand that we be less passionate in our advocacy, but it will not come without each side feeling respected and valued.

JR: It is often said that people have become too isolated from one another, which warrants a need of more sense of community. How true, and how futile, this harping is without ensuring a desirable way to bring people together. Understanding that you are also part of the problem and trying to understand the other side are key. No wonder so many people wish to be alone—relationships can be troublesome when not approached respectfully. When our communication and relationships become compassionate, a conducive community spirit will surely follow.

PP: Think of one of your primary relationships. What is the problem with it, and how are you part of the problem? Admit it to yourself (or, better yet, to the other) and see what you can do to move towards resolving it.

March 29

*The question is how
to stay rooted.*

We must be brave enough to love one another, to tolerate one another's religion, even prejudices and superstitions, and to trust one another. This requires faith in oneself.

> *Love never claims, it ever gives. Love ever suffers, never resents, never revenges itself. Our ability to reach unity in diversity will be the beauty and the test of our civilization.*

JR: How do you stay rooted and firmly believe in yourself, particularly in a world enveloped with several competing perspectives? The person who is able to feel the oneness of life in the midst of such diversity is the one exhibiting a strong faith and is not afraid of those who are different. Rather, she shows her faith in word and action and also inspires others. She never tries to raze another's faith, realizing that it can lead to a spiritual crisis in the other, but encourages people of every faith to move towards its firmly-grounded goodness.

PP: What is it that keeps you rooted in this complex world? How can you make this foundation stronger?

March 30

River and rock—the symbiosis of opposites

Charter for Compassion

The principle of compassion lies at the heart of all religious, ethical, and spiritual traditions, calling us always to treat all others as we wish to be treated ourselves.

Compassion impels us to work tirelessly to alleviate the suffering of our fellow creatures, to dethrone ourselves from the center of the world and put another there, and to honor the inviolable sanctity of every single human being, treating everybody, without exception, with absolute justice, equity, and respect.

We urgently need to make compassion a clear, luminous, and dynamic force in our polarized world. Rooted in a principled determination to transcend selfishness, compassion can break down political, dogmatic, ideological, and religious boundaries. Born of our deep interdependence, compassion is essential to human relationships and to a fulfilled humanity. It is the path to enlightenment, and indispensable to the creation of a just economy and a peaceful global community.

JR: Water is so soft but, over time, can smoothen even the most jagged of rocks. Likewise, compassion can temper the hardest of souls. When more and more people flow in the river of compassion, even the roughest character can be softened, and the subsequent realization of our interdependence moves us into calmer waters.

PP: What is the main barrier that prevents you from being more compassionate? How can you start tearing it down?

March 31

So pleasing to the eye of the beholder

"All the joy the world contains
Has come through wishing happiness for others;
All the misery the world contains
Has come through wanting pleasure for oneself."

JR: Pleasing others is often considered as denying oneself, and self-sacrificial. Making yourself happy while pleasing another is ideal, but when immediate gratification isn't possible, witness how delighting another brings goodness into your life in a more significant way. At the same time, reflect how doing something pleasurable only limited to yourself typically provides a fleeting, good feeling rather than a deep-seated joyful sensation.

PP: Think of something pleasurable you did only for yourself vs. something you did both for yourself and for another. Which one had a greater overall effect?

APRIL

Nonviolence & Sustainability

The concept of non-violence includes an outer and an inner dimension, simply understood as not harming others (or yourself) deliberately, physically or intangibly.

Both within the self as well as in the physical world, the opposite of non-violence, i.e. violence, diffuses bitterness and creates a threatening environment that necessitates an aggressive spirit. It drives living beings (or the variant aspects of the self) apart, and is most often caused by the lack of empowerment. On the other hand, a non-violent spirit and society encourages creativity and cooperation, appealing to the unity of our existence. Non-violence doesn't imply not hating evil actions, but it does mean engendering a spirit that does not hate the person. It doesn't mean denying your anger (which always leads to its coming out in other violent ways), but rather transforming it into a force for good. A vital component of non-violence is to learn forgiveness since, as long as you are unable to forgive, you are letting the past control you and engendering a spirit full of bitterness and remorse—in effect, committing violence to yourself.

Non-violence is closely connected to the concept of sustainability. A life which is sustained by violent acts, including the destruction of other people and/or lifeforms (deliberately or not), is unsustainable as it destroys the foundation of its very existence. While it is impossible to completely eliminate violence from life, moving increasingly towards a life-engendering, non-harmful way of life is both more sustainable and, in the long run, more fulfilling.

For those of us leading a materialistic lifestyle, living more simply can be a way to decrease damage to the physical world at the same time as help us to focus more on what is truly important (relationships, self-actualization, love), making us encounter life more directly. The increasing enjoyment of these delights influences a decreasing desire for more material things. Subsequently, our lifestyles, in turn, become more sustainable, creating more "space" for other living beings (poor people, plants, and animals) to flourish as well. Significantly, with this change, our being no longer needs more outside material goods to become fulfilled, but comes to find its own ways to produce self-fulfillment. You become your own master!

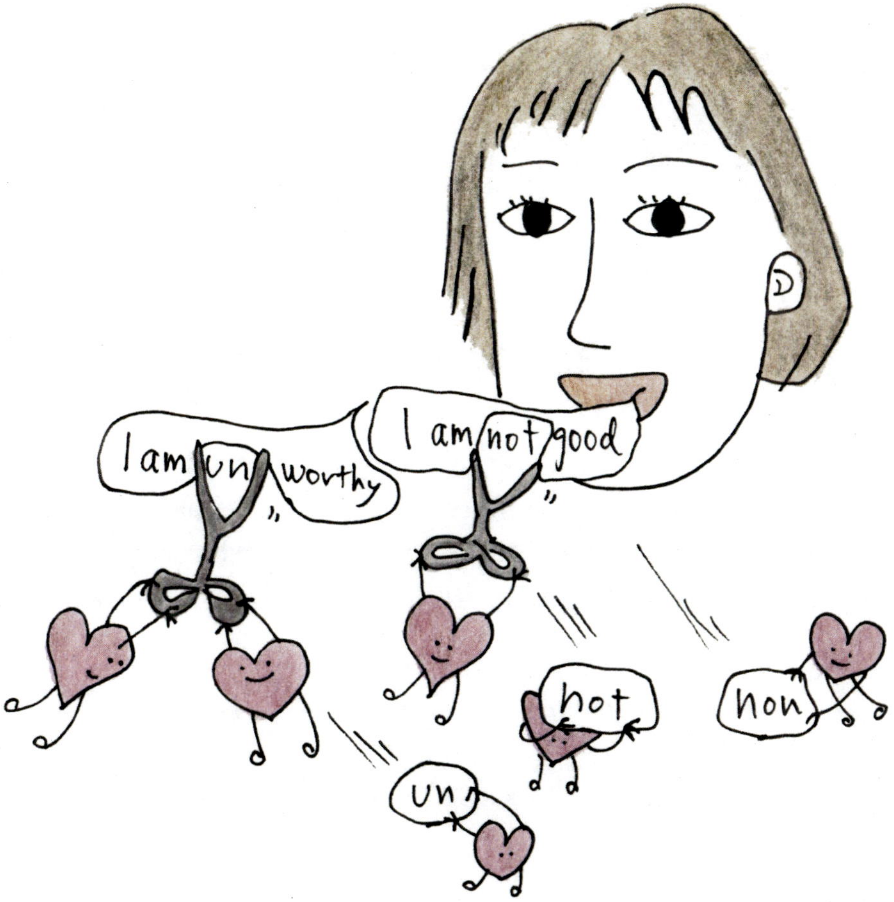

I am not good
I am un worthy
not
un
non

April 1
Love peace

"Instead of hating people you think are war makers, hate the appetites and disorder in your own soul, which are the causes of war. If you love peace, then hate injustice, hate tyranny, hate greed—but hate these things in yourself, not in another."

JR: It is much easier for us to hate others and to criticize their cruel intentions and evil ways than to look within and introspect. It's easier because there is usually little, if anything, we can effectively do about it, which justifies our inaction. On reflection, when we see those things in ourselves, it is more difficult to pardon a do-nothing attitude, since we do have the capacity to work on ourselves.

PP: What attitude do you have that you don't like? Don't condemn it, but rather contemplate how it would be possible to start transforming it into something desirable to you.

April 2

Living life with open arms

Always remember that your state of mind and the resulting goal you will achieve are in your own hands, because there are really only two things you can do—judge as an expression of fear, or forgive as an expression of love. One perception leads to the peace of God and the other perception leads to war.

JR: When your emotions are aroused, it is difficult, if not impossible, to guide your state of mind, which makes it that much more important to train it at other times. Constant judging and fighting against others whom you are most likely unable to exert an effect upon leads to an eternal and internal struggle. When you are able to cultivate a forgiving state of mind, you advent peace within your core. Which would your rather have?

PP: What (who) can't you forgive? Why not? What are you afraid of?

April 3

The epitome of nature's transmutation

"I have learned through bitter experience the one supreme lesson to conserve my anger, and as heat conserved is transmuted into energy, even so our anger controlled can be transmuted into a power that can move the world."

JR: Look at the wisdom of these cherry trees, which shed their leaves in autumn, conserve their energy in the cold of winter, and then, upon the return of the warm days of spring, explode with flowers and the leaves which sustain them. We can benefit much from their humble example, through finding ways to release our pent-up energy in ways that make us grow rather than cause us to self-destruct. Anger is a powerful force, and it is up to you whether or not to direct it into a constructive channel.

PP: When was a time that you couldn't control your anger and you let it fly with no holding back? What was the result? Looking back, could you have better transmuted it into a beneficial force?

April 4

Your mindset is reflected in your life deeds.

Forgiveness is crucial to our well-being and to our integrity.

It says in A Course in Miracles, "The Holiest place on earth is where an ancient hatred has become a present love."

Remember, forgiveness is for you. It's about releasing the past, so it no longer has control over you. It is a commitment to your own well-being and to your own peace of mind. Ultimately, forgiveness is a choice.

When you recognize how holding on to old resentments has affected the quality of your life, you'll be ready to let go of your role as victim.

JR: Harboring resentments against others and holding onto past hurts negatively affect the beholder most. Why do you continue to hurt yourself? While forgiveness may be good for the forgiven, through forgiveness, primarily the forgiver is relieved of carrying a load burdening his life. Getting rid of this baggage which pulls him back, he is then able to move on and improve his life and relationships, less hindered by the bitterness of his past.

PP: What resentment do you hold about the past? How can you release it, forgive it, and move on towards a more spirit-liberating future of your own making?

April 5

All mixed up? Please try to understand why

The very pragmatic necessity of nonviolent social change was expressed eloquently by Martin Luther King, Jr.:

The old law of an eye for an eye leaves everybody blind. It is immoral because it seeks to humiliate the opponent rather than win his understanding; it seeks to annihilate rather than to convert. Violence is immoral because it thrives on hatred rather than love. It destroys community and makes brotherhood impossible. It leaves society in monologue rather than dialogue. Violence ends by defeating itself. It creates bitterness in the survivors and brutality in the destroyers.

JR: When we refuse to make a sincere effort to understand the other and find constructive ways to settle conflict, we adopt the less mentally strenuous method of destruction and violence. Each one of us is mixed up and confused to some degree, so rather than criticizing others, it is imperative to understand. This could possibly shine a light on some of your own confusion in addition to initiating the first step towards peaceful resolution.

PP: In what part of your life does confusion reign? Find someone who has struggled with similar confusion (a personal friend, writer, public figure) and seek out her wisdom.

April 6

This can pave the way for a rewarding future, or you can squash it.

"We kill at every step, not only in wars, riots, and executions. We kill when we close our eyes to poverty, suffering, and shame. In the same way, all disrespect for life, all hard-heartedness, all indifference, all contempt is nothing else than killing. With just a little witty skepticism we can kill a good deal of the future in a young person. Life is waiting everywhere, the future is flowering everywhere, but we only see a small part of it and step on much of it with our feet."

JR: Killing is typically considered as the physical termination of life. But through harsh words, discouragement, and mocking, we kill a soul's dreams and fruitful energy. As a society, we commit these horrendous acts to such an extent that many people accept a life of "just getting by," lacking any hope for something better. Fortunately, nature shows that life springs up whenever a seed is planted in the fertile earth. It is up to us to provide such a productive soil where good-hearted hopes and dreams can take root and grow abundantly.

PP: Encourage someone you know to try out something he is excited about, but hesitant to do.

April 7

Rigidified—permanently on guard

1) Remember that in a threatening environment, the human brain becomes permanently organized for aggression. Has this happened to your enemy?

2) "The most potent weapon in the hands of the oppressor is the mind of the oppressed."

JR: *Our minds are conditioned by the surrounding environment. If there is constant war and violence around us, how can we not be programmed to be constantly on the defensive and daring to lash out at any time? Fighting against an opponent with such a mindset will only reinforce it, resulting in a cycle of violence. Finding ways to make his environment safer and, in effect, dismantle his aggressive tendencies is a much surer road to peace.*

PP: Think of "an enemy," near or far, who seems permanently aggressive. Is there anything you can do personally, or as a member of society, to create conditions to pacify his mindset?

April 8

How much more must I give before you are satisfied?

The roots of violence are both external and internal, the environmental and psychological. Yet the two are not separate. They interconnect and feed one another, just as external sense objects interconnect with the senses, giving rise to consciousness and psychological processes. If a people's environment is unhealthy, corrupt or unjust, the seeds are sown for violent resistance, through the growth of motivating ideologies which take on a life of their own as they grip the minds of those who are being oppressed. If the environment is excessively competitive, consumer-oriented and materialistic, an "aggressive personality" (tanha) will quickly arise, develop and expand into obsessive patterns of greed, taking over and dominating the perception of people who find themselves victims of craving rather than masters of their own perceptual processes.

The step to violence is then small. If other elements are present, such as a group without access to the wealth visible in others, discrimination against minorities or racism, then the drive towards violence will be more rapid.

JR: As a society, we must constantly question as to how we are contributing towards augmenting and creating the violence around us. Blaming others is fruitless, as we can only truly change ourselves. On a personal level, becoming more grateful and satisfied with what you are and what you have leads to a more serene spirit abetting a more non-violent lifestyle.

PP: When do you most feel at peace? How can you bring more of these moments into your life?

April 9

Live harmoniously— that's the only way we can survive

Peace as a state of lasting harmonious relations between nations is only possible when the having structure is replaced by the being structure. The idea that one can build peace while encouraging the striving for possessions and profit is an illusion, and a dangerous one, because it deprives people of recognizing that they are confronted with a clear alternative: either a radical change of their character or the perpetuity of war.

JR: When we live and lead our lives aligned to achieve more and more (materially), we can't help but to create a violent social structure. Our constant grasping inevitably leads to conflict with those who are barely surviving or others who are trying to achieve the same thing. However, when we focus on "being good" and seek out ways to share and care, our relationships become stronger and more harmonious, diminishing violent confrontations.

PP: Which do you choose—having more or being more? If you choose "having more," question yourself as to why you want more. If you choose "being more," ask yourself how you can become a better person with the people/situations currently in your life.

April 10

Remain centered and firm—refuse to be polarized

The first requirement of war is polarization. In peacemaking, a third party suddenly stands outside that framework; he or she dissolves that simple polarization by embodying the longing for peace that is above all labels and hatreds.

JR: In the heat of battle (interpersonal or international), it is natural to get fixated on our rightness and their wrongness. It is this polarized perspective which allows the conflict to fester and spiral out of control. When we can step back and acknowledge the other side's perspective, and the possibility that we are not always 100% right, we have taken the initiative and made the first move towards breaking out of the cycle of violence and moving towards peace.

PP: Contemplate an ongoing conflict that you now have; it may either be interpersonal or within yourself. Try to understand both perspectives, find common ground, and move towards a mutually acceptable resolution or, if that's not possible, a peaceful co-existence.

April 11

Choose your focus wisely

1) Thinking of violence as disease takes blame out of the picture. It puts our focus where it belongs, where efficiency and compassion want it to go—on prevention.

2) The only way to take the inevitability out of war is to give young people something else to do with their restless energy.

JR: Where you focus your thoughts and energies largely determines the direction of your life. Looking at the United States and its politics, the focus is clearly on presenting a tough guy image and developing weapons and a strong military, as is reflected in the use of the nation's funds. The result is constant war. Shifting the focus to the creation of good and building a caring society would do much to eliminate the root causes of war.

PP: What is the primary focus in your life? Is that leading you in the direction you wish to go?

April 12

The fog sometimes hides the glory.

Violence is keyed to the lowest image of the human being. Nonviolence is keyed to the most exalted. This is one of the reasons violence drives us apart, while nonviolence appeals directly to the mysterious unity among all of us, which is the hidden glory in each of us. It is one of the reasons that a nonviolent attitude leads to works that confer a sense of meaning while a life of violence confers, at best, fleeting and shallow satisfactions.

JR: Our society has often come to equate power with the ability to exert more violent force, and marking it as something deserving of respect. Concurrently, we criticize the adolescent's lashing out against society as a waste of youthful energy. Isn't our use of force the same? When we are able to use our appeal on others with soft power, and draw them to us with our ideas and ideals, our lives are venerated far more than by manipulating them with physical coercion.

PP: Who do you know from the people around you who is floundering, unsure of himself and "wasting his energy" in destructive pursuits? Tell him about a good (creative and uplifting) quality he has and share your respect for him underpinned by that quality.

April 13

It's tough to grow into such natural beauty.

Lincoln knew the tendency of victors in a grueling conflict was to seek vengeance, and of the vanquished to turn bitter. He argued that both sides should bear in mind their shared wrong and see their common opportunity. He concluded: "With malice toward none; with charity for all; with firmness in the right, as God gives us to see the right, let us strive on to finish the work we are in; to bind up the nation's wounds; to care for him who shall have borne the battle, and for his widow, and his orphan—to do all which may achieve and cherish a just and lasting peace among ourselves, and with all nations."

JR: How tempting it is to rub the loser's face in the dirt after a tortuous victory. And how good it feels to the victor. Yet, the enlightened soul, like Abraham Lincoln (in the writing above), is aware that this simply plants the seed for future conflict. Contrarily, showing compassion and healing the wounds bring about the possibility of a glorified society which currently exists only in our ideals.

PP: Think of a recent victory you "scored" in a personal relationship and how you reacted. Consider how the other must have felt and express caring and compassion towards her to heal the rupture the conflict may have caused.

April 14

Time to understand "why?"

The entire training program (for civil disobedience) was to get people to think about how to put yourself in another person's position and see the world through their eyes. That was so helpful for me in being able to embrace nonviolence.

We practiced "loving, not judging" your opponent, but thinking about the fact that there was a reason your opponent behaves the way they do.

JR: The only way we can move towards a firmly grounded and peaceful society is to deepen our capacity for understanding others' viewpoints and actions. This doesn't imply that you necessarily agree with what they are doing, but rather, through understanding, find ways to co-exist harmoniously and build on the shared commonalities.

PP: Think of a friend or family member who has some idea or does something that really irks you. Try to understand why he thinks (or does) so. If you have no idea, ask him (in a non-judgmental tone of voice), stating that you simply want to understand.

April 15

No question where the impact is here

The dynamics for principles of classic nonviolence are the same: the consciousness-raising impact of the "new" force, the way non-violent resisters mobilize that force by refusing to identify the humanity of the individual aggressor with his intention (the sin is not the sinner), and finally the dramatic declaration that success is primarily spiritual and long-term rather than visible and immediate. These are all familiar landmarks of nonviolence, and each of these principles has been known to work.

JR: Nature has no problem creating an impact with its multitude of colors, shapes and unique living characters which it is constantly molding and re-configuring. IF WE ONLY STOP TO TAKE NOTICE. Nonviolence, too, is most effective when people notice, which they do when the action is uniquely carried out and makes people feel a sense of "the divine made earthly."

PP: Commit a nonviolent act (or a random act of kindness) that will leave a deep impression on someone.

April 16

Create loving relations

Studies conducted in 1972 showed that 24 US cities, each with populations over ten thousand, experienced a statistically measurable reduction in crime when as few as one percent (one hundred people for every ten thousand) of the population participated in some form of meditative practice. This became known as the "Maharishi Effect."

For centuries, prophets and sages have suggested that one-tenth of one percent of humanity, working together in a unified effort, may shift the consciousness of the entire world.

JR: Rare is the individual who creates a great effect on the world by herself. Her vitality and charisma may be a trigger, but it is the combined work of innumerable co-conspirators that amplifies the influence she exerts. Finding the right people to work with to help spread your good ideas or good action will generate a deeper and longer lasting effect.

PP: Who is someone who you resonate with, in terms of your ideals or good actions? Talk with him about what you can do together to better live them out and project yourselves as exemplars in your community. Eventually, bring others in as well.

April 17

With true empowerment, there is no violence.

1) "In violence, we forget who we are."

2) Andrew Schneider describes violence as an issue of power. People become violent when they feel powerless. Violence is used as an inappropriate way of attempting to re-establish one's own sense of power over whatever or whomever is perceived as a threat.

The antidote to violence in ourselves and in society is empowerment. We need to empower people to live out their best without fear. When people feel strong and able within themselves, they do not see themselves as potential victims. They do not have to struggle against others in order to feel secure. The curriculum for empowerment is learning and loving.

JR: This passage runs counter to what many of us believe—that violence is used by the powerful. This belief begs the question "What does power mean?" When it implies the ability to force people to obey you, violence can be considered as an important form of power (at the expense of destroying another's). However, correspondingly, a lot of energy is required to feed that strength. When one develops the ability to lure people towards her way of thinking and way of life with the inspiration she provides, both the giver and the receivers are vitalized, and this leads to the cultivation of empowerment all around.

PP: What can you do to empower yourself (without exerting power over others), so that you are more actively choosing (rather than passively enduring) the life you truly wish to live?

April 18

How difficult to overcome the ego, especially when you are so beautiful

"Islam means 'in peace.' For us, peace is paramount. When we meet someone we greet each other by saying 'Peace be with you.' So peace is the essence of Islam."

"Jihad does not mean war, it means struggle. What is our struggle? Our first and foremost struggle is to fight against our ego and overcome our pride. We must defeat the forces of anger. That is jihad. Then we struggle against injustice, against the exploitation of the weak by the strong."

JR: All of the world's major religions are manipulated to a certain extent by some of the power holders, particularly those for whom holding the power is more important than following the true message of the religion. One of the fundamental teachings of Islam, as with the other world religions, is to strive towards peace. This is achieved when we overcome our ego, our separateness, and become conscious of our unity, which then directs us towards creating a just society where exploitation is taboo. How much better off we'd all be if we focused on embodying this unity in our lives rather than ceaselessly harping on the abuses in our own and in others' religions.

PP: In what ways has your ego hijacked your soul? How does your desire for status, sex, power, or money destroy your capacity to do good to others (and, ultimately, to yourself)?

April 19

What can be more important than preserving this?

The speed of today's production, driven by an insatiable desire for more, virtually guarantees us no time to care about important issues (i.e. about the painful slaughter of animals).

Asceticism is not a flight from society and the world, but a communal attitude of mind and way of life that leads to the respectful use, and not the abuse of material goods. Excessive consumption may be understood to issue from a world-view of estrangement from self, from land, from life, and from God. Consuming the fruits of the earth unrestrained, we become consumed ourselves, by avarice and greed. Excessive consumption leaves us emptied, out-of-touch with our deepest self. Asceticism is a corrective practice, a vision of repentance. Such a vision will lead us from repentance to return, the return to a world in which we give, as well as take, from creation.

JR: In today's world, an efficient accomplishment of things and being busy are considered valuable. And there is an established direct relationship between our emphasis on these two "values" and our lack of caring, loving, and playing. We should ask ourselves how we can come to love someone, when our priority is to be busy and focus singularly on efficiency? Demonstrating love to another necessitates time and energy. From a "work efficiency" viewpoint, this, as well as some forms of morality (like treating animals humanely) and the joy of play, would be considered as wasteful and fruitless.

PP: How much sway does staying busy and being efficient hold in your life? If it's too much, how can you engender more balance (between them and the caring, playful parts of your life)?

April 20

The less you carry herein, the higher your spirit can soar.

Once we change our possessions we have a very hard time going back down. Ownership simply changes our perspective. Suddenly, moving backward to our pre-ownership state is a loss, one that we cannot abide. And so, while moving up in life, we indulge ourselves with the fantasy that we can always ratchet ourselves back if need be; but in reality, we can't. Downgrading to a smaller home, for instance, is experienced as a loss, it is psychologically painful, and we are willing to make all kinds of sacrifices in order to avoid such losses.

JR: *We seldom consider how our income level traps us into a certain lifestyle and way of thinking. It's natural to mingle with others belonging to a similar socio-economic class; therefore, if we find ourselves suddenly getting a significantly lower income, we either feel ashamed or end up grudgingly changing our friends aligned to our "lowered status." However, the few who purposely downsize hold out a ray of hope, in that they generally express a freedom and joy in escaping from their previously materialistic lifestyle.*

PP: *How does your socio-economic level effectively shape your lifestyle and acquaintances? Does this concur with your deeply held values? If not, how can you better integrate them?*

April 21

Want a treat? Open your eyes and soak it in

We fail to realize how many of our modern amenities are the outcome of boredom. The basic rule of the affluent society is: when bored, go out and buy something; so our homes are full of gadgets we seldom use. Man of the Golden Age found everything so interesting that he felt no need to spice his life with variety. When he wanted to give himself a treat, he went and sat on a hilltop or looked at the stars.

JR: Why is it that many of us turn on the TV when we're bored? Or start to play video games? Or go shopping to fill our emptiness? And why is it that these things provide immediate gratification and stimulation which quickly fades? It is because the thrill is so addictive that we forget those less intense but much more gratifying pleasures which soothe the soul. Re-experiencing and soaking in these pleasures make it impossible to feel bored.

PP: What do you do when you get bored? How long does the thrill last? What soulfully uplifting activity can you do instead to fill the emptiness?

April 22

Tough to sustain integrity—but marvel at the incredible result

We invest in organic-food companies but have kitchens stocked with processed foods. We give money to Greenpeace but drive an SUV. We understand the risks of mad cow disease, but don't think we are related to it in any meaningful way by the cheeseburger on our plate.

We reckon such dissonance to be an unavoidable consequence of the scale and complexity of modern life. Yet this reckoning is what makes violence possible. Disconnecting our personal actions from the world theater, we unleash the power of impersonal institutions to act in ways that we would never act ourselves. We let institutions do the dirty work for us.

It is only by addressing this dissonance, by beginning to reduce it, that we can begin to effect a systemic change that is the only hope of lasting peace. Peace depends on nonviolent economies. Nonviolent economies depend on nonviolent households.

Reducing violence, not maximizing growth, would be the primary goal of an economy that was oriented toward enhancing human well-being. Reducing dissonance, not maximizing financial return, would be the primary goal of investments that were oriented toward reducing violence.

JR: *Our global society makes it nearly impossible to understand the way our lifestyle and consumption choices affect other people, living things, and natural environments. Ah! What a wonderful excuse to avoid any responsibility. Yet, our every purchase has an effect, and we ignore that at our own peril. The very unethical behaviors we so often criticize could well be a result of what we are buying. Our words are completely worthless until we become more dedicated to backing our purchases with what we say.*

PP: *Think of one product that you love and try to identify the "ethical standing" of the company that makes it. Does it satisfy you, or do you feel like you should start looking for a different company's product?*

April 23

No need to work in order to be

An American businessman was at the pier of a coastal Mexican village when a small boat with just one fisherman docked. Inside the small boat were several large yellow fin tuna. The American complimented the Mexican on the quality of his fish and asked how long it took to catch them.

The Mexican replied, "Only a little while."

The American then asked, "But what do you do with the rest of your time?"

The fisherman said, "I sleep late, fish a little, play with my children, take siesta with my wife, stroll into the village each evening where I sip wine and play guitar with my amigos."

The American scoffed, "You should spend more time fishing and with the proceeds buy a bigger boat. With the proceeds from the bigger boat you could buy several boats, eventually you would have a fleet of fishing boats."

The fisherman asked, "But senor, how long will this all take?"

To which the American replied, "15-20 years."

"But what then, senor?"

The American laughed and said, "That's the best part. When the time is right you would sell everything and become very rich. You would make millions."

"Millions, senor? Then what?"

The American said, "Then you would retire. Move to a small coastal fishing village where you would sleep late, fish a little, play with your kids, take siesta with your wife, stroll to the village in the evenings where you could sip wine and play your guitar with your amigos."

JR: What a wonderful story demonstrating the importance of exploring the question "What do I really want in this life?" We work hard to make money, but to what purpose? Could it be that the Mexican was much more in tune with his life force, choosing to live as he wanted here and now rather than sentencing himself to 20 years of "hard labor" before doing so?

PP: What do you most crave in this life? How can you start to move towards it here and now?

April 24

At times, staying buttoned-up is better than getting carried away by expectations.

1) The most important finding of all is that happiness does not really depend on objective conditions of either wealth, health or even community. Rather, it depends on the correlation between objective conditions and subjective expectations.

2) If happiness is determined by expectations, then two pillars of our society—mass media and the advertising industry—may unwittingly be depleting the globe's reservoirs of contentment.

JR: If I expect to get a salary increase, but don't get it (while others do), I become unhappy. On the other hand, an unemployed person is delighted at landing a minimum wage job. As a society, we fashion unrealistic expectations and cultivate a discouraged population. A perfect example is the many young women who feel excessively insecure due to the beautiful models who are seen all over the mass media. Advertising companies then profit from this insecurity by selling beauty products; however, it is nearly impossible to be as physically enticing as a model, thus leading to frustration. What an insane world, and it's one that nearly all of us are complicit in making.

PP: What expectation of yours is not being met? How does it make you feel? How can you adapt it so that it becomes more attainable and pleasing for you?

April 25

Let it ring

The Bicycle:

- Encourages you to use your senses—smelling the freshly mowed grass, listening to the birds sing, seeing the changing contours of the land, and feeling the coolness of the breeze
- Allows you to have direct contact with your surrounding environment, not being trapped within the confines of a vehicle's glass and metal
- Makes you smile
- Provides prime time for personal reflection
- Saves you money, since there is little maintenance and no fuel cost
- Doesn't pollute the environment
- Is good for mind (good meditation time) and body (exercise)

JR: Something as simple as a bicycle can accord several benefits. Our problem is that we don't let ourselves truly experience life. On the contrary, most of our everyday work lives prevent us from getting out and contacting other life forms outside of our work environment. We lock ourselves in buildings and vehicles for most of our lives and cut ourselves off from the rest of the living world. What a joy it can be to go out and reconnect!

PP: Go out for a ride on your bicycle or take a walk, and feel how refreshingly different it is than speeding about in a vehicle that walls you in, separating you from the environment surrounding you.

April 26

Take it all in and come alive

When you have enjoyed something intensely, you need very little.

Slow down and taste and smell and hear, and let your senses come alive. If you want a royal road to mysticism, sit down quietly and listen to all the sounds around you. You do not focus on any one sound; you try to hear them all. Oh, you'll see the miracles that happen to you when your senses come unclogged. That is extremely important for the process of change.

JR: The problem for many of us is not that we have too little, but that we actually sense too little. In order to get our work done or because of our addictions, our senses become underutilized and dull. Just like a junk food addict who can no longer appreciate healthy food, our junk culture prevents our senses from experiencing the uplifting natural pleasures of life. Enliven the senses to nourish your spirit.

PP: Take 10 minutes sometime today to go out, preferably to a natural area, and take in the whole environment with all of your senses. Feel how it invigorates your spirit.

April 27

True wealth fears neither rust nor moth.

With regard to things, total renunciation of the having structure is demanded. The oldest community insisted on the radical renunciation of property; it warns against collecting riches: 'Do not lay up for yourselves treasures on earth, where moth and rust consume and where thieves break in and steal. For where your treasure is, there will your heart be also'.

JR: Pretty radical stuff this is! One can justifiably argue that giving up all possessions in today's world is not possible, especially when others are dependent on you. Yet, the emphasis of the message here is to most treasure those things which can't be owned—namely, the gifts of the spirit—and devote time and energy towards the spirit's development over the accumulation of material goods.

PP: For what do you devote most of your time and energy? Is it what you really most treasure in life?

April 28

Give thanks for nature's visual banquet

The philosopher Diogenes was sitting on a curbstone, eating bread and lentils for his supper. He was seen by the philosopher Aristippus, who lived comfortably by flattering the king.

Said Aristippus, "If you would learn to be subservient to the king, you would not have to live on lentils."

Said Diogenes, "Learn to live on lentils, and you will not have to cultivate the king."

JR: Learn to live simply. Enjoy simple food and drink, and you can bask in a spiritual uplifting that is otherwise unattainable. Rather than feeling forced to cozy up to undesirable people or act against your morals to achieve more of what you want, you become free to integrate word, belief, and action while enjoying the banquet which nature presents free of charge.

PP: What simple, wholesome foods do you like? Why not make them an essential part of your diet?

April 29

Keep it simple—and feel the ultimate joy

Gandhi was once asked: "Can you tell me the secret of your life in three words?

He replied, "Yes—Renounce and enjoy."

We fool ourselves if we believe that nonmaterial needs can be met through the consumption of goods. Instead, love, self-esteem, and self-actualization are best gained through personal, social, and cultural interactions.

Not only is modern development unable to meet these higher needs; it may actually block people from attaining them. There is "an impressive body of opinion suggesting that materialism inhibits the satisfaction" of non-material needs. Much of today's advertising sends an implicit message that is patently false: your self-worth depends on what you own. The car in your driveway, the electronic gadgets in your house—these externals have nothing to do with self-worth, but advertising works relentlessly to convince us otherwise. To the extent that advertising steers us toward false sources of self-esteem, it might be described as a promoter of faux development, or even as a source of developmental decay.

JR: When you spend excessive time, money and energy acquiring and taking care of more and more material goods, you necessarily withdraw time from building a more loving and self-actualised character. The mistaken idea that more goods will bring more happiness and love is one of the root causes of many of our global problems, from extravagant development projects which hurt the poor to environmental destruction.

PP: What material goods do you hardly ever use? How about giving them away or throwing them out, freeing yourself from the burden of holding on to them?

April 30

Even rocks are found intriguing by the enlightened one.

1) To live more voluntarily means to encounter life more consciously. To live more simply is to encounter life more directly.

2) We consciously trivialize the human experiment with shallow pursuits of money and social status that mask rather than celebrate the magnificence of the human being. All the while a miracle of creation surrounds us and intimately infuses every particle of our existence.

JR: Living simply is often mistakenly seen as painfully sacrificial. But a life of voluntary simplicity is quite the opposite. We increasingly discover more and more joy and augmented pleasure in the miracle of our existence and the creation around us. It is the life of nourishing soulful delights, in contrast to the materialistic-based lifestyle which focuses on the accumulation of "dead things" and a dependence on outside influences to find temporary pleasures—a life where we unwittingly give up our capacity to create our own pleasures.

PP: Celebrate your being. Take five minutes simply to appreciate the countless miracles responsible for your existence (breath, blood flow, the whole shebang).

MAY

Universal Ideals & Unity

The majority will claim that spiritual precepts are beautiful although they cannot practically be lived out in our dog-eat-dog world. On the contrary, the most fallacious "fantasy" is that we can continue to live on a relatively benevolent planet without their full implementation. Fortunately, there are some basic universal values on which the majority of the world's people can agree. The disagreement arises on the optimal application and achieving the proper balance between these values.

On achieving an understanding of the essence of these universal values and their benefit to all of humankind, our society can become more unified to find ways of implementing and integrating them into our everyday lives. Surely, great differences of opinion will exist on the best incorporating mechanisms of these values into our communities. However, the conflicts will be steeped in a spirit of unity, discovering ways that can benefit all, a kind of spirit which lives by, "More for you means more for me." This way of thinking is nothing new, rather it is drawn from ancient wisdom embodied in all of the world's main spiritual traditions.

The exploration of different paths in moving towards these universal ideals in such a multi-cultural world can be frustrating and stressful. Yet, when you approach the search with a sense of curiosity, and share your ideas and learn from others, you are humbled by your own ignorance of the diverse ways of life around the world, which can also be a source of great delight. And, in the process, you become much wiser towards learning new ways of living in unity that you might have never before considered.

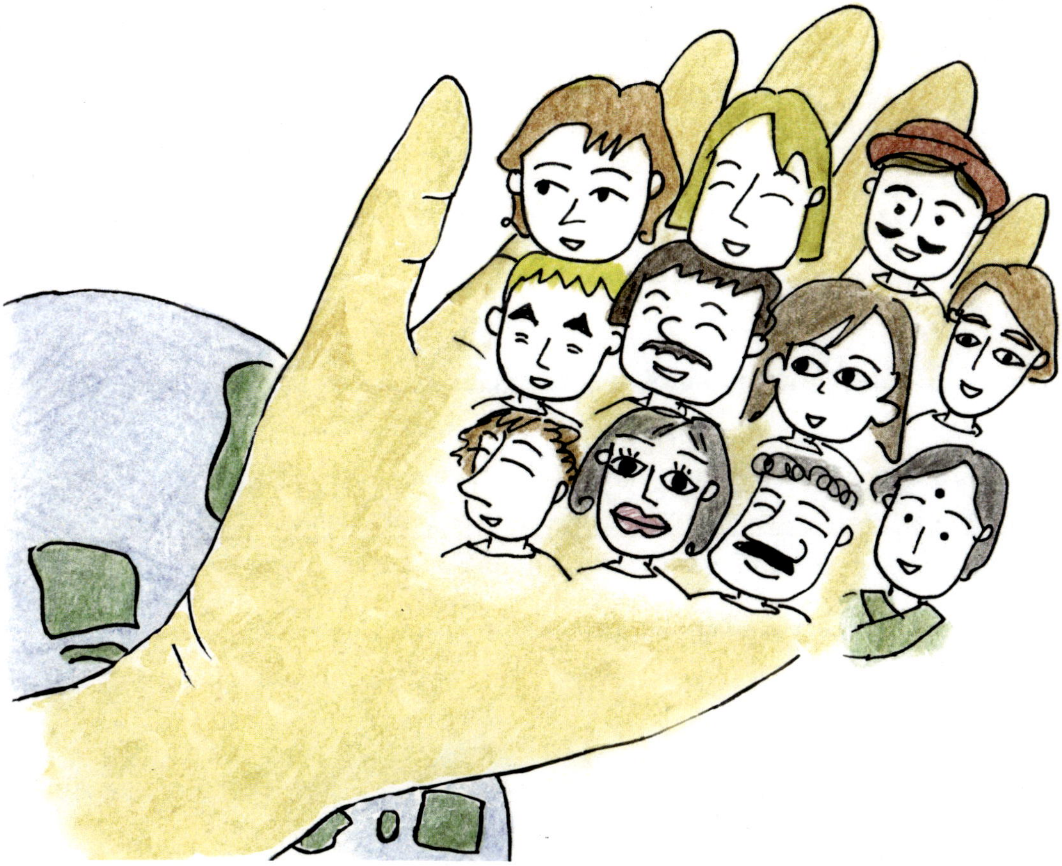

May 1

How worthy we all are of true appreciation—each of us

Universal moral values—such as treating all people justly and respecting their lives, liberty, and equality—bind all persons everywhere because they affirm our fundamental human worth and dignity. We have a right and even a duty to insist that all people behave in accordance with these universal values.

JR: A completely relativistic attitude of "Anything goes" cannot lead to and structure a peaceful society. First and foremost, we must begin by acknowledging diverse universally desirable values necessary to living lives that are accepted by all civilized cultures. There will be disagreements as to how to live them out and in what balance, but without first establishing such a foundation, no discussion on moving towards a peaceful world can result in durable solutions.

PP: What do you think the values are which should be upheld by civilized societies throughout the world?

May 2

At your service

All true religions and spiritual paths teach the universal values of compassion, unity, truthfulness, fairness, tolerance, responsibility, respect for, and service to, all life.

JR: *It is a travesty that many religious conflicts are igniting fear and hatred in humanity, in sharp contrast to these religions' most fundamental teachings. Each and every world religion teaches the universal values as stated in this passage, but how is it possible to enact them when those who claim to believe in them are fighting each other? Obviously, other factors bear more weight in most of our lives than trying to live up to these worthwhile ideals.*

PP: When are you most able to live in accordance with these universal values? Can you increase the frequency of such times?

May 3

Discovering and living by our common values beautifies the world.

The world's major religions—Western Christianity, Orthodoxy, Hinduism, Buddhism, Islam, Confucianism, Taoism, Judaism—share key values in common. If humans are ever to develop a universal civilization, it will emerge gradually through the exploration and expansion of these commonalities. For peace in a multicivilizational world, the commonalities rule is needed: peoples in all civilizations should search for and attempt to expand the values, institutions, and practices they have in common with peoples of other civilizations.

JR: *A universal civilization does not imply that everyone is living in an analogous fashion under a totalitarian ruler forcing his application of these ideals on others, as some fear-mongers would have us believe. It is understood that the universals are simply goals to aspire to, with innumerable ways of implementing and balancing them. They provide us with a strong foundation, a shared set of common, humane values to navigate from into a multitude of ways of living nestled in the warmth of these cherished ideals. When we are able to achieve this, a diversity of flourishing cultures set in a world of peace becomes possible.*

PP: Find the common values which you share with a friend belonging to a different religion (or who isn't religious).

May 4

Focus—Don't let your ego override you and divert your attention

Jesus had direct and clear teachings on issues such as nonviolence, a simple lifestyle, love of the poor, forgiveness, love of enemies, inclusivity, mercy, and not seeking status, power, perks, and possessions: throughout history, all have been overwhelmingly ignored by mainline Christian churches, even those who call themselves orthodox or biblical.

This avoidance defies explanation until we understand how dualistic thinking protects and pads the ego and its fear of change. Notice that the things we ignored above require actual change of our lifestyle, our security systems, or our dualistic thought patterns. The things we emphasized instead were usually intellectual beliefs or moral superiority stances that asked little of us: the divinity of Christ, the virgin birth, the atonement theory, and beliefs about reproduction and sex. After a while, you start recognizing the underlying bias. The ego diverts your attention from anything that would ask you to change to righteous causes that invariably ask others to change.

JR: What a tremendous insight this passage provides! Furthermore, we fear to undertake any meaningful discussion on these issues since any such discussion exposes our weaknesses (failure to live according to these clear teachings) and "justifies" blame (towards oneself). We can shape an encouraging dialogue when, instead of criticizing each other on our shortcomings, we learn to discuss ways to better live according to these teachings, and consequent dialogue can even contain a playful sense of adventure.

PP: Find someone willing to have a discussion with you on how to better live out your shared values. Initiate the dialogue with her.

May 5

Find the right balance

Western fundamentalism echoes what it finds so repulsive in its enemy, Bin Laden: first, a sense of unquestioned superiority; second, an assertion of the universal applicability of its values; and third, a lack of will to understand anything that is profoundly different from itself.

We are all prisoners of our subjectivity. Liberalism is right to assert that there are universal moral principles (such as the rights of women and free speech) but wrong to insist that there is only one interpretation. Rights come into conflict, and every culture negotiates trade-offs.

To understand those trade-offs is sometimes complex. But no single culture has cracked the perfect trade-off. There is a huge amount we can learn from Islam in its social solidarity, its appreciation of the collective good, and the generosity and strength of human relationships. Islamic societies are grappling with the same challenge as the West—how to balance freedom and responsibility—and we need each other's help, not each other's brands of fundamentalism. If we are asking Islam to stamp out its fundamentalism, so must we.

JR: It is convenient to find and blame the world's problems on "the epitome of evil." It offers a great way to escape any personal responsibility and avoid taking notice of the "evil" that lurks within each one of us. Each society acts in a manner that contradicts the ideals which it claims to uphold and embody. Therefore, it would be much more effective to take notice of our own hypocrisies and make an effort to right them and provide others with a worthy example to emulate.

PP: What is that one hypocrisy in your life which bothers you most? What can you start doing now to eliminate it?

May 6

Respecting diversity allows all kinds of life to flourish.

On the "heart level" there are basic needs and aspirations every human being has in common. We all have a need for community and service; we have an inalienable, universal need for respect—both to be accorded one's basic human dignity and to respect others ungrudgingly.

JR: The cause of our frustration or anger with others often stems from a feeling of not being respected. Our need to feel respected demands of us that we respect others in turn. If we can keep a feeling of respect for each other deep down, even while we are bubbling with anger on the surface, we can feed one another's basic needs and, in so doing, find ways to calm the rough waters when they inevitably encroach.

PP: Who is someone you're feeling frustrated with now? Think of one thing you respect about him, and keep this in mind when you meet him again.

May 7

Individuals rarely have much influence, but together with others, the effect is greatly expanded.

There are 3 major philosophies upon which we have constructed our modern culture.

The first of these practical philosophies is individualism. When most people today are faced with a decision, the question that seems to dominate their inner dialogue is, "What's in it for me?" This question is the creed of individualism, based on an all-consuming concern for self. No community, whether as small as a family or as large as a nation, can grow strong with this attitude. Individualism always weakens the community and causes the whole to suffer.

"Pleasure is the supreme good" unmasks hedonism as the second philosophical mark of our age. Hedonism is not an expression of freedom; it is a passport to enslavement by a thousand cravings and addictions. And in the end it produces not pleasure, but despair.

The third philosophical mark is the creed of minimalism, which is always asking, "What is the least I can do?" Minimalism is the enemy of excellence and the father of mediocrity.

JR: Integrating often conflicting ideals into your life requires constant balancing. In many human societies, the community structure projects a feeling of binding like a chain holding a person back from her aspirations. In many societies, the reaction against this entrapment has become an extreme form of rugged individualism that has severely weakened community. Regaining a healthy balance will be necessary in order to heal the social problems of today.

PP: Do you have a good balance between individualism and community? If not, what can you do to achieve a more comfortable and fulfilling balance?

May 8

To be proud or to feel ashamed for standing out?

One evening an old Cherokee told his grandson about a battle that goes on inside people.

He said, "My son, the battle is between two "wolves" inside us all. One is Evil. It is anger, envy, jealousy, sorrow, regret, greed, arrogance, self-pity, guilt, resentment, inferiority, lies, false pride, superiority, and ego. The other is Good. It is joy, peace, love, hope, serenity, humility, kindness, benevolence, empathy, generosity, truth, compassion and faith."

The grandson thought about it for a minute and then asked his grandfather: "Which wolf wins?"

The old Cherokee simply replied, "The one you feed."

Food for thought for today

* Which wolf are you feeding?
* How's that working for you?

JR: The feelings that you focus on largely determine the type of person you become. When you constantly think of revenge and project anger at having been wronged, it's easy to harbor hatred for the world and lash out against others. If you choose to try to build a serene spirit through regular meditation, you are more likely to treat others (and yourself) more generously. Only you can build your core foundation based on the qualities that you are feeding.

PP: What is your basic attitude towards others and towards life? Do you find it pleasing and beneficial to you? If not, how can you strengthen the sentiment which you most desire to embody?

May 9

Explore nature's wonders and create anew

Teachers emerging from the New Spirituality will understand that asking children to memorize facts is asking them to re-create the past, but that inviting children to explore concepts and ideas—such as fairness, tolerance, equality, and honesty—invites them to create a new future, for their ideas may be different from yours.

JR: Memorization and rote-learning of past events require no active thinking on the part of the learner. At best, it is a waste of time: at worst, it is complicit in destroying a child's ability to think creatively. Rather, learning how ideas have shaped the past and analyzing their good and bad results while developing a strong moral character used day in and day out to build a good future can provide the high quality and very useful education which the youth are both deserving of and inspired by.

PP: What learning most inspired you when you were in elementary school? Why? How can you encourage others to learn in a similar way?

May 10

Stand up for your ideals

We must make students aware that there is a core of uncontroversial ethical ideals that all civilizations worthy of the name have discovered.

Have them read almost any great work, and they will encounter the basic moral values: integrity, respect for human life, self-control, honesty, courage, and self-sacrifice. All the world's major religions proffer some version of the Golden Rule, if only in its negative form: not to do unto others as we would not have them do unto us.

JR: Why is it that the literary classics continue to be read by the masses for centuries? Why is it that the stories of enlightened people and those who do good continue to inspire generation after generation? They strike a chord in the "average" person, causing her to reflect on the ethical ideals which have guided civilized societies throughout history, and often nudge her into finding ways of better implementing them into her own life.

PP: What is a classic book or film that has really inspired you? Think about why it moved you. Better yet, read it or watch it again and stop at those points where you are especially touched, reflecting on why they impress you.

May 11

Living for the common good leads to flourishing.

While the call for a social covenant acknowledges the great diversity of global values, it puts forward three that express a consensus across cultures and religions. They are: 1) the dignity of the human person, 2) the importance of the common good, which transcends individual interests, and 3) the need for stewardship of the planet for posterity.

As the covenant says, "Together these offer a powerful unifying ideal: valued individuals, committed to one another, and respectful of future generations."

Contracts have been broken, but a covenant adds a moral dimension that is now essential. The social covenant's many contexts and results will vary from place to place. But they should all include shared principles and features: a value basis for new agreements, an emphasis on jobs that offer fair rewards for hard work, security for financial assets and savings, a serious commitment to reduce inequality between the top and the bottom of society, stewardship of the environment, an awareness of future generations' needs, an accountable financial sector, and the strengthening of both opportunity and social mobility. Such a covenant promotes human flourishing, happiness, and well-being as social goals.

JR: The social covenant as mentioned herein recognizes that the uplifting of the individual, the commons, and the natural environment go hand in hand. In the long run, it cannot be otherwise, for any damage to one factor inevitably leads to a worsening of the others. Our movement towards a sustainable society necessarily acknowledges such a social covenant.

PP: What is one action that you take which elevates all three of these values simultaneously? How can you put this into practice more often in your everyday life?

May 12

Optimal balance creates a wonderful environment.

Ever since the French Revolution, people throughout the world have gradually come to see both equality and individual freedom as fundamental values. Yet the two values contradict each other. Equality can be ensured only by curtailing the freedoms of those who are better off. Guaranteeing that every individual will be free to do as he wishes inevitably short-changes equality. The entire political history of the world since 1789 can be seen as a series of attempts to reconcile this contradiction.

JR: It is easy to talk about universal values while ignoring the fact that, surely, each one clashes with certain others. Revolution is frequently an attack against extremely corrupt systems, and the universal values hold great appeal to and hope for the masses. In the process, they easily become idealized. Yet, as history bears witness to all too often, another corrupt system arises from the ashes of the previous one UNLESS the women and men who take control after the revolution lead lives of great integrity and transparency in their efforts to harmonize conflicting ideals.

PP: Reflect on how the individuality vs. equality conflict is enacted in your own life. Do you feel this is well-balanced?

May 13

True love, true joy

To be the sort of person who helps move the world toward shared, sustainable flourishing will require a strong set of virtues:

- A sense of wonder, to perceive and value the extraordinary beauty and mystery of the thriving world
- Compassion, to feel the suffering of both human and nonhuman animals caused by climate change and ecological collapse
- Imagination, to envision new and sustainable ways to provide for human needs without plundering the planet
- Independence of mind, to distinguish true from false, to distinguish real needs from created markets, to understand how to make good moral decisions under conditions of uncertainty
- Integrity, to do what one thinks is right, even if it means making decisions that are radically different from the decisions one's friends and neighbors make, decisions contrary to what is well-advertised or easy
- Justice, to honor the needs of other people and other species as highly as one's own, and to respect in others the rights one claims for oneself
- Courage, to do what needs to be done even if the lonely odds are against you

JR: This insightful list of virtues functions as a foundation on which to base your life. As you optimally and fully integrate them into your life, they can instill your life with true love and passion. Living virtuously is a great challenge, made even more difficult by the great number of cynics who claim that even attempting such a life is a fruitless endeavor. Yet, the joyous and loving figures who have inspired us throughout the ages prove the cynics wrong, and demonstrate to us that the virtuous life is not only attainable, but also one which can reap great rewards.

PP: Which of these virtues do you most lack in? What can you do to strengthen them?

May 14

Such distinct beauty isn't possible without the many disparate parts.

This is the mark of great ideas: they unify people and they also act to unify the disparate parts of the human being; they speak of a social order that is possible on the basis of an ordering within the individual self.

JR: Many of the influential ideas which have taken hold in the contemporary world focus on fear and the differences between us, and are a root cause of many modern day conflicts. Rediscovering the benign power of ideas that bring together and harmonize the disparate aspects of the self as well as different peoples, and developing creative ways of implementing them would be an important step towards moving to fully integrate these contrasting elements both within ourselves and, from there, throughout the society.

PP: What two ideas do you hold that clash with each other and make you feel disintegrated? How can you adapt them in order to feel more accepting of both?

May 15

Reflect your glory

It is our light, not our darkness, that most frightens us.

We ask ourselves, who am I to be brilliant, gorgeous, talented, fabulous?
Actually, who are you NOT to be?

You are a child of God.
Your playing small doesn't serve the world.

There's nothing enlightened about shrinking so that other people won't feel
insecure around you. We are all meant to shine, as children do.

We were born to make manifest the glory of God that is within us. It's not just
in some of us; it's in everyone.

And as we let our own light shine, we unconsciously give other people permission to do the same. As we're liberated from our own fear, our presence automatically liberates others.

JR: Even people who live in darkness can draw encouragement from Nelson Mandela (whom this passage is often mistakenly attributed to), who was imprisoned for 27 years and literally lived in darkness (solitary confinement) for long stretches. The adverse experience, rather than crushing him, fortified him with a strong, humble spirit which will forever be a light unto the world. Each one of us also has hidden potential beckoning to make an appearance, only if we are willing to seek it out and build it up in preparation for its debut on the stage of the living.

PP: What is a talent/ability that you have but haven't "made public?" What can you do NOW to start making it shine for you and those around you?

May 16

Inseparable

We must overcome the torture of absolute separateness in some way: by submission or by domination or by trying to silence reason and awareness. Yet all these ways succeed only for the moment, and block the road to a true solution. There is but one way to save ourselves from this hell: to leave the prison of our egocentricity, to reach out and to one ourselves with the world. If egocentric separateness is the cardinal sin, then the sin is atoned in the act of loving.

JR: While our egos long to keep us "unique" and separate, our spirit longs to bring us together with others and the natural environment. It is often mistakenly assumed that "one-ing yourself with the world" translates as you being a social butterfly. Yet, there are people who are naturally introverted or shy. What about them? There are many ways of liberating the spirit by connecting with life without socializing with a large number of people. In fact, the restoration of the natural world requires doers much more than talkers. It is up to each one of us to find the way that is right for her.

PP: Are you an introvert or an extrovert? How can you more actively demonstrate your love of other living beings based on your type of character?

May 17

Why are you afraid? Is the threat so real?

Why does the feeling of separateness cause anxiety? Because anything or anyone that we perceive as separate, foreign, or alien to us is a potential threat—potentially anxiety producing. To the degree that we feel oneness or union with anything or anyone we can feel comfortable, accepting, and loving—the opposite of anxiety.

From a Macro perspective, all human suffering, fear, hate, pain, and disease are the result of lack of faith that all is one—all is love—all is what you might call God—all is perfect.

JR: When we are taught to be wary of those who are different from us, by default our defences are built up to keep them away from us. Our world closes in on us and our connections become restricted. And we unknowingly become the creators of much of the suffering that we claim to be caused by others. Why would anyone reasonably cause himself to suffer?

PP: How do you suffer emotionally or spiritually? Can you see how this may be due to your perception of another (others) being a threat to you and your happiness? How can you make him (them) an ally in creating happiness for both of you?

May 18

Some things are naturally worthy of praise.

All human beings share a fascinating taboo against selfishness. Selfishness is almost the definition of vice. Murder, theft, rape and fraud are considered crimes of great importance because they are selfish and spiteful acts that are committed for the benefit of the actor and the detriment of the victim. In contrast, virtue is, almost by definition, the greater good of the group. Those virtues (such as thrift and abstinence) that are not directly altruistic in their motivation are few and obscure. The conspicuously virtuous things we all praise—cooperation, altruism, generosity, sympathy, kindness, selflessness—are all unambiguously concerned with the welfare of others. This is not some parochial Western tradition. It is a bias shared by the whole species.

JR: *How intriguing it is that there is a universal disgust towards the purely selfish individual, in contrast to the great respect towards the one who shows concern and acts for the good of others. And it is extremely perplexing to observe that many of today's teachings turn this deeply ingrained belief on its head, making selfishness virtuous and criticizing those who help others. This flip unquestionably forms one of the main causes of today's social and environmental problems.*

PP: *What does your religion, or the ethical path you follow, teach you about selfishness? Do you take it to heart and practice it in your everyday life?*

May 19

Integrating and blending in naturally

1) The non-discriminating nature of suffering can sometimes help us to get over our discriminating nature.

2) Money is the most universal and most efficient system of mutual trust ever devised.

3) Money is the only trust system created by humans that can bridge almost any cultural gap, and that does not discriminate on the basis of religion, gender, race, age or sexual orientation. Thanks to money, even people who don't know each other and don't trust each other can nevertheless cooperate effectively.

JR: Funny how two completely different things bring people closer together, i.e. suffering and money. Everyone suffers, and it is through this suffering that we can develop compassion for others. And while money is often derided as evil by many of the pure of heart, it cannot be denied that financial transactions bring together otherwise totally unrelated people. In this sense, money has the potential of being a force for good.

PP: How do you view money? How can you better use it as a source of unity (bringing people together more beneficially)?

May 20

No way to escape

Some of our society's hunger for drugs may be related to our yearning for this unified state of mind, body, and nature. Recreational drugs, or drugs used in a religious context, are present in nearly every society, including those of tribal peoples who live closer to nature. But the purpose and context is more often than not about transcendence, not escape. In Western society, drugs and alcohol are more likely to be used to blunt pain, to block the static and noise—the excess, often meaningless information that comes our way every day. By contrast, the high achieved through deep green exercise opens the senses; this high is about transcendence, about natural ecstasy.

JR: We often use drugs (including alcohol) to escape the reality in which we find ourselves, resulting in an enslaving dependence on this superficial high. If we focus on either changing our reality or our perception of reality, finding healthy ways (meditation, contact with nature, etc.) of making it not only bearable, but enjoyable, and then moving towards delight, the addiction to the drug dissipates.

PP: What gives you a natural and healthy high? Find ways of doing this more often to bring more joy into your life.

May 21

Losing ground

In a time of increasing disruptions related to a changing climate and economic dislocation, our challenge will be to create the conditions that encourage us to turn to each other in hard times, not turn on each other. We are far more likely to achieve that in a more equitable world, where we are mindful of the many blessings we have and skilled at discovering sources of happiness that don't cost the planet, but are abundant and free.

JR: *While we have certainly been losing ground both literally (with much of our good topsoil being washed away) and figuratively (in terms of losing large areas of the natural environment), the subsequent development of human networks which have ensued to deal with these issues is extremely encouraging. Expanding these connections to eventually include even those who have opposed preservation or restoration efforts, and swelling the numbers of people active on the ground to better the environment, will build a strong mutual support system needed during difficult times.*

PP: *What is one thing you can do now to build a stronger bond between you and an acquaintance you'd like to know better?*

May 22

Broaden your horizons

While spite, hatred, envy, and ingratitude shrink our horizons and limit our creativity, gratitude, compassion, and altruism broaden our perspective and break down the barricades we erect between ourselves and others in order to protect the frightened, greedy, insecure ego.

***JR:** Knowing that we are capable of either shrinking or broadening our perspective based on the feelings we harbor empowers us to choose our direction. "Easier said than done" you may say. Maybe, but by cultivating "the loving arts" and becoming more open, the ego starts to lose its grip and you become more comfortable in many situations which would have previously caused distress and anxiety.*

***PP:** Think of five things you are grateful for in your life now, and feel how this thought alone lifts you up.*

May 23

*Be open to the world—
then there's no need
for greed*

The essential teachings of all the great humanist religions can be summarized in one sentence: It is the goal of man to overcome one's narcissism.

Only if man can do away with the illusion of his indestructible ego, only if he can drop it together with all other objects of his greed, only then can he be open to the world and fully related to it. Psychologically, this process of becoming fully awake is identical with the replacement of narcissism by relatedness to the world.

JR: What does it mean to be open to the world? It means indulging yourself by taking the time to experience nature in all its variations, consciously using all of your senses to truly feel the experience, and feeling appreciation for being a part of this creation. When you become aware of your deep connection with the living world, you become a religious and humanist ideal, losing your narcissism and greed to the delight which is created by opening and uniting with other living beings.

PP: What do you need to boost your ego (praise, money, status, etc.)? How can you become more open so you no longer need any of these drugs?

May 24

Dance it up—you're here only a short time

1) "Beliefs separate. Loving thoughts unite."

2) Our ego focuses on how we are different from the rest of the world. Our soul lives when we experience how we are the same.

Any time you separate yourself from other people or from situations, you know your personality is in control. At such times, shift your perspective to build connection and you will move into soul.

As our picture of life becomes larger, more things make sense and we have a greater playing field for life to unfold—naturally.

3) "As a holistic being you shatter the illusion of your separateness and reveal your connection to everything. This empowers you in a way that the ego-driven self could never contemplate."

JR: The beautiful feelings of loving and connecting with others make you feel joyous, and you want to live it up. When you start to feel this way, you realize the imprisoning nature of the confinement of egoistic living that prevented you from the freedom of connecting with others and fully enjoying this dance of life.

PP: What is something you can do that makes you feel like uninhibitedly dancing with joy? DO IT!

May 25

Cheers to the integration of human ingenuity with the natural environment

ENVIRONMENTAL INTEGRATION—This is the keyword of JAMBO. As individuals feel more integrated internally, they seek to create the same in the external environments (social and natural). In the same way, improvement in the external environments encourage spiritual growth and contentment. This creates a "cycle of benevolence." JAMBO has been in existence since 1996 and has now focused its activities to work on bettering these three parts of the environment (internal, social, and natural) consistently, offering a variety of programs each month.

JR: In today's world, working for the good of society tends to be separated from bettering the natural environment, and there is almost no attempt to connect either of these activities with people's spiritual development. This separation inevitably results in many problems, as one "environment" is improved usually at the expense of another. All three MUST be worked on in a synchronised manner to create a better world.

PP: Think of and carry out one activity that betters society, nature, and your spirit simultaneously.

May 26

Re-uniting the elements of spirit, nature and humanity

Promiscuity is so often a mark of dislocation, of boredom, alienation and despair. One very seldom realises that when one's young, of course, because the transient pleasure's so overwhelming. But later the pleasure no longer heals, and then, as in all cases of alienation, one yearns for the putting-right, the making-whole, the unification of the fragmented self. This is the theology of atonement—At-one-ment!

JR: Our society inculcates in us a learning to remain like promiscuous teenagers, deepening our desires so they become overpowering, and then feeding them with ever-changing entertainments and goods which results in our never growing up. As people mature, they strive for integration, and find that moving towards uniting the different parts of self is a much more long-lasting and stable pleasure compared to the satisfaction of the fickle whims of yesterday.

PP: What harmful pleasure do you indulge in regularly? Can you find a way to slowly replace it with a healthier delight?

May 27

*No judgment here—
only forgiveness*

Whereas judgmentalism focuses on flaws, forgiveness focuses on wholeness. As we learn to act from the sphere of forgiveness in all our relationships, we become conduits for a greater energy, a lifeforce that we vibrantly "feel" as love, peace, compassion, power, wisdom, and an enthusiastic gratitude for life.

JR: Whenever we judge others, we erect emotional barriers between ourselves and them. Whenever we forgive, we connect with them and move towards unity. This does not mean that we live without values and say "anything goes," but rather that, even if we disagree with another's behavior, we seek to understand it and, through such understanding, forgive.

PP: Who are you judging negatively now? Try to understand why the person acts as he does and move towards forgiveness.

May 28

Identity crisis—Am I one or two?

So widespread is this experience of the supreme identity that it has, along with the doctrines that purport to explain it, earned the name "The Perennial Philosophy." There is much evidence that this type of experience or knowledge is central to every major religion—Hinduism, Buddhism, Taoism, Christianity, Islam, and Judaism—so that we can justifiably speak of the "transcendent unity of religions" and the unanimity of primordial truth.

This type of awareness, this unity consciousness or supreme identity, is the nature and condition of all sentient beings; but we progressively limit our world and turn from our true nature in order to embrace boundaries.

JR: How would we behave differently if we truly felt this unity consciousness—that we are all one? While this is a fundamental teaching in every major religion, our egos fight relentlessly against such awareness. However, if more and more people ever do come to experience it, our world would certainly be drastically transformed for the better.

PP: Imagine how different your life would be if you truly believed and felt that "all is one."

May 29

Capturing and feeling the whole is pure delight.

1) "Love is but the discovery of ourselves in others, and the delight in the recognition."

2) "I destroy my enemies when I make them my friends."

JR: It is impossible to transform bad relationships into good ones when we feed our hatreds and jealousies. Only through the cultivation of a spirit of love can we make more and more people our lovers (in the spiritual sense) and feel comfortable and delighted in their company. In the process, our relationships grow to become increasingly inclusive.

PP: Focus on some common interest or characteristic you share with someone who you don't care for, and witness the seed of caring for her being planted in your soul.

May 30

A transformed landscape—a new paradigm

Truly, empathy is the fastest form of communication. Deep understanding of the other person's story inevitably inspires compassion. When we truly see through the tears, when we finally feel what's in the heart of a loved one, we are transformed. Our paradigms change radically.

JR: By transforming the internal landscape of your emotions, your entire worldview changes. Rather than focusing on someone's terrible behavior, that would lead to a feeling of disgust, make an effort to understand his reasoning for behaving that way so you can start to feel an empathy which is the first step towards loving him. Such compassion is the strongest agent for true change, in both the giver and the receiver.

PP: What is one of your behaviors that others dislike? Seek to understand why you behave that way and be compassionate towards yourself.

May 31

Nature is all-inclusive.

Only when our sense of self expands to include others, through love, is the truism "More for me is less for you" replaced by its opposite: "More for you is also more for me." This is the essential truth embodied in the world's authentic spiritual teachings.

JR: Our economic systems and social relationships are full of greed and envy because we think that more for you is less for me. So we fight to get and keep whatever we can. When our sense of self becomes increasingly inclusive, it naturally follows that more for you is also more for me. With this new perspective, you come to wish to do good to others since acting so is also doing good to yourself.

PP: Do something today that makes you feel like you are receiving something wonderful in the act of giving.

JUNE

Purpose & Persistence

Seeking out and finding a purpose in life can be one of the most difficult and also most rewarding endeavors you can undertake. Peripherally, though it may sound easy to "have an ultimate goal," most of us simply accept earning money, getting married, being beautiful or one of the countless other messages given to us in our schools, advertisements and the media as being "our purpose." We fail to seriously consider or understand the reason why we wish for them. Then, on attaining what we thought we so desired, we wonder why the initial exuberance doesn't last, not realizing that it was only a step to something else, which still hasn't been acquired.

At a deeper, life-engendering level, very few of us know what our purpose is, what we truly want, and then continue to live unhappily without knowing why.

It requires a lot of persistence and discipline to first find your purpose (through constant soul-searching and reflection) and then still more to embody and live it out. Scary words—persistence and discipline—and they sound like as much fun as going to boot camp for intensive training. Yet, it is through making tireless efforts at "creating and implementing" your true purpose that a long-lasting and steady contentment permeates your entire being. And when that happens, you will look back and wonder how you could have wasted so much time chasing those ephemeral desires, like money and beauty—the comings and goings over which you have limited control. Determining your true purpose and moving towards it tenaciously grants you mastery over your life's direction—even if the final goal is unattainable—giving you a passion for living.

June 1

Beautiful flowers flourish in a well-weeded garden.

1) "Everything you are against weakens you. Everything you are for empowers you."

2) "Don't water your weeds."

JR: Whenever you ponder about the terrible things happening around you or ideas which you oppose, you are actually robbing yourself of time and energy which could be spent appreciating the good in your life and moving towards those things which excite and uplift you. If you move towards doing more of the latter, the weeds lose their nourishment and die out, making your internal garden a beauty to behold for those around you.

PP: What is something you are against? Change your thought pattern by considering what it is you are for in this case.

June 2

Sharing beauty with all

Nietzsche made the pronouncement: "He who has a why to live for can bear almost any how." When Dorothy Day gave up her lover, she gave up an intensely tangible private affection for another for a broader love, of God, but also of purposefulness, meaning, involvement, and community, without which she had been miserable even in her menage. She gave up her how for a why. The joy in disaster comes, when it comes, from the purposefulness, the immersion in service and survival, and from an affection that is not private and personal but civic: the love of strangers for each other, of a citizen for his or her city, of belonging to a greater whole, of doing the work that matters.

These loves remain largely dormant and unacknowledged in the contemporary postindustrial society.

JR: Love is often seen as a passionate and focused connection between two people which excludes others. This is much closer to the intense desire of lust, while love (in the meaning here) is opening up to others, and filling your life with purpose. Our society makes little effort to cultivate this kind of enriching love, yet it is evident at times of disaster when people "are forced or moved" towards a common purpose. How can such a sense of love and feeling as a part of the greater whole be instilled on an everyday basis? Finding the answer to this question would move us into a new, enlightening paradigm.

PP: What is something which you gave up with difficulty, but resulted in bringing more love into your life? Is there anything now that you could give up to achieve the same?

June 3

Am I dreamy or am I dreaming?

Out of our relationship with the earth and the universe arises our capacity for dreams, visions, and spirituality. When that relationship is open, uninhibited, and wild, our dreams are powerful, dramatic, and energy-giving; when that relationship with nature is damaged and diminished, our capacity to dream shrivels too. We are losing the original dream of spiritual well-being to a narrower dream of material ambition. Dreaming is a source of the lost gospel.

JR: We have today come to place higher importance on the dream of acquiring more and more material things than on the much more life-fulfillling dream of creating a soulful life for ourselves and others. By limiting our dreams to more acquisitions, we destroy our capacity to create and live out our visions for the more well-grounded and spiritually-uplifting endeavors.

PP: Which dream of yours fills you with hope for the future? Can you ignite this flame and move towards living it out now?

June 4

C'mon—just one little smooch

When healthy avenues for the expression of our meaning-needs are blocked, our life energy will seek other, sometimes destructive, means of expression. Our spiritual energy, banned from the respectable institutions of public life by liberals determined to keep them value-free and "scientific," resurfaces in distorted forms, such as excessive consumerism and fetishization of sports, sex, drugs, and rock and roll. Because spiritual energy, like other forms of energy, cannot be destroyed, its repression in one area of our lives ensures its emergence in other areas of our lives, sometimes in other forms.

JR: Whatever need you have that instills your life with a sense of purpose is a meaning-need. When you either feel like you don't have such needs or feel like they are impossible to attain, you settle for those "desires" that give you temporary delights or thrills at the expense of meeting your meaning-needs. Even connecting to a loved one with a "little smooch" can propel you towards improved purpose in your life.

PP: What desires do you focus on that take you away from potentially meeting your "meaning-needs?" How can you give the meaning-needs an improved priority in your life?

June 5

Find your center, identify your focus, and go for it

Most of us imagine that most people are motivated primarily by material self-interest. So it is surprising to discover that average people often experience more stress from feeling that they are wasting their lives doing meaningless work than from feeling that they are not making enough money. Middle-income people are deeply unhappy because they hunger to serve the common good and to contribute something with their talents and energies, yet find that their actual work gives them little opportunity to do so. They often turn to demands for more money as a compensation for a life that otherwise feels frustrating and empty.

How frequently the deprivation of meaning in daily life is at the root of many of our individual and social problems!

JR: What a powerful insight! It's true that, in the long run, most people get tired of work in which they find no meaning, as they are doing it only for material benefit. There is an inherent yearning in the human spirit to work for the common good and give to others. Unfortunately, this need is downplayed or simply ignored in much of our media and advertising. No wonder we end up taking out our frustrations, which are rooted in our inability to live meaningfully, on others or on ourselves through self-destructive practices.

PP: What can you do to better serve the common good? How would doing this make you feel?

June 6

Be content in knowing exactly what you want

It is not that someone else is preventing you from living happily; you yourself do not know what you want. Rather than admit this, you pretend that someone is keeping you from exercising your liberty. Who is this? It is you yourself.

JR: Wouldn't it be nice to be like the bee, knowing exactly what it wants, i.e. the flower's pollen? We have so many desires which are often in conflict with one another, and so much so that we don't know what we really want. Instead of making an earnest effort to carry on the true search by ourselves of those things we truly long for (that would bring us a deep-seated happiness), we blame others, our circumstances or life for not being able to get them. But get what? In the majority of cases, we don't even know what we are looking for. Realizing what you MOST WANT deep down is the first step towards acquiring it.

PP: What one personal attribute do you most desire? Envisage what you can do to get it and how your life would change if you had it.

June 7

The water's ceaseless flow transforms and shapes the landscape.

1) The greatest enemy of education is not a lack of funds, though that hurts; it's a lack of purpose.

2) Positive change begins when we ask ourselves what we have become too comfortable with and what feels safe to us yet lies in conflict with the change we wish to seek and the person we wish to become. Only by manifesting profound inner change and beginning our own migration towards greater effectiveness and peace can we create positive outer change that is durable and beautiful. In essence, it is essential that we stir up conflict within ourselves as we begin the journey down the change-making path. Viewed this way, conflict can be seen as a vital and healthy part of any change—inward or outward.

JR: What does positive change mean? It means moving in the direction of your purpose. Without a purpose, you get stuck in a rut or change according to your whims, thus sometimes going this way and sometimes that with no definite direction. With a sense of purpose, you can find ways of moving towards it, and constructively engage in the conflicts that help to mold you to progress towards attaining your goal.

PP: What change do you need in order to move towards one of your life-enriching goals? Find a way to initiate making and effecting that change.

June 8

Not wasting creativity, but being creative with waste

Unknown numbers of people were suffering dangerously from an "existential vacuum:" the loss of an ultimate meaning to existence that would make life worthwhile. As Frankl saw it, "The consequent void, the state of emptiness is at present one of the major challenges to psychiatry."

Carl Jung agreed. During his long professional practice as a psychoanalyst, he was consulted by people "from all the civilized countries of the earth." Among all his patients in the second half of life, "there has not been one whose problem in the last resort was not one of finding a religious outlook on life. It is safe to say that every one of them fell ill because he had lost that which the living religions of every age have given their followers, and none of them has been really healed who did not regain his religious outlook."

JR: Having a meaningful belief system (religious or otherwise) and hope for the future fills one with energy and also repositions her to use her creativity to live out that faith. Losing, or simply not being able to feel, a sense of hope not only drains your energy, but scatters it in seeking the fulfillment of a host of temporary, fleeting desires which provide no long-term contentment. Regaining a sense of hope can resurrect those who are trapped in the dungeon of meaningless despondency.

PP: What do you despair about? How can you shine a ray of hope therein to start dispelling the darkness contained within?

June 9

Appealing to our nobler nature

What sort of science is it that must, for the sake of its predictive success, hope and pray that people will never be their better selves, but always be greedy social idiots with nothing finer to do than getting and spending, getting and spending?

We need a nobler economics that is not afraid to discuss spirit and conscience, moral purpose and the meaning of life, an economics that aims to educate and elevate people, not merely to measure their low-grade behavior.

JR: The messages in our mass media and advertisements to buy more, look after only yourself, and be a success nearly drown out the intermittent chirping that may faintly be heard to live a moral life of purpose and cultivate a joyful spirit. Herein, through focusing on our selfish desires at the expense of doing good to others, we are creating a hell on earth. However, when committed groups of people choose to enhance both simultaneously, heavenly places emerge.

PP: What is one way you can start living out a "nobler economics" in your own life?

June 10

The door leading to another world

The further we proceed in diminishing our narcissism, our self-centeredness and sense of self-importance, the more we discover ourselves becoming not only less fearful of death, but also less fearful of life. And we become more loving. No longer burdened by the need to protect ourselves, we are able to lift our eyes off ourselves and to truly recognize others. And being able to experience a sustained, underlying kind of happiness that we've never experienced before as we become progressively more self-forgetful and hence more able to remember God.

This is the central message of all the great religions: Learn how to die. Again and again they tell us that the path away from narcissism is the path toward meaning. Buddhists and Hindus speak of this in terms of the necessity for self-detachment, and, indeed, for them even the notion of the self is an illusion. Jesus spoke of it in similar terms: "Whosoever will save his life (that is, whosoever will hold on to his narcissism) will lose it. And whosoever will lose his life for my sake will find it."

JR: Death opens the door to other possibilities that are previously unimaginable. For example, when your job "dies," you may wither in misery, or feel the freedom to do what you've always wanted and get trained to move into a completely novel area of work. When you can do so, you have "learned how to die." And when you train yourself to consistently be renewed in the wake of trying times, you cultivate a generative attitude in which the suffering that accompanies each death in your life provides a fertile soil which gives rise to new life.

PP: What is something (someone) that would devastate you if you lost it (her)? Try to imagine a way you could create a renewed life for yourself after such a loss.

June 11

Seek and identify signs as to where you want to be heading

The greatest danger in our society is hardly self-delusion about the possibility of creating the "perfect society!" It's the opposite—feeling so cut off from power to shape our society that we lose any vision of where we are headed as a people. This loss violates our very nature because, as human beings, we are creative. Being part of making the world better is as much a part of being human as is the pain of disappointment.

Psychologists confirm that most people have a greater sense of well-being when they contribute to something they care about beyond themselves. In fact, they say, our mental health depends on it.

JR: Our education system, and today's society, focuses its energy on molding obedient and submissive people willing to sacrifice their own creative urges for a secure job with a steady income. Most of us surrender the effort to shape our own paths, and blindly follow the herd. There are certainly numerous opportunities for each of us to search for and shape her own life course; however, as a whole, the main thrust of our lives subordinates this need to that of material security and the acceptance of others.

PP: What area of creativity would you like to develop? Do it just for a little while today and see how you feel.

June 12

Cutting through all obstacles and carving a path

Teach, don't Preach

1) "Happiness is the joy that comes from positive activity.

You never keep that which has not been obtained through personal development."

2) "Positive affirmation without discipline is the start of delusion.

Make changes from inspiration, not desperation.

We all need long-term powerful goals to get us past the short-term obstacles."

JR: Some people may shy away from the words "goals" and "purpose" since, in today's world, they are often directed towards describing success, becoming popular, or striking it rich—aims towards which many are either ill-equipped for or not predisposed towards. In this case, however, long-term goals can indicate anything which mobilizes you towards what you truly believe in, and affect a firmly grounded happiness and fulfillment. Only you can determine that. When you find that purpose which is uplifting to you, reaching for it is a joy (even with the struggles it entails) and you create the energy needed to get around the roadblocks along the way.

PP: Without thinking of others' expectations, contemplate one long-term goal you'd like to move towards, something that fills you with happiness in just considering it.

June 13

Find the best course

A friend once inquired if Gandhi's aim in settling in the village and serving the villagers as best he could was purely humanitarian. Gandhi replied, "I am here to serve no one else but myself, to find my own self-realization through the service of these village folks."

JR: Quite a paradox—serving others is a selfish endeavor in that it is pleasing to oneself. In other words, we help ourselves by helping others. While doing things only for yourself may provide immediate happiness, doing things for others engenders a deeper, longer-lasting, and fulfilling contentment. Ah, the selfishness of altruism—the world is indeed a strange place!

PP: What course of service is fitting for you? How can you incorporate more time for it in your life?

June 14

Lasting happiness lies in love and service to the sacred.

A plump Indian businessman, dripping with gold and diamonds, came one day to visit Mother Teresa, fell at her feet and proclaimed, "Oh my God, you are the holiest of the Holy! You have given up everything! I cannot even give up one samosa for breakfast!" Mother Teresa started to laugh so hard her attendant nuns grew scared. Eventually, she stopped laughing and, wiping her eyes, leaned forward to help her adorer to his knees.

"So you say I have given up everything?" The businessman nodded. Mother Teresa smiled. "Oh, my dear man, you are so wrong. You have given up the supreme sacred joy of life, the source of all lasting happiness, the joy of giving your life away to other beings, to serve the Divine in them with compassion. It is you who are the great renunciate!" Mother Teresa got down on her knees and bowed to him. Flinging up his hands, he ran out of the room.

The tremendous and simple secret that Mother Teresa was trying to communicate is the message at the core of all the world's spiritual revelations—that lasting happiness springs only from true love of the Divine, the world, and others, a true love that expresses itself tirelessly in wise and compassionate action.

JR: The sacred, the Divine, a higher consciousness—it is so easy to get lost in the words themselves and the various connotations they imply. But with a singular focus on the experience, the "supreme joy of life" as something we all seek, we find a resonance that ties us all as one, irrespective of your faith. In addition, it can move us towards lives of true love, wherein lies the hope of an enlightened society.

PP: What is one personal attribute that would make you feel spiritually joyful and is within your power to cultivate?

June 15

Join me in the worshipping dance of benevolence

The whole mission of Volunteerism is to engender a kind of deep happiness which becomes the basis of our being. And isn't this what each and every one of us wants in our lives?

In this sense, volunteerism can be considered "selfish." It clears away the illusion that pleasing myself while ignoring others can bring about a grounded sense of contentment. This hallucination fades away as one comes to realize that pleasing oneself while pleasing others creates a longer-lasting, deeper joy. Previous feelings of despair and emptiness disappear as you experience yourself as a catalyst of happiness in others' lives, which circulates back and creates the same in your own life. You become a constructive agent for change, bringing about a better world and infecting others with the goodness in yourself, and making them aware that they, too, have the same within themselves waiting to be released. And others do the same for you in a "circle of benevolence." It is this kind of joyous spirit which people can look forward to when they make volunteerism a part of their lives, doing something they truly believe in and blessing themselves with the gift of purpose, meaning, and deeper joy.

JR: Such beautiful words, but hardly applicable to someone who is withdrawn, depressed, or introverted—or are they? Volunteerism is sometimes mistakenly stereotyped as social activities for outgoing people. However, there are many things that a loner can enjoy while being of service— like planting trees or providing free editing or translation online for do-good groups. Such help is much needed in today's world, and can also be a great way to help rise above the murkiness of depression.

PP: What skill or interest do you have that you enjoy putting into practice? Find a way to use it in some kind of service work.

June 16

Experiencing enlightenment requires some standing back.

A sense of meaning is our strength. When we can see meaning clearly, we know exactly what we are supposed to do, and our energies respond. When we cannot perceive meaning, we yawn with boredom, and our energies fail. This explains one of the chief problems of everyday life. We can be perfectly comfortable, in an enviable situation, and yet thoroughly bored. We can be uncomfortable, in a highly dangerous situation, and yet feel intensely alive. Danger forces us to make a mental effort. We `stand back' from life, like a painter standing back from his canvas, and see over-all meanings. The result is a flood of vitality. It begins to look as if civilization is man's downfall, since it subjects him to increasing comfort. Healthy spirits usually dislike it and may actually go out and seek discomfort. This explains the apparently paradoxical actions of so many `Outsiders' like Gauguin, Van Gogh, Lawrence, who turned their backs on comfort. But man possesses an instrument for adjusting the balance. It is called imagination.

JR: The capacity of humans to create meaning in our lives is such a beautiful gift! And, contrary to expectation, excessive comfort often leads to a feeling of boredom with lives which have lost any sense of meaning. Instead of being forced to use our energies for simple survival, as in the past, the current trying times warrant the invigorating challenge of vitalizing ourselves through creating our own purpose.

PP: Imagine being told that you MUST define your life purpose in one sentence. Write it down. (Even if you don't have one, just make one up and see how it feels.)

June 17

Sustainable wellbeing

We can engage in a global dialogue to envision "the future we want" (the theme of the UN's Rio+20 conference), and then devise an adaptive strategy to get us there, or we can allow the current system to collapse and rebuild from a much worse starting point. Obviously, the former strategy is better.

To do this, we need to focus more directly on the goal of sustainable human wellbeing rather than merely GDP growth. This includes protecting and restoring Nature, achieving social and intergenerational fairness (including poverty alleviation), stabilising population, and recognising the significant non-market contributions to human wellbeing from natural and social capital. And to do this, we need to develop better measures of progress that go well beyond GDP and begin to measure human wellbeing and its sustainability more directly.

Balancing and investing in all our assets to achieve sustainable wellbeing requires that we pursue three dimensions in an integrated way: ecological sustainability, social fairness, and efficient allocation of resources.

Social fairness means that these resources are distributed fairly within this generation, between generations, and between humans and other species.

JR: There is little, if any, discussion conducted in our schools about the kind of future we truly desire for our future generations on earth. Rather, the focus is on learning a variety of subjects, most of which are futile for use in later life. Why don't we structure education as a powerful force for envisioning and creating a sustainable wellbeing for all, making it more intriguing to teachers and students alike?

PP: What three factors do you consider to be most important in creating a truly sustainable world?

June 18

*All life
seeks contentment.*

Paul Raskin and his colleagues in the Global Scenario Group envisioned a future when human values are realized. 'Here is a civilization of unprecedented freedom, tolerance and decency. The pursuit of meaningful and fulfillling lives is a universal right, the bonds of human solidarity have never been stronger and ecological sensibility infuses human values. Preferred lifestyles combine material sufficiency with qualitative fulfillment. Conspicuous consumption and glitter are viewed as vulgar throwbacks to an earlier era. The pursuit of the well-lived life turns to the quality of existence—creativity, ideas, cultures, human relationships and a harmonious relationship with nature. The economy is understood as the means to these ends, rather than an end in itself.' A new consciousness such as this breaks with anthropocentrism and contempocentrism and embraces a perspective on life and the world that prizes the two central ideas of environmental ethics: the protection for their own sake of the living communities that evolved here with us and our trusteeship of the earth's natural wealth and beauty for generations to come.

JR: A bit idealistic, wouldn't you say? Yes, as it's supposed to be. We limit ourselves by saying "it can't happen." The purpose of envisioning a perfect future is to identify and understand the direction we want to move towards. When that is determined, then, and only then, can the discussion begin on how to progress on that path. "Progress" nowadays simply refers to changing and moving forward into an unknown future, as if we are automatons with no conscious input on where we wish to go.

PP: What do you think about the Global Scenario Group's vision? What can you do to advance the points you most agree with?

June 19

Reawakening your sense of awe

The denial and inability to stay focused on the ecological crisis, one of the great historical instances of collective denial, is easier to understand if we recognize that most people are in such immediate pain in their lives (caused by the frustration of their meaning-needs) that they are unable to pay attention to this larger but less pressing problem. If people feel terrible about themselves and their lives, and they internalize those feelings in the form of self-blame, they develop what I call "surplus powerlessness."

Ironically, it is precisely the de-meaning and the disenchanting of the world that has created the context for the ecological crisis in the first place. It is only because we have suppressed our natural tendency to respond to the world with awe, wonder, and radical amazement, that current environmentally destructive practices are tolerated. We have replaced these sentiments with a willingness to see the earth as a resource to be exploited for the benefit of anyone who has the economic or technological capacity to do so.

JR: By discovering ways of dealing with their own issues constructively, people feel empowered and can become positive change agents for larger issues such as climate change. In addition, through cultivating a sense of wonder for the natural world, we engender a spirit of caring towards it. Empowerment and awe—these are two of the most important qualities to cultivate among the masses for dealing with the environmental crisis.

PP: How can you instill more of a sense of "radical amazement" in your own life?

June 20

You owe me—for all I bring to your world.

There is a pervasive pattern of contextual strangulation we are seeing in the media, in which long-term consequences are eliminated from discussion or thought by focusing on some fabricated controversy about short-term events. It's the same kind of contextual decimation that has been used in official discussions of climate change, deforestation, and the extreme poverty of 2 billion people. We are systematically encouraged to forget that we have any moral obligation to any other lives than our own. And the mainstream publishers and producers, who know where their advertising and investment revenue is coming from, remain mute. Other cultures, other generations, and other species aren't at the table. In this shift of context, the concern we might have for the future of life on Earth is grotesquely transmuted into a fear that gasoline prices might rise, or that illegal immigrants might start camping out on our lawns.

JR: Our focus on short-term solutions while ignoring their long-term (and often harmful) aftereffects results in many of the intractable environmental and social issues plaguing us today. How can we generate a genuine concern for the way we are influencing future generations and other forms of life? The majority of people are unlikely to be "threatened" into really caring about the large issues of climate change and poverty UNLESS they can understand how their concern and action will better their own lives. Frequently reminding a person of the pertinent issues and the consequences is important, but more important is showing the positive improvement of taking action now on their own lives (and those of their descendants).

PP: Where do you get your news? How about finding an additional source that shows positive actions people are taking to deal with today's issues?

June 21

The peak of the cycle is blessed by such beauty.

The eternal enemy of civilization is complacency.
From bondage to spiritual faith,
From spiritual faith to great courage,
From courage to liberty,
From liberty to abundance,
From abundance to selfishness,
From selfishness to complacency,
From complacency to apathy,
From apathy to dependency,
From dependency back again to bondage.

JR: It is interesting, and somewhat disheartening at the same time, to see this cycle repeating itself throughout history. How can we break the cycle, and move from abundance to more emotional caring? Rather than becoming complacent and apathetic, we need to proceed so that we consciously stimulate ourselves into creating more goodness and beauty in the world. It will surely take a mammoth effort to encourage people to become sources of their own stimulation and creators of good, but if we do move forward in this way, the descent into complacency can be effectively halted.

PP: Plant a seed, either literally or figuratively (like a seed of hope), and water it, bearing witness to the goodness you've nurtured.

June 22

Freedom lies in designing your own path.

Some observers argue that people are inhibited from accepting a vision of expanding leisure because of the threat of having to be responsible for structuring and self-managing their time. Fromm maintained that rather than welcoming the opportunity to be responsible for managing their own lives, people want instead to rely on some external agent. In medieval times it might have been the church, and today the corporation and paid work. The liberation of time so that it becomes useful to the individual and to society alike will be a major undertaking for those used to having time scheduled and organized externally by others.

JR: People make paths in the woods and take responsibility to manage them; otherwise, the paths will be overtaken by plant growth. Yet, few people choose to take control of their own life path, making others responsible for most of their time-management. When others determine how our time is used, it lifts a great burden from us, i.e. taking on the responsibility of setting our own course. While much of your time may be set by your company, school, family and the like, seeking out the best ways to use your free time, the time that you can use as you like, is a good start towards taking control of this precious resource.

PP: What do you do in your free time? Is it nurturing what you wish to see and feel in your life?

June 23

Wonderful to see what happens when nature and humanity work in tandem

1) If you want to be abundant in money, love, or anything else, you have to show up consistently. Persistence will win out over creativity and talent just about every time.

2) "I haven't failed, I just found 10,000 ways that don't work."

JR: The whole history of evolution is underpinned by trial and error. This implies attempting new things and constantly altering them. As some die out in the process, others achieve their niches on this diverse planet. Without this tenacious "effort" of the natural world, the earth would have been a dead planet long ago. How much we have to learn from this living example of persistence and healthy survival.

PP: How can you become more consistent in showing up more often for the person or ideal you treasure most?

June 24

Cultivating anything worthwhile takes time.

The 22 cantons, or counties, of Switzerland clashed relentlessly with each other for a thousand years, but with the Constitution of 1848, when all the Swiss people at last felt their voices would be heard, a remarkable transformation overtook the country.

The educational system actively emphasizes the creative unity they share and de-emphasizes old resentments. At heart, the success of Switzerland is due to "the ethic of respect." Successful ethnic coexistence is dependent on a significant amount of equality between groups.

JR: What we focus on is what we are most likely to bring into our lives. When we feed our indignations, we likewise attract others who are resentful; however, focusing on living cooperatively with others will bring like-minded individuals into our lives. By centering our education system on that which we want to bring into our lives, we take an important step in making it a reality. Switzerland serves as an inspiring example.

PP: What value do you want to bring more into your life? How about watching programs or reading books about people who are actively putting that value into practice?

June 25

The individual and the collective—beautiful when in balance

The reason we have not achieved our potential for happiness or behaved like an enlightened society is because we have not understood that real happiness is attained not in the pursuit of material things but in the quest for enlightenment.

When we understand that it is possible to attain perfect enlightenment ourselves, our sense of meaning of our lives changes. Enlightenment is an evolutionary goal. It is perfect freedom—a freedom so total it cannot be lost. It is perfect security, certain of its reality, perfection, and eternal bliss—it is the goal in the quest for happiness.

In the US we have a government built on democratic principles that could support the growth of individual and collective enlightenment. We have access to the teachings of the Buddha and other enlightened beings to guide our evolution. As individuals we must make enlightenment our primary goal, and as a country we must emphasize the development of resources to help the individual attain true happiness. An America built on the principles and practices of enlightenment would be the greatest country in the world.

JR: While it is doubtful whether perfect enlightenment is attainable for anyone, striving to move towards it has great merit for the individual and for society as a whole. The ideological system in the United States operates against any kind of collective enlightenment as it encourages people to gain more riches and live for #1 (the self). How can we start moving away from our self-centeredness and towards a society that cares for all? And remember, the only way you can truly care for others is to also care for yourself.

PP: In what way don't you care for yourself, or even hurt yourself? How can you change that so you treat yourself better?

June 26

Complete dedication made all the difference.

1) "There is only one thing in this world which is worth dedicating all your life. This is creating more love among people and destroying barriers which exist between them."

2) "Many persons have a wrong idea about what constitutes real happiness. It is not attained through self-gratification, but through fidelity to a worthy purpose."

JR: Blessed is the one who is able to identify the singular dedication of one's life and does so with a joyous heart. A lot has been written about how a sense of purpose advents fulfillment, yet few of us critically question the ultimate purpose of our life. One of the true joys for a mother is her complete devotion towards her children, which is a wonderful exemplar model for those in search of their life's purpose.

PP: What is one way you can break down a barrier that separates two important people in your own life?

June 27

Being just right

Emotional health isn't about finding the right person, but being the right person. To let go of negative thoughts and emotions and to discover inner peace, joy, and happiness—these are the goals. You will find life so much more enjoyable.

JR: Developing a realization that you yourself are responsible for your happiness makes you focus on how to become the right person, and empowers you to move towards that happiness. The opinion that "When I find the right person, everything will be all right" completely robs you of your power, making you dependent on another for your happiness. As you flourish to become the person you wish to be, you find that you fit in more easily wherever you go, with "the right people" naturally gravitating towards you.

PP: For you, what does it mean to be the right person? How can you cultivate the qualities to become that person?

June 28

When your heart is passionate about it, you flower.

There's a difference between something that stimulates you for a year and something you can be passionate about for ten years. What is the difference? One thing is not ten times more stimulating than the other. The difference is whether your heart's in it.

The traditional search for a career begins with the question "What am I good at?" But that's often not the right starting point for finding a calling.

The true search is for what you believe in. When your heart's engaged, the inevitable headaches and daily annoyances become tolerable and don't derail your commitment. Let your brain be your heart's soldier.

JR: Why do many people nowadays feel de-energized and burnt out? Very often, it is because they choose a life path that is practical or that others are also following, rather than a path that excites them deep down. Choosing to do something that has captured your heart so that the path and the passion become one fills you with an energy which makes you willing to try to overcome any obstacle which may present itself. The challenge and stimulation entailed in taking up such a course provides a fuel that never stops burning and keeps you alive.

PP: Is there something you used to do that your heart was completely absorbed in? How can you bring that activity and feeling back into your life?

June 29

Some things are stuck in the status quo—luckily, you have the capacity to take action.

"How do we keep our inner fire alive? Two things, at minimum, are needed: an ability to appreciate the positives in our life—and a commitment to action. Every day, it's important to ask and answer these questions: 'What's good in my life?' and 'What needs to be done?'"

JR: Some of you will say "WHAT—a commitment to action—it's hard enough simply to get up in the morning." That indeed may be the case, but once most of us achieve this feat, the question then becomes "What next?" Perhaps you feel as if you have no goal to commit action towards. If this is the case, think of the good things in your life now, and what you'd like to see more of in your future. Then, design ways of bringing more of these into your life.

PP: What needs to be done to bring in more of what you want into your life?

June 30

*Find yourself first
and then reach out
to others*

The greatest contribution you can make to the world is to grow in self-awareness, self-realization, and the power to manifest your own heartfelt dreams and desires. The next greatest thing you can do is to help others do the same.

JR: Becoming self-aware, of what makes you tick and what makes you truly happy, provides you with the rudder needed to steer the right course in your life. Understanding your "passion" and finding ways to live it out instill within you an energy which excites you and, in turn, inspires others. On the other hand, without this knowledge, we often accept what others say we should be doing and burn ourselves out in the process, eventually coming to need others' help rather than being able to be helpful to others. The best thing you can do for anybody is to first discover, and then cultivate, your own essence—THE REAL YOU.

PP: What can you do to find your essence or, if you have already found it, help others to find theirs?

JULY

Dignity & Inclusion

The concepts of dignity and inclusion are necessarily intertwined, for those who are excluded from a circle of any kind lose their sense of dignity and their feeling of being worthy as human beings. Correspondingly, those who experience a deep sense of worthiness feel as if they are a part of something bigger—a group which they value, the larger society, or feel a strong connection to nature or a spiritual discipline. When society comes to perceive each person and all of life as being inherently valuable, extremism has no place to wrap its tentacles around and eventually withers away. When we treat people with dignity, they naturally come to treat others in the same way, creating a strong bond that becomes increasingly all-inclusive.

The meaning of "all-inclusive" herein entails the idea of all life as being fundamentally valuable and encourages individuals to act on that, while encouraging others to do the same. At the same time, when we blindly accept individual behaviors damaging to our universal ideals, like someone who insists on his right to downgrade others, we destroy our own sense of community and inclusiveness, for such a person drives a wedge between people. Continuing to treat such people with dignity while refusing to accept such behavior helps to undermine potential acts of cruelty, understanding that people resort to meanness and crime largely because of the feeling of being disrespected and unloved. We treat all people with respect with the realistic hope that our treatment will be a seed for others to do the same.

Looking at dignity and inclusion from this perspective, we must be wary of our well-intended charitable actions that may actually be detrimental. By making others more dependent on handouts for simple survival, we are destroying their dignity and secluding them from the "functional" society. But through investing our time and money towards empowering these people to better care for themselves and, going a step further, personally working with them in the spirit of true kinship, making them a part of our lives, we move more towards a society where the spirit of dignity and inclusion prevails.

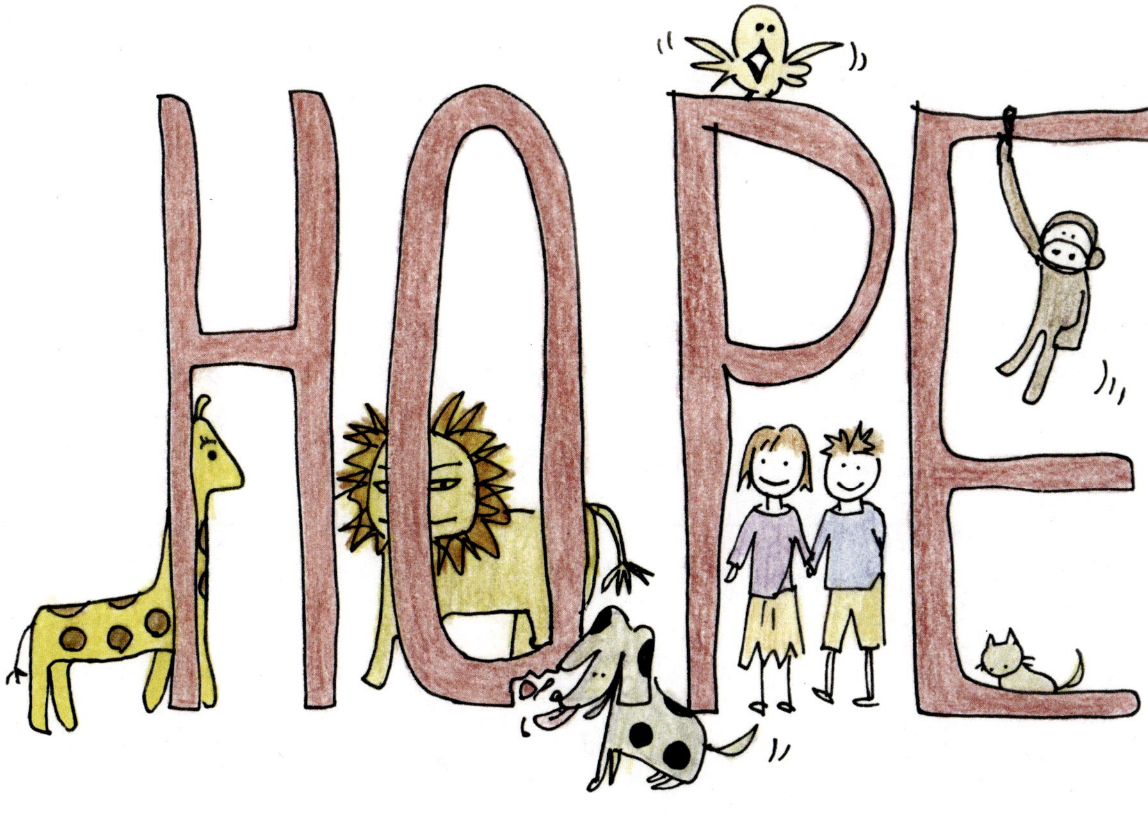
HOPE

July 1

All creatures share the will to live.

Which concepts are most desirable to the people of various countries? Among the words offered were liberty, freedom, independence and human dignity. Dignity was chosen first in all countries.

JR: While charity work is filled with good intentions, it too often treats the receivers as being helpless and thereby robs them of their power. The best kind of good works towards the disadvantaged is that which gives them a sense of dignity, the power and capacity to help themselves and others in the process. Put yourself in their shoes and imagine how you'd like to be treated.

PP: Rather than simply giving something to a homeless (or other disadvantaged) person, what can you do to make them feel more dignified?

July 2

Talk about insecure—
Just one wrong move
and down we go

No wonder people feel insecure today. When we live in a world in which people are not able to see each other as fundamentally valuable, as created in the image of God—as mini-miracles who should elicit our sense of awe and wonder—then everyone starts to feel less safe. The selfishness that fills our economic world begins to shape every other part of life, too. Families and relationships begin to fall apart. You can't live in a society that teaches selfishness, materialism, and "looking out for number one" all day in the world of work and then expect that people won't act this way when they get home. As a result, there is a huge spiritual and ethical crisis in this society—a crisis rooted in the bottom-line consciousness of the world of work.

Spirituality refers to an orientation to reality in which we respond to the universe (and to each other) with awe, wonder, and amazement, as opposed to looking at the universe (and each other) primarily from the standpoint of how we can use it (or each other) to advance our own economic, political or ego goals. Right now, it's virtually impossible to get workplaces or government or media to create space for us to integrate our spiritual insights or sensitivity into our daily lives.

JR: "Every man for himself." "It's a dog-eat-dog world." "What's in it for me?" These kinds of messages dominate the public discussion on the kind of world we live in. Spirituality—the cultivation of a sense of wonder and caring for yourself and others—loses out, yet it is the only thing which can bring a deep sense of security to the individual and society as a whole.

PP: Contemplate on how giving to and caring for others makes you feel more secure.

July 3

Feeling nostalgic at day's end with the anticipation of a new dawn

What do I have in common with people who regard their religious and political convictions as so authoritative that they feel no need to listen to anyone who sees things differently—especially that small subgroup of extremists who would use violence to advance their views? Perhaps we share an abiding grief over some of modernity's worst features: its mindless relativism, corrosive cynicism, disdain for tradition and human dignity, indifference to suffering and death.

JR: Denouncing "those incorrigible extremists" may instill a sense of righteousness and make you feel like the good person you are. But aren't you also saddened about the misguided path which society is following, at least in some ways? Harping on others' evilness will do nothing to better them. It is essential to understand why they have become that way—the anger and grief they feel towards a world gone awry—and be more aware of this in yourself as well. This initiative can be a stepping stone to finding a way to eventually work together on rooting out the cause of the problem and smashing the foundation on which violent extremism now stands.

PP: What is one of modernity's features which you despise? How can you constructively work towards its healing?

July 4

Difficult to perceive the real fault line

The great fault line in the world is not between Americans and Arabs or Muslims and Christians. It is between the moderates of all traditions and the extremists who belong only to one—the tradition of extremism.

JR: Our world would be much better if we spent more time on overcoming our own faults than focusing on finding fault with others. By criticizing a whole group of people, refusing to distinguish the good from the bad within that group, we simply increase the hostility and ill-feelings which we righteously claim to be trying to stomp out. Finding and working together with others who share our basic sense of universal values, against those who wish to destroy them, will achieve more towards cultivating a peaceful world than the righteous hypocrisy which now feeds the extremists.

PP: Read a newspaper or magazine piece that is sympathetic to some group which you don't like, and try to understand their point of view.

July 5

Rise up and better your world

For most of the poorest people in the world, their hard work doesn't matter. They are trapped within social, cultural, political, and economic systems that do not reward their labor. The result of this entrenched futility is devastating to the human spirit. A person, no matter how gifted or determined, cannot escape the trap in which he finds himself. He has lost the one thing that every person needs to thrive: hope—hope that he will somehow overcome his circumstances, that tomorrow can be better than today, and that his children might someday have a better life than his. Such people discover that they are in an economic and social prison from which there is no escape—unless something happens to change their circumstances and to restore the link between effort and their reward.

JR: How would you feel if the only work available paid so little that you and your family had to live on a dirt floor and were malnourished for lack of money? Or if you had to prostitute yourself in order to survive? There would be no escape since there would simply be no other paid opportunities. Can you feel the despair and the agony that so many people are living in today? If you can indeed really feel it, you will make an effort, however small, to correct this unforgivably cruel flaw in our global system.

PP: How about buying some fair trade good(s) as one way of restoring the link between effort and reward?

July 6

Place your trust where it is reciprocated

People who cannot trust themselves become the fugitives of society. They punish themselves indirectly by putting their trust in the people who are least likely to return it. Then they parade the fact that they have been betrayed. This eases their own burden. In place of personal integrity, they rely on the grand absolution of sin: everybody does it. Their personal lives are a whirlpool of bad relationships and failed projects. In the end, pretense strengthens the fear it was meant to conceal.

JR: Similar to what untrusting people do in unconsciously building relationships that are bound to fail, we do as a society in our relationship with nature. We trust more in our technologies—willing to inflict "collateral damage" on our living fellows (plants and animals alike) for increasingly more development—than in nature and her bounty which has provided for our livelihoods since time immemorial. Are we not making the same mistake as the untrusting soul?

PP: Who are you putting your trust in? Is your relationship with her fruitful, or is it filled with a sense of distrust that justifies your suspicious attitude towards the relationship?

July 7

Sharing beauty delights one and all.

Money is like manure. If you pile it up, it stinks. But if you spread it around, it can do a lot of good. If we do not use our wealth and resources to help lessen the gap between rich and poor, when the world looks back on us, people with money who didn't do anything will be remembered as war criminals.

JR: Accumulating more and more goods with the attitude that you are deserving (while others are not) or as security against a hostile world is critically damaging not only to society (in that it is taking away from the whole) but also to your own soul (in that you pit yourself against others). By sharing your wealth, others become your supporters and a deeper sense of security is created than any great wealth could ever bestow.

PP: How can you use some of your wealth to build stronger relationships with people near and far?

July 8

Each element shapes its surroundings.

1) The intolerance we feel towards others is always a reflection of how intolerant we are of ourselves. Whenever we judge, hate, humiliate, or ostracize another, it is always because we fear being judged, humiliated, rejected, or stigmatized ourselves.

2) The way you see people is the way you treat them, and the way you treat them is the way they become.

JR: Perceiving intolerance as a symptom of your own fear gives you a chance to deal with it constructively. It is easy to despise a woman who you are frightened of and who judges you negatively. However, if she constantly shows loving acceptance towards you, the fear disappears and it becomes increasingly difficult to hate her. This awareness moves you towards dissipating your narrow-mindedness and, in the process, transforming your relationships, for then you can truly understand the value of demonstrating love even towards the despicable.

PP: Who are you intolerant of? Can you see how your own fear of being unacceptable to others causes this intolerance?

July 9

Human habitation in nature's embrace

1) Have the courage to go against the tide of this culture of efficiency, this culture of waste. Encountering and welcoming everyone, solidarity—a word that is being hidden by this culture, as if it were a bad word—solidarity and fraternity: these are what make our society truly human.

2) To sustain a lifestyle which excludes others, or to sustain enthusiasm for that selfish ideal, a globalization of indifference has developed. Almost without being aware of it, we end up being incapable of feeling compassion at the outcry of the poor, weeping for other people's pain, and feeling a need to help them, as though all this were someone else's responsibility and not our own. The culture of prosperity deadens us; we are thrilled if the market offers us something new to purchase; and in the meantime all those lives stunted for lack of opportunity seem a mere spectacle; they fail to move us.

JR: Solidarity can be a scary word—after all, it is difficult to commune with, much less to befriend, others of different beliefs, races, and customs. It is easier to mingle with those who think and do the same as us because then our sense of righteousness is unchallenged. It is our indifference and our separation from others who are different that causes many of today's ills. By reconnecting, we allow ourselves to feel what others are going through, open up the doors to understanding, and find spaces where constructive solutions become feasible.

PP: FEEL what the poor go through by giving up just one meal and experiencing hunger for a short time. Many are stuck in this state of deprivation. How can you provide support (through donating or volunteering, for example) to them?

July 10

Stand up and express yourself

Hate and punishment never cured anything, only love can cure.

If humans were born with an instinct for criminality, there would be as many criminals from fine middle-class homes as from slum homes. But well-to-do people have more opportunities for expression of the ego. The pleasures money buys, the refined surroundings, culture, and pride of birth all minister to the ego. Among the poor, the ego is starved.

The youths who are called delinquents are trying to express power that has been suppressed. I have generally found that the antisocial child, the leader of a gang of window breakers, becomes under freedom a strong supporter of law and order.

It is only thwarted power that works for evil in a child. Human beings are good; they want to love and be loved. Hate and rebellion are only thwarted love and thwarted power.

JR: In many spiritual writings, it may be mistakenly assumed that the ego is bad. On the contrary, a healthy (not inflated) sense of ego is necessary for spiritual growth. The disempowered person whose ego has been thwarted is more likely to express his frustration in destructive ways. Through finding ways of constructive expression of himself and empowering his life, his ego is fed and his desire to "fight against" is changed into "living for."

PP: When did you feel completely powerless? How did you feel? Try to understand that this is the road on which many of today's poor and rejected are stuck.

July 11

Take a close look

Most crime arises from the despair of the disrespected and the unloved. This fact does not excuse lawbreakers in any way, but it is still a fact. The antidote is to truly see one another, to seek to understand one another, and to create 3rd Alternative solutions to hopelessness.

JR: Many people feel a sense of hopelessness because they feel that nobody truly hears or cares for them. Feeling alone and outside of the fold, they feel that societal rules no longer apply to them. Overcoming this sense of futility requires being listened to closely and feeling the doors of hope opening, transforming the outcast into a constructive contributor to society.

PP: Think of someone who has committed an atrocious crime, and read a passage or watch a short video told by him, or someone sympathetic to him, to try to achieve an understanding as to why he did it.

July 12

Sharing is a joy when there is no exploitation.

We will never learn to live in balance with the biosphere until we value human justice—and we will never achieve human justice until we realize that we cannot sublimate our exploitative urges onto the environment. When we see the world, or other people, only as useful tools, we enter into exploitative I-it relationships, spiritually crippling both victim and victimizers. Exploitation is one of the worst forms of idolatry and self-worship; kinship with creation, a humble acknowledgement of God's ownership of and sovereignty over all, is one of the highest forms of prayers.

JR: For the believer in a personal God, the kind of prayer that communicates with Her "out there" while granting a license for you to destroy creation is a slap in Her face. However, showing respect and appreciation to your fellow living creatures, the different manifestations of the Divine, is a kind of prayer which uplifts the soul and makes you capable of no longer seeing them as things to be used, but rather as your kin in this life's journey.

PP: Say a prayer of thanks to the various life forms around you, and feel your kinship with them.

July 13

There's a time to protect yourself and a time for opening up.

People are only mean when they're threatened, and that's what our culture does. That's what our economy does. Even people who have jobs are threatened, because they worry about losing them. And when you get threatened, you start looking out only for yourself. You start making money a god. It is all part of this culture.

JR: Why do we find so many people wishing to live alone nowadays? One reason is that it's easier and more stress-free than the complicated ups and downs of a live-in relationship, and the associated insecurities. We fear being rejected because of our faults and feeling of not being good enough. Likewise, in the larger society, it's hard to feel that our existence is being treasured in a throw-away culture that treats people as things. Bringing love and universal values back into the center of our lives is the way to entice people out from their shells.

PP: How do you feel threatened in your everyday life? How can you "relieve" this feeling?

July 14

The hell with what others think—I'm living it up!

"Dying is only one thing to be sad over. Living unhappily is something else. So many of the people who come to visit me are unhappy."

"Why?"

"Well, for one thing, the culture we have does not make people feel good about themselves. We're teaching the wrong things. And you have to be strong enough to say if the culture doesn't work, don't buy it. Create your own. Most people can't do it. They're more unhappy than me—even in my current condition. I may be dying, but I am surrounded by loving, caring souls. How many people can say that?"

JR: Culture shapes us, but we also shape our culture. When you blindly follow the culture without questioning it, you are designating it more power while giving up your power to control your life. Search for what makes you dance with joy, and find ways of doing it more frequently in your life.

PP: Which cultural habit or teaching doesn't fit you? Think of how you can stop following it and create a way that is right for you.

July 15

Getting personally involved makes all the difference.

Tough Love with a Vengeance

Sister Connie opened the St. Martin de Porres House of Hope for women in a tough South Side neighborhood in Chicago. And her shelter is not a place where homeless women are coddled. Residents must accept a strict regimen that includes rising at 6:30 A.M. Mothers must clean their children and their rooms before breakfast. Classes in parenting and life skills are mandatory. So are the daily twelve-step programs for substance abusers. Those without a high school diploma have to work toward one.

It's tough love with a vengeance—and it works. Since 1982, more than 10,000 women have passed through the shelter, and thanks to Sister Connie's tough-love approach, 95 percent of them leave the shelter system—and welfare—for good. That's a far higher success rate than government-funded shelters can promise.

Sister Connie's secret, of course, is the moral demands she adds to the assistance she gives. If assistance is to make a long-term difference, it has to come with moral strings attached. It involves making people learn how to behave responsibly.

We need to help people understand that the best way to solve entrenched social problems is to offer what Sister Connie offers: compassion—and a sense of moral responsibility.

JR: What a powerful combination—compassion shown through personal involvement with others' issues and demanding that they assume responsibility for their own lives! There is no better way to provide hope to individuals who have given up on life.

PP: Find a person or organization that provides practical hope with this effective combination, and offer your support in some way.

July 16

Be constructive, not destructive

Gandhi's trust for the future lay mostly in steady, constructive work—steady rather than occasional, work rather than protest; self-uplift rather than the obstruction of others; practical and concrete rather than symbolic.

JR: Gandhi is best known for his resistance against colonialism and advancing India towards independence. However, it was his emphasis on steady, constructive work, discipline, and empowering the poor that made the resistance so potent. A strong foundation built with persistence and the provision of hope makes a movement most effective.

PP: What do you (want to) protest against? What constructive action can you take that would lessen its attraction and encourage others to support your alternative?

July 17

Break through, and brighten up the world

Right after WWII the US initiated the Marshall Plan.

People tried to rethink after WWII, and what they came up with was that they would help to rebuild the industrial countries of Western Europe and make them self-sufficient, to rebuild those societies so there would be trading partners, other people who were productive. And they came through. Instead of giving them loans, they gave them grants. It worked. They took what had been the most horrific event in the history of humankind—WWII—and they came out of it with a plan to build on the foundations of human dignity and local self-sufficiency. They made it possible for France to build a new France, not an American France—and on and on. The idea behind that model, the enlightened self-interest of that model, could change things in the Middle East, in Afghanistan, in Pakistan, in all of central Asia.

JR: In the aftermath of war, the victors usually are known to punish the losers. And this action plants the seed of another conflict since it leads the defeated into a downward spiral of feeling humiliated, resenting their conquerors, and eventually seeking revenge. However, through restoring human dignity to the defeated, the victors can effectively champion an even greater path of mutual support, peace, and the possibility of a world free of war.

PP: Who is someone you know who "feels defeated?" What can you do to help her regain her dignity?

July 18

The feeling of exclusion can be so devastating.

Poverty is being excluded from community. It is internal exile. But if poverty is exclusion, then it's not enough just to help people get "things;" to bring people into the economic fold through microcredit, for instance. The mores, the norms must change so that it is no longer acceptable to exclude, to leave people out of what they need if they are to be members of the community.

The root of poverty is exclusion!

JR: How would it feel to be living in a society where everyone ignores you? They look through you rather than at you. You are invisible to them or simply ignored because you have nothing to offer to them. If they acknowledge your existence, they are pained with a sense of guilt, or must seek justification as to why you are in that state. That is the life of many of today's poor, homeless, and others. Would feel pretty miserable, wouldn't it?

PP: Who is excluded from your family or acquaintances? Imagine how he must feel.

July 19

Abandon me and I will unleash my fury

Public abandonment and disapproval of homosexual sons and daughters drives them away from the family and makes the irresponsible behavior of their subculture almost predictable.

JR: In abandoning those of who we disapprove, we become unknown accomplices to their further destructive behaviors. Lack of recognition of homosexual union makes clandestine promiscuity the norm. Ignoring or simply disapproving of terrorists, refusing to acknowledge their complaints, pushes them to even more violent acts of fury, in their search of doing anything to be seen and heard. Listening does not mean accepting, but it does mean opening up enough so that such desperate acts of futility are no longer seen as desirable to anybody.

PP: Who have you abandoned in the past? What could you have done (or can you do now) to lessen her despair in having been "discarded?"

July 20

Even the best of us feel hostile at times.

All the sages preached spirituality of empathy and compassion; they insisted that people must abandon their egotism and greed, their violence and unkindness. Not only was it wrong to kill another human being; you must not even speak a hostile word or make an irritable gesture. Further, nearly all the Axial sages realized that you could not confine your benevolence to your own people: your concern must somehow extend to the entire world. In fact, when people started to limit their horizons and sympathies, it was another sign that the Axial Age (a 700 year period dating from 900–200 BC, during which much of the world turned away from violence, cruelty, and barbarity) was coming to a close.

If people behaved with kindness and generosity to their fellows, they could save the world.

JR: Feelings come and go. Even the holiest have waves of anger or jealousy that seethes through their being at times. What makes them special is not that they don't have such feelings, but that their sense of compassion and benevolence rises above and flows out to everyone, friend and foe alike. Spirituality for them means the persistent cultivation of such kindness, which expands to all of life.

PP: What group is your spirit of compassion limited to? How can you expand it a bit to others outside your current boundary?

July 21

Focus on what really matters

A new consumer consciousness and behavior is needed, one where desires are reigned in and people create more time and mental space in their lives, by simplifying and concentrating on what really matters to them. Also, making upscale purchasing uncool because of its inegalitarianism and exclusivity could be the beginning of reforming society the way we want to.

JR: Simplifying life is seen by most people to involve sacrifice and austerity. We fail to see how a luxurious lifestyle full of material goods necessarily diminishes the fulfilling pleasures of deep relationships, loving, connecting with nature, and creating from the heart. This can be attributed to the excessive time and energy needed to acquire and take care of so many goods. Simplifying your life opens up space for these treasures of the spirit to re-emerge and eventually form the focus of your existence.

PP: What dear possession (physical, spiritual, or emotional) have you sacrificed in order to maintain your materialistic lifestyle? Was it worth giving up? If not, how can you simplify your life so that it can again bless your life?

July 22

Feeling secure nestled among friends

The basic building block of peace and security for all peoples is economic and social security, anchored in sustainable development. It is a key to all problems. Why? Because it allows us to address all the great issues—poverty, climate, environment, and political stability—as parts of a whole.

JR: In the days of old, economic and social obligations so burdened people that they came to reject them in favor of today's reigning individualism. Yet, we discover that taking individualism to the extreme leaves us feeling insecure, for what will happen when we can no longer fend for ourselves? The search for a sustainable path which balances the dependence on others for our security with a degree of individuality would surely move us towards being able to deal better with the major issues of our time.

PP: In what way do you feel most insecure? What would make you feel more secure in that respect, and how can you start moving towards that?

July 23

Impossible to feel as separate entities when we're one

Zen master Dogen, the founder of Soto Zen in Japan, declared, "to be enlightened is to be intimate with all things."

Only in the intimacy of the timeless present can we awaken. This intimacy connects us to one another, allows us to belong and, in this belonging, we experience love. In this we move beyond our separateness, our contraction, our limited sense of ourselves. If we investigate what keeps us from intimacy, what keeps us from love, we will discover it is always an expectation, a hope, a thought, or a fantasy. It is the same expectation that keeps us from awakening. Awakening is not far away; it is nearer than near.

JR: How can we live in the present when our minds are so befuddled with thoughts of the past and dreams for the future? More consciously experiencing the present moment fully, even with your remembrances and hopes, can make you feel connected—in unity with all around you—living in a spirit which all of the major religious paths consider desirable.

PP: When did you feel completely connected and "in love" with life? Find ways of "re-creating" such an experience.

July 24

Kinship at the margins

Pema Choldron, an ordained Buddhist nun, writes of compassion and suggests that its truest measure lies not in our service of those on the margins, but in our willingness to see ourselves in kinship with them.

JR: Most of our "do-good" organizations and activities focus on serving others, but it is much more challenging and healing for all to move beyond that and feel in kinship, as one, with them. This is a difficult step to take when we spend day-in and day-out with those of our own ilk. Finding ways of being with those at the margins provides a great boost towards developing a deeper sense of compassion.

PP: Who is "on the margins" where you live? Can you find a way to share a good time with them as you would with a friend (in contrast to serving them)?

July 25

Making boundaries obsolete

1) Jesus was not a man for others. He was one with others. There is a world of difference in that.

2) Jesus eats with tax collectors, touches a dead body, and is touched by a bleeding woman. This healing is not fixing the defective, or endorsing a particular kind of body as holy or whole. It is restoring relationship, creating community, and transgressing boundaries that exclude people.

JR: The life of a true Christian is much more difficult than most Christians would care to admit. Hanging out with the rejected? Befriending the riffraff? Be for real. Yet, this is what it means to follow Jesus. So very different from what is seen and experienced in most examples of Christianity today.

PP: What can you do to help create a stronger, more inclusive community where you are here and now?

July 26

Feeling trapped really sucks!

Whenever we Christians are enclosed in our groups, our movements, our parishes, in our little worlds, we remain closed, and the same thing happens to us that happens to anything closed: when a room is closed, it begins to get dank. If a person is closed up in that room, he or she becomes ill!

JR: This passage could be applied to any group of people—whenever you remain only with your own kind, the same ideas, habits, lifestyles are reinforced and growth becomes severely limited, or completely stops. Exposing yourself to different kinds of people and environments forces you to open your shell and, in the process, you come to see yourself more clearly as well.

PP: Go out and experience something completely new (it could be as simple as going to a restaurant that serves food you've never had).

July 27

Even an ugly seed can blossom into a beautiful flower.

One day, when I was a freshman in high school, I saw a kid from my class walking home from school. His name was Kyle. It looked like he was carrying all of his books. I thought to myself, "He must really be a nerd."

Then, I saw a bunch of kids knocking all his books out of his arms and tripping him so he landed in the dirt. He looked up and I saw this terrible sadness in his eyes. I jogged over and saw a tear in his eye. I said, "Those guys are jerks." He looked at me and said "Hey thanks!"

Over the next four years, Kyle and I became best friends. When we were seniors, Kyle was valedictorian of our class, giving the graduation speech. He cleared his throat, and began.

"Graduation is a time to thank those who helped you make it through those tough years. I am here to tell all of you that being a friend to someone is the best gift you can give them. I am going to tell you a story." I just looked at my friend with disbelief as he told the story of the first day we met. He had planned to kill himself over the weekend. He talked of how he had cleaned out his locker so his Mom wouldn't have to do it later. He looked hard at me and gave me a little smile. "Thankfully, I was saved. My friend saved me from doing the unspeakable."

Never underestimate the power of your actions. With one small gesture, you can change a person's life.

JR: Always remember that the way you deal with others can have a great effect on them. Do you have a negative effect on others due to your bad treatment of them, or engender a positive influence through your kind consideration and action towards them?

PP: Think back on someone who "saved" you or really helped you out in a time of need. Feel the gratitude you have towards her and, if possible, tell her directly.

July 28

Welcome the outlier

In 2009 in Cordova, Tennessee, Heartsong church pastor, Steve Stone, learned that the Memphis Islamic Center had bought land adjacent to this church. Rather than protest the plans, he put up a large sign that said: "Heartsong Church Welcomes Memphis Islamic Center to the Neighborhood." The Muslim leaders were floored. They had dared to hope only that their arrival would be ignored. It had not occurred to them that they might be welcomed.

The Islamic Center's new building was still under construction, so its members used Heartsong Church for Ramadan prayer services. Heartsong's community barbecues served halal meat and the two congregations planned joint efforts to feed the homeless and tutor local children.

Stone also got a call from a group of Muslims in a small town in Kashmir. They said they had been watching CNN when the segment on Heartsong Church aired. Afterward, one of the community's leaders said to those who were gathered, "God just spoke to us through this man." Another said, "How can we kill these people?" A third man went straight to the local Christian church and proceeded to clean it, inside and out.

JR: There is no more long-term, sustainable way of positively influencing others than loving kindness, especially when it blows people out of the water, coming unexpectedly. Those who are outcast often have never felt this kind of truly compassionate kinship and, in turn, are most likely to be strongly affected by it.

PP: Do a completely unexpected "act of kindness" for someone, and delight in the joy it gives to you and to him.

July 29

The magical triad: Air, Land, and Water

A 3 part framework for pluralism: a society characterized by respect for people's religious (and other) identities, positive relationships between people of different religious backgrounds, and common action for the common good.

JR: A pluralistic society can flourish only by respecting each other's differences, carving out a set of common universal values, and working together to move towards creating a community that attempts to live by those values. In such a community, as you become more open and inclusive, taking action with people of very different backgrounds for the common good becomes a delight.

PP: Get together with someone who has a very different belief system than you, and ask her to tell you about it. Try your best to listen simply in order to understand, without interfering and without judgement.

July 30

Mutual well-being

Any solution that does not place the well-being of nonhumans—and indeed the natural world, which is the real world—at the center of its moral, practical, and "realistic" considerations is neither moral, practical, nor realistic. Nor will it solve global warming or any other ecological problem.

Do we want a living real world, or do we want a social structure that is killing the real world? Do we want a living real world, or do we want a dead real world, with a former social structure forgotten by everyone, because there is no one left alive to remember? You choose.

JR: The culture in which we are engrossed focuses on the short term and compartmentalizes everything. These are two of the primary reasons why we are soiling our nest. Who cares what happens in the next 20 years as long as we're making money now? Let's cut down and clear a forest and make a golf course to make the golfers happy, with no worry about the natural environment we're destroying. When we start to develop concern for the long term and seek well-being in a holistic way, for the good of all life, real sustainable solutions become possible.

PP: Reflect on what you do, or what can you do, that supports the well-being of people and nature simultaneously.

July 31

Nature is inclusive of humans, but humanity often fails to reciprocate.

The kingdom of God, then, seeks a 3rd way: not exclusiveness and rejection on the one hand, and not foolish, self-sabotaging inclusion on the other hand, but rather purposeful inclusion. In other words, the kingdom of God seeks to include all who want to participate in and contribute to its purpose, but it cannot include those who oppose its purpose.

JR: PURPOSEFUL INCLUSION is the key! Critics of inclusion and plurality justifiably claim that by letting everyone in, the criminals and saboteurs of a well-functioning society have a place to roost. Without an agreed-upon sense of purpose and accepted values, inclusion becomes self-destructive. Purposeful inclusion welcomes all who wish to move towards "the kingdom" and invites those who work against it to change their ways and join in.

PP: Play with the thought of what purposeful inclusion means to you.

AUGUST

Integration & Connection

Here are another two concepts which go hand in hand. Within the individual, the quest for integrity means striving for a harmonious fitting together of the different aspects of the self—mind, spirit and body. In your integration with the life community, you find ways of promoting your own growth at the same time as positively cultivating your natural and human communities. To do so means that you must make an effort to connect with all of the aspects of the self in order to become whole. In becoming whole and matching your beliefs with your actions, you become fully alive and can proceed to develop and live out visions for the good of life. You seek to find those things that you believe are good and build on them.

It is believed by some that they must reach perfection before acting. RUBBISH! Not only does this never happen, but such a belief leads to making the perfect become the enemy of the good.

Forging the connections that are best will vary greatly from one person to another, depending on your character and your environment. The more extroverted may prefer to connect with other people through organizing fun get-togethers or volunteering. The more introverted may connect with famous writers of forgone times and share them with others through writing, develop technological applications that cultivate compassion, or take care of animals and plants. There is no one and only correct way of connecting with life, but everyone benefits when any one person finds her own right way. And when you truly find the way that is right for you, the connections breathe life into your spirit as your integrity inspires those around you.

247

August 1

Pity those who have to make a conscious effort to be well-aligned

When your external actions reflect your internal code, you are in alignment with your morality. This is how an individual gains integrity. Integrity is important because without it you are living with a sense of division within yourself; you feel incomplete and conflicted.

JR: There is no use in talking about a life of integrity without first developing an understanding and realizing what values are most important to you. By experiencing the process of determining the moral priorities in your life, you establish an underlying foundation for a code of ethics which can become your life guide. Then you know what actions are needed to feel integrated (the matching of deeds and morals), which makes it possible to move consistently towards a more holistic life that forms the bedrock for a deep, inner contentment.

PP: What action do you undertake that closely harmonizes with a value you hold dear? How does it make you feel?

August 2

Learn to develop good vision

Through a number of steps, eighteenth-century capitalism underwent a radical change: economic behavior became separate from ethics and human values. The development of this economic system was no longer determined by the question: What is good for man? But by the question: What is good for the growth of the system? One tried to hide the sharpness of this conflict by making the assumption that what was good for the growth of the system (or even for a single big corporation) was also good for the people. This construction was bolstered by an auxiliary construction: that the very qualities that the system required of human beings—egotism, selfishness, and greed—were innate in human nature. People refused to recognize that these traits were not natural drives that caused industrial society to exist, but that they were the products of social circumstances.

Not least in importance is another factor: people's relations to nature became deeply hostile. Being 'freaks of nature' who by the very conditions of our existence are within nature and by the gift of our reason transcend it, we have tried to conquer nature, by transforming it to our own purposes until the conquest has become more and more equivalent to destruction.

Industrial society has contempt for nature—as well as for all things not machine-made and for all people who are not machine makers. People are attracted today to the mechanical, the lifeless, and ever increasingly to destruction.

JR: Without reconsidering what is truly good for humankind and for the natural environment at large, we continue to blindly follow the path marked with frequent episodes of violence and destruction. Good vision includes the capacity to perceive and understand that what we do to nature is what we do to ourselves.

PP: Read about a group or tribe where egoism and selfishness are (were) minimized. How can we better cultivate such a spirit in the society of today?

August 3

We all get lost at times.

Imperatives to spend in consumer society are numerous, and the incentives to save are weak. But something else unique to the work-and-spend dynamic is that rising incomes create social pressures to spend. A more leisured, lower-spending lifestyle does not emerge. Instead, people get more money and put in long hours on the job. As long as a few fashion-minded or highly consumerist households take on the role of innovators, spending their increased income on new, better, or more consumer items, the impact of their consumption ripples through the system.

JR: Think about this. The more you make, the more you spend. Most of us hang out with people in the same income bracket and feel peer-pressured to keep up with them purchase-wise. We lose sight of the direction that we really wish to go, unencumbered by the demands of our peer group and society as a whole. Getting back in touch with what you really want at the "soul" level will probably relieve your financial pressures and make you feel better about regaining some control over your life.

PP: What things do you buy because you really want them and which do you buy because of expectations from people around you? Are you willing to break out of the expectation trap and fly in the direction of your own choosing?

August 4

If you're bored even with all of this, you've got a problem.

Boredom is as likely to be caused by an excess of stimuli as a vacuum of sensory input.

Perhaps more than half of boredom in America is the result of stimulus satiation rather than stimulus hunger. The American psyche is overloaded with poor-quality mass-produced stimuli.

As a diet of junk food generally suppresses our taste for what is nourishing to the body, so junk values gradually destroy our taste for what is satisfying to the whole person. As Erich Fromm says, in the bored character "there is a lack of appetite for life, a lack of any deep interest in anything or anybody, a feeling of powerlessness and resignation; personal relations—including sexual ones—are thin and flat, and there is little joy or contentment."

JR: *In a world where we suffocate our own creative prowess by taking in ever greater amounts of passive consumption entertainment, we become increasingly bored. We come to rely on outside stimuli to get temporary arousal which quickly dissipates rather than depend on our vast inner resources, which hold the potential of granting us long lasting and fulfilling enjoyment.*

PP: *Think of one creative endeavor you used to do that really excited you. How about taking it up and doing it on a regular basis?*

August 5

Can't help feeling that something is missing

When we experience the loneliness, isolation, and emptiness of societies that value wealth and power above all, and devalue ethical and spiritual reality, we often feel desperate, angry, and ready to embrace any alternative. Economic collapse becomes so terrifying precisely because, without a community of meaning and purpose, each one of us must face the possibility that there will be absolutely no one to help us get basic food or shelter should we lose our job and savings.

JR: How can it be that people of great wealth suffer from the same feelings as the rest of us, and go through similar ups and downs of what everyday existence brings to them? After all, isn't more money what we all wish to have? Still, something's missing even when we are financially well-off. And in many cases, when we continually weaken our connections with others to make more money, that internal emptiness brought about by that "missing something" expands and grows ever darker.

PP: Who could you depend on if you suddenly lost your job and your house? What can you do now to deepen that relationship? Or, if you don't have one, how can you build one?

August 6

All that is holy is not sacred.

In the name of modernity we are creating dysfunctional societies that are breeding pathological behavior—violence, extreme competitiveness, suicide, drug abuse, greed, and environmental degradation—at every hand. Such behavior is an inevitable consequence when a society fails to meet the needs of its members for social bonding, trust, affection, and a shared sacred meaning. The threefold crisis of deepening poverty, environmental destruction, and social disintegration is a manifestation of this dysfunction.

JR: What do we wish to do when we modernize? Ideally, we would build on new ideas which make our societies function more smoothly while retaining past values which instill us with loving concern and spiritual joy. Somehow though, we have chosen "modern" values which separate us and encourage us to fight against each other, often through cutthroat competition, creating a dysfunctional society in the process.

PP: What is one dysfunctional societal value you have incorporated in your life? How would you like to change this into a functional, life-giving value?

August 7

Cultivate life—there are innumerable forms to choose from

The machine, so far from being a sign in our present civilization of human power and order, is often an indication of ineptitude and social paralysis. Any appreciable improvement in education and culture will reduce the amount of machinery devoted to multiplying the spurious mechanical substitutes for knowledge and experience now provided through the channels of the motion picture, the tabloid newspaper, the radio, and the printed book. So, too, any appreciable improvement in the physical apparatus of life, through better nutrition, more healthful housing, sounder forms of recreation, greater opportunities for the natural enjoyments of life, will decrease the part played by mechanical apparatus in salvaging wrecked bodies and broken minds. Any appreciable gain in personal harmony and balance will be recorded in a decreased demand for compensatory goods and services. The passive dependence upon the machine that has characterized such large sections of the Western World in the past was in reality an abdication of life. Once we cultivate the arts of life directly, the proportion occupied by mechanical routine and by mechanical instruments will again diminish.

JR: Machines unquestionably provide us with greater convenience, comfort, and pleasures previously unknown. Yet, over-dependence on the machine leads to our increasing lack of concern for the many forms of life, plant and animal alike, which we necessarily depend on in order to live, as they provide us with nourishment, companionship, and the very air we breathe. Making them a larger part of our everyday lives will move us towards a culture that is actively supportive of life.

PP: How much time do you spend with machines every day? How can you make more time to be with and appreciate the plants and animals which inspirit your life?

August 8

Connecting the spiritual and the earthy

Whatever stands in the way of a conscious contact between the spiritual and the material in human life, only that is truly evil. The desire from physical things, family, safety, comfort, sex—none of that is evil. These are all aspects of one of the great forces of the universe in the human animal.

No, the real evil in our lives is now, and has always been, the cloud of human ignorance and fear which prevents experiential contact between the two levels.

JR: What is it that you desire? Is it spiritually uplifting or soul destroying? Does it move you towards the kind of person you want to become or lead you away from the path of your dreams? The answers to these questions determine whether the desire is to your benefit or actually works against your innermost desire.

PP: What desire do you have that fills you with positive energy, is life-promoting, and moves you towards the person you wish to be? Design your life to better meet this desire.

August 9

Mist-ery

Sin is when you turn away from God—or, in the other language, alienation occurs when the ego, that erratic, unreliable driver of the personality, temporarily turns aside from the great quest for integration with the inner self, the self that's authentic, the self that contains the potential to be fully human, fully fulfilled and fully alive. You don't become fully human by exploiting others; you don't realise your full potential by being insensitive and uncaring. You miss the mark. You fall short of bringing to life your unique personality blueprint designed by the living God who dwells as a spark in the very core of it. The quest for integration—for self-realisation—for the start of what religious language calls eternal life—has been thwarted. Sin/alienation is psychological disease which if unhealed can lead to the living hell of lost hopes and blighted lives.

JR: It's difficult to understand what is right for you when you are being bombarded by so many conflicting messages from others, the media, ads, and so on. It's easy to get caught in the fog of ever-changing expectations. But when you invest time in finding your own unique gifts, develop them, and use them in your everyday life for your own good and the good of others, you will feel the contentment of harmonizing the real you with your surroundings. This is the sinless life, the truly holy life.

PP: What is that something, sinful or otherwise, that makes you feel disintegrated and alienated from yourself? Why does it make you feel so?

August 10

The power of living in the now

Non-polarity thinking teaches you how to hold creative tensions, how to live with paradox and contradictions, how not to run from mystery, and therefore how to actually practice what all religions teach as necessary: compassion, mercy, loving kindness, patience, forgiveness, and humility. It allows you to live in the naked now and to resist the pulls toward any shameful past or any idyllic future.

JR: The temptation to escape from tough situations is strong, but where can you go that doesn't have tension of some kind? Bear in mind that much of the stress in your life is brought on by the baggage you carry with you. So the most effective thing you can do is to "become religious" in the sense of living with mystery and finding creative ways of dealing with difficulties through cultivating these spiritual attributes.

PP: What is a point of tension in your life? How can you deal with it more creatively (by applying one of these spiritual traits)?

August 11

Our perception of the world is all too often a reflection of what we are.

What do you do with someone like Hitler?

In practical terms you fight him. And in spiritual terms you pray for him and remember that there's a divine spark in every human being.

JR: How should you deal with a person bent on wreaking havoc and destruction in the world? Letting him continue with his rage implies effectively granting him permission to destroy you. You must fight against him however you can—either by changing him or, if this is not possible, destroying him in order to save yourself and others and preserve a world where compassionate spirituality can thrive.

PP: Who commits atrocious acts that must not be permitted? What do you think is the best way to fight against him?

August 12

Sleepwalkers beware

Integrity must precede vision. History has shown us the awesome cost of vision without integrity. A charismatic leader such as Hitler gets his people excited about a vision but leads them to doom because the vision is unsupported by integrity, rotten at the core. If your vision does not have a strong integrity base, expect disaster down the line. Begin by focusing on integrity, and your visions have a great deal of positive power in the world.

JR: The dream of the idealist—so beautiful—and so potentially destructive. A vision of a good future gives one a sense of hope, but too often people try to adopt it without first developing in themselves the discipline needed to move towards it effectively. A group of fairly integrated people, whose lives closely correspond to the positive values they proclaim, has great potential towards living out the vision which they share.

PP: Do you feel that your walk matches your talk about "the good life?" What is needed to bring more harmony between the two?

August 13

A good path guides us in the right direction.

1) If we try to solve these challenges in isolation—cutting carbon without addressing the toxicity, habitat impacts or social justice implications of our decisions—we only solve one problem by exacerbating another

2) Getting several billion of us to behave differently—to behave morally—means guiding market forces in the right direction, making it in our interest to do the right thing. It's the only way to make the planet notice.

JR: A good trail must take into account many factors: the terrain, the kind of vegetation, the climate, and so on. Similarly, a good solution to each environmental woe needs to consider other issues which it affects, working to come to the aid of these other problems rather than worsening them.

PP: Think of a major problem in your own life that you solved. What other consequences did the resolution bring about? Did they serve you well or could another solution have been more holistically beneficial?

August 14

*Sometimes a change
in course is necessary.*

There are 3 "bads" that our tax code should be redesigned to address, and in doing so support our transition to a more healthy and sustainable economy: 1) Extreme concentrations of income, wealth, and power that undermine social cohesion and a healthy democracy; 2) Financial speculation, such as the activities that destabilized our economy in 2008, and profligate consumption and waste; and 3) Pollution and the depletion of our ecosystems.

JR: One of the most effective ways to make our societies healthier is to take a close look at how the taxes are acquired and separate the good taxes (which move us towards more sustainability) from the bad ones (which reward activities which destroy the environment and worsen societal integrity). Then, find practical ways of phasing out the bad ones and increasing the good ones. Just like the people who give life to our government through our support, we taxpayers have the responsibility to make our elected leaders work towards such a beneficial tax system.

PP: What is one "bad" in your life you'd like to address? What policy can you adopt to start realistically dealing with it now?

August 15

Build a healthy, well-integrated environment step by step

1) "Spirituality is a search for completeness within ourselves— mind, body, and emotions— and a connectivity with others."

2) "It is no measure of health to be well adjusted to a profoundly sick society."

JR: How do we build a healthy environment which sustainably harmonizes nature and humanity? If development implies destroying nature in order to "better" people's lives, we are effectively spreading a cancer to obtain temporary relief. It's as if we are addicted to drugs—going for short term highs while killing our future. We must break out of such self-destructive patterns in order to move towards a sustainable and invigorated society.

PP: What is one thing we can do, as a society, which benefits both nature and the "common" people?

August 16

No wonder I am so guarded—this dude seems like trouble

When we're being honest with ourselves and true to our values, we will admit it when we're being greedy, guarded, intolerant, stubborn, self-absorbed, or deceitful and get the help we need. Integrity leaves us a trail to follow when we've lost touch with our higher self. Where deceit guarantees a life of fear, shame, and uncertainty, the spiritual antidote of integrity delivers peace of mind and a joyous heart.

JR: How can we not feel guarded in a dog-eat-dog world? As long as we perceive the world with this mindset, the feelings of selfishness, intolerance, cutthroat competition and Us vs Them will determine the course of our lives. Then, conflict and struggle will reign. However, when we are able to start seeing our unity and cultivate compassion, conflicts are transformed through finding ways of bringing about a peaceful integrity between opposing camps which lifts them both beyond the turbulence.

PP: How do you view the world, and your role in it? How does this affect your approach to life?

August 17

Our lives become murky with a lack of connection.

1) What blocks connection?

We experience soul when we really connect with life—when we stop and consciously experience what is happening.

We lose soul with:

- resistance – to anyone or anything
- superficiality – we avoid depth of experience
- control – we try to control the relationship
- selfishness – we remain self-centered

Each of these attitudes fosters separation rather than connection. Once again, soul lives in relating. Take time to become aware of how you relate to other people and things in your life.

2) "People are lonely because they build walls instead of bridges."

3) "We have to decide for ourselves what's nourishing to our souls, and do those things over others."

JR: Sometimes, the world can seem like a scary place and, at times, we need to protect ourselves against those forces that seek to destroy us. Yet, when you are good to yourself and to others, developing connections with your deep inner self and with others who resonate with you can give you spiritual nourishment which enriches the soul and serves to open channels where positive forces in your life can be strengthened, and detrimental elements can be diminished.

PP: What skill do you have (or can you develop) that could be used as a bridge between you and other people who have the potential to nourish your soul?

August 18

Bringing joy into public spaces

As the pressures on private spending have escalated, support for public goods, and for paying taxes has eroded. Education, social services, public safety, recreation, and culture are being squeezed. The deterioration of public goods then adds ever more pressure to spend privately. People respond to inadequate public services by enrolling their children in private schools, buying security systems, and spending time at Discovery Zone rather than the local playground. These personal financial pressures have also reduced many Americans' willingness to support transfer programs to the poor and near-poor. Coupled with dramatic declines in the earning power of these latter groups, the result has been a substantial increase in poverty, the deterioration of poor neighborhoods, and alarming levels of crime and drug use.

JR: We tend to forget how much a fulfilling private life is dependent on the many public services we too often take for granted—education (learning), policing (security), parks (recreation and connecting with nature), and more. When we can more fully understand and appreciate how our taxes are used to help us, as individuals and society as a whole, we become more willing to provide our support. Transparency is necessary for this to happen, for lessening financial mismanagement, decreasing suspicions, and gaining the public's favor.

PP: What other ways can you find (besides paying taxes) to support a public service which you consider to be extremely important?

August 19

It is becoming increasingly difficult to escape the trap we've set for ourselves.

It is becoming harder and harder for most of us to have the kinds of personal lives we want—blessed with loving friendships, health, and strong family ties—in a world that is dominated by escalating levels of selfishness and cynicism. Yet, it is sometimes hard to see other people as really deserving of our love and caring when we have so deeply internalized a materialistic and reductionist account of what it means to be a human being.

JR: The overemphasis on ME at the expense of WE leads a man to close in on himself to a point where the life force is smothered and only a heartless, materialistic shell remains. He forgets the significance of the relationships (with people and other life forms), however many or however few they may have been, that fed him the loving energy that vitalized his existence. The "human" has disappeared from his "humanity," and he becomes an "ity"—an it-like thing unable to feel the true joy of life.

PP: What relationship (to any living being) energizes you most? Spend more time with that to invigorate your spirit.

August 20

Talk about complete connection with the Earth

When we focus our lives on consuming more and more and increasing our possessions, we necessarily have less energy to develop our sensitivity to the Earth and her living forms. In becoming wealthy, we all too often become lonely because of our alienation from the human society and earthly community of beings. Whether or not we are willing to face it, we are completely dependent on each other and on nature. Without them, no matter how much money we have, our chance of survival is nil.

JR: Drinking a lot of alcohol feels good, and dulls our pains. However, done too frequently, it kills us. Over-consumption does the same whenever we get so addicted to it that our relationships fall to the wayside. To stay healthy, all people—introverts and extroverts alike—need living relationships, albeit to different degrees and of different kinds.

PP: How do your consumption patterns enhance or hinder your relationships with others? What can you do to make them promote better relationships?

August 21

The multi-sensory experience of nature

By respecting our desire for multi-sensory attraction relationships and the supportive community they promote, we discover that our discomfort from:

Loneliness is really an attraction for responsible sensory relationships.

Depression is an attraction for stronger multi-sensory satisfaction.

Abandonment is a strong attraction to being reconnected to a supportive sensory community.

Shame is an attraction to live in a supportive new-brain story.

JR: Experiencing the web of relationships which form the bedrock of our earth-bound existence is best done out in nature. By providing yourself with multi-sensory connections to other life forms, your desire for relationship is at least partially fulfilled, and any feeling of isolation and sadness relieved. And the best part of these nature relationships is that they are completely non-judgmental, with no concern of your unpopular/popular, reserved/outgoing, or negative/positive nature.

PP: Especially when you feel pained with loneliness, go outside and feel how you are a part of all creation, just like everyone else.

August 22

*Seeking
healthy nourishment*

A child's electronic stewards—television, videos, computer games—occupy attention and mental space without nourishing. An ironic revelation of the television-computer age is that what people want from machines is humanity: stories, contact, and interaction.

Today's machines deliver not a limbic connection but imprecise simulations. Small wonder that Internet use in adults actually causes depression and loneliness.

JR: It is a well-known fact that rather than nourishing the physical body, junk food burdens it with excessive salt, fats, and sugars, leading to disease. In the same way, junk entertainment, which is passive and time-consuming, robs the mind and the soul of the nourishing endeavors of active play and creation.

PP: How much time do you spend with passive, mind-numbing entertainment? How can you move away from that towards a nourishing form of recreation?

August 23

Another member of the earth community

Crime will be reduced when people feel a social bond toward one another. That bond cannot be imposed by government or social programs or education. It is the cumulative product of a society that validates the spiritual and ethical dimensions of human reality, that embodies in all its actions a respect for every human being, and that encourages and rewards mutual recognition and caring among all members of the society.

JR: When we feel connected to others, combined with a sense of community, committing a crime against them becomes unthinkable. Today's emphasis on individualism and our separateness has torn this bond apart. By rebuilding this affinity, not only with our human counterparts but with all living beings, we are co-creators of a world where purposely harmful violations against any other living being (which is not inflicting harm on us) are so repulsive to the great majority of people that they become prohibited by law.

PP: How can you support some program that strengthens the social bonds in your community?

August 24

Remain centered in a floating world

Beneath—indeed driving—our system of competitive consumption are deep class inequalities.

At all levels, a structure of inequality injects insecurity and fear into our psyches. The penalties of dropping down are perhaps the most powerful psychological hooks that keep us keeping up, even as the heights get dizzying.

JR: Our current economic system creates a nagging fear that a person has to keep his job, his house, his lifestyle, or something comparable, or live in danger of losing his socio-economic status, friends, or even the support of the government. Even if he is miserable at his work, it is better than the insecurity of losing everything that he considers important. As a society, we shape people who are willing to live lives of boredom or misery rather than people who are fully alive and willing to take the risk to passionately follow their dreams.

PP: Where does your security lie? Can you feel "safe" even if you lose that source of security?

August 25

Feeling strangely disconnected from my source

If participants in a financial transaction can be more visible to each other—if they can understand each other's needs and intentions, and sustain a personal connection whenever possible—then risk decreases and fulfillment increases. We believe this is nothing less than an antidote for the adverse impacts of modern finance.

For most of us, we simply don't know where our money is going anymore; we are almost completely disconnected from the real consequences of our economic and investment activity.

As a result, we are experiencing a multi-layered spiritual crisis. Not only are natural resource depletion and climate change creating anxiety, not only is severe income inequality creating conflict, but we must now also come to grips with the fact that, until many of us make significant changes in what we buy, where we bank, how we invest, we are all contributing to these problems.

JR: *In a globalized world, it becomes increasingly difficult to feel any connection to the places from where our products come and the people who make them. As a result, we unknowingly become accomplices to environmental destruction, slave wages, and a host of other social ills. Through finding ways of re-connecting with those who make the products we consume, either by buying local or better understanding how producers are treated, we can choose the people and companies we wish to support and, in the process, become co-conspirators in creating a more equitable world.*

PP: **What is a local company or retailer whose values you respect? How about showing your support by buying from them?**

August 26

Truly astonishing!

Small circles, mostly of women, are bound together to shoulder responsibility for repaying each member's loan—resulting in an impressive 96.7% loan recovery rate. "Solidarity lending" is the fancy term professionals have given to this most natural of human impulses: groups of peers sitting in a circle together, turning to one another for support. The results of these friendship circles have been astonishing: As of March 2010, 68% of Grameen Banks's eight million borrowers have crossed out of poverty. What's even more surprising is that, from the beginning, Grameen Bank has passed along ownership of its equity—95%—to the borrowers themselves.

JR: *It is incredible what can happen when a group of committed people come together, offer mutual support to each other, and pool their resources, however limited, towards the betterment of the individual and for the group as a whole. Today, there are many kinds of micro-lending models, with the most successful being those that cultivate strong mutual support networks, which drastically reduce the possibility of failure.*

PP: *Check out such micro-lending networks online. If you have the resources and find one appealing to you, offer some financial (or service) support.*

August 27

Crossing paths creates a colorful mosaic.

Democracy requires not perfect equality, but it does require that men and women from different backgrounds and classes and ethnic groups encounter one another, bump into one another, have occasions to meet and learn to respect their differences. This only happens if there are public institutions that gather people together, despite different backgrounds. As inequality deepens, this will be less and less the case. And this makes democracy difficult to sustain because it becomes harder to think of ourselves as citizens sharing common purposes. I call this corruption of civic virtue. It's an erosion of the sense that we're in it together. What's corrupted by growing inequality is the basis of social solidarity.

JR: *We come to understand our deeper common purposes—for love, for growth, for a degree of security—when we share them in speech and action with diverse people. However, when we have no contact with people of different backgrounds and colors, we become susceptible to believing in only the stereotypes and the differences which separate us. Creating ways to increase our contact with those of different persuasions, whatever they may be, would be a step towards developing a stronger web supporting and respecting all peoples.*

PP: Do you tend to stick with those of your own kind? How can you connect with someone from a very different background (if not physically, then through the written word or the visual arts)?

August 28

Find a good guide, and then become a light unto yourself

"We cannot win this battle to save species and environments without forging an emotional bond between ourselves and nature as well—for we will not fight to save what we do not love."

JR: How do we cultivate a "loving feeling" with nature, feeling a deep sensitivity and connection with it? There are inspirational guides from all faiths and cultures who can point the way, people who fell in love with nature and devoted their lives to it. Each person must eventually find the way that best fits her, but these guides provide an encouraging starting point.

PP: Find a person (living or deceased) who inspires a deep love for nature. What is it about her that enlivens you? Go out and do something similar to deepen your love of nature.

August 29

*Connect deep within
and far beyond*

The enjoyment of gardening or walking in nature comes because past and future fade away. Only the immediate connection to the earth and its beauty remain. The peaceful, loving quality of life's Source floods through our connection to the moment. "Ah, I love the woods," we think. But the peace is not inherent in the forest or the garden, the "beloved" that temporarily holds our attention. It is present within us. And when we connect to this inner wellspring, we feel our connection to all of life so much more strongly.

JR: Do you notice how difficult it is to appreciate and love when your spiritual condition is running amuck? On the other hand, how easy it is to feel compassion and love for all whenever you feel connected to your life source. Being in and with nature connects us to the source of life (being life itself), while cultivating a loving spirit within reinforces the connection with a strong bonding force.

PP: What plant, animal, or natural phenomenon makes you feel most connected to your life source? Where can you go to experience it?

August 30

Healing ourselves and healing the world

Since all minds are connected, then the correction of anyone's perception is on some level a healing of the entire racial mind. The practice of forgiveness is our most important contribution to the healing of the world. Angry people cannot create a peaceful planet. Forgiveness is the world's only real chance to begin again. A radical forgiveness is a complete letting go of the past, in any personal relationship, as well as in any collective drama.

JR: Carrying a grudge and harboring resentment in any form not only corrupts your spirit by making it spiteful, but also consumes energy that could be used fruitfully and creatively elsewhere. In this sense, the inability to forgive is doubly harmful. To forgive does not mean to forget, but rather to release the stranglehold that anger holds on you and choosing to use that newly liberated energy for doing something spiritually uplifting.

PP: Who or what haven't you forgiven? How can you move towards forgiveness and feel the burden diminish?

August 31

Respecting each other's existence makes the whole flourish.

The first person to recognize the Prophethood of Muhammad was a Christian and the primary protector of Muhammad during those brutal early years in Mecca was a pagan. Interfaith cooperation was written into the very founding of my faith tradition. There is a story of the Prophet hosting a Christian delegation in Medina. The Muslims and Christians had a heated debate on the differences between their respective traditions. At one point, the Christians asked for the Prophet's protection so they could leave the city and perform their prayers. The Prophet surprised them by inviting them into his mosque to pray, saying that just because their traditions had differences did not mean that they should not respect and show hospitality to the others' practices.

JR: How is it that we have become so lazy that we let others (people, media, etc.) determine for us what another religion or group of people is like? Worse yet, look at how we all pick and choose those parts of our own "holy books" that are "appropriate" for us and ignore those that are not. Especially with regard to Islam, so many consider it evil and full of terrorist ideologies without looking at the vast majority of good Muslims and the origins of the religion, which preach peace and respect for others.

PP: Look at your own holy book. Which parts don't you accept as being applicable to you? Do you have a good reason for this or is it only because you are not "disciplined" enough to follow it?

SEPTEMBER

Nature & Spirit

What is this mystery called life? Most often, it is defined as all things having the spirit of breath and carrying out continuous processes whereby they relate to the outside world through giving and taking therefrom—in other words, all animals (humans included) and plants that constitute nature. In this sense, spirit and nature are one and the same.

Nature is often seen in today's world as a resource, which is to be exploited for our selfish good, leading to the environmental ruin which we see today. Yet, it is the most integrated, productive system known to us, and one that could lead us towards a far more sustainable world if closely imitated. And much more than that, our direct experience with nature stimulates our imaginations which, in turn, provide the seeds for our creativity to blossom. Nature's beauty provides unfathomable inspiration for the arts, which uplift our lives. When we destroy nature, we are destroying our own creative and artistic capabilities.

Closer contact with nature blesses us with spiritual experiences which "naturally and spiritually" engender within us a desire for less material goods (since the pleasure of contacting "holy life" gives us much more contentment than any superfluous goods ever could). In addition, it offers hints towards finding ways of developing technologies which make our lives better while also benefitting the natural environment of which we are an intricate part.

Spiritual work, including frequent contact with nature and anything else that bring us closer to the source of life, results in a gratification and joy which we bring to our everyday lives. Surely, there will be dark days and down cycles, but the overall trend of your life will move you towards a self-created serenity that consistent spiritual work brings. This is precisely the reason why one of the main points of this whole paradigm is that spirituality is uplifting and fun!

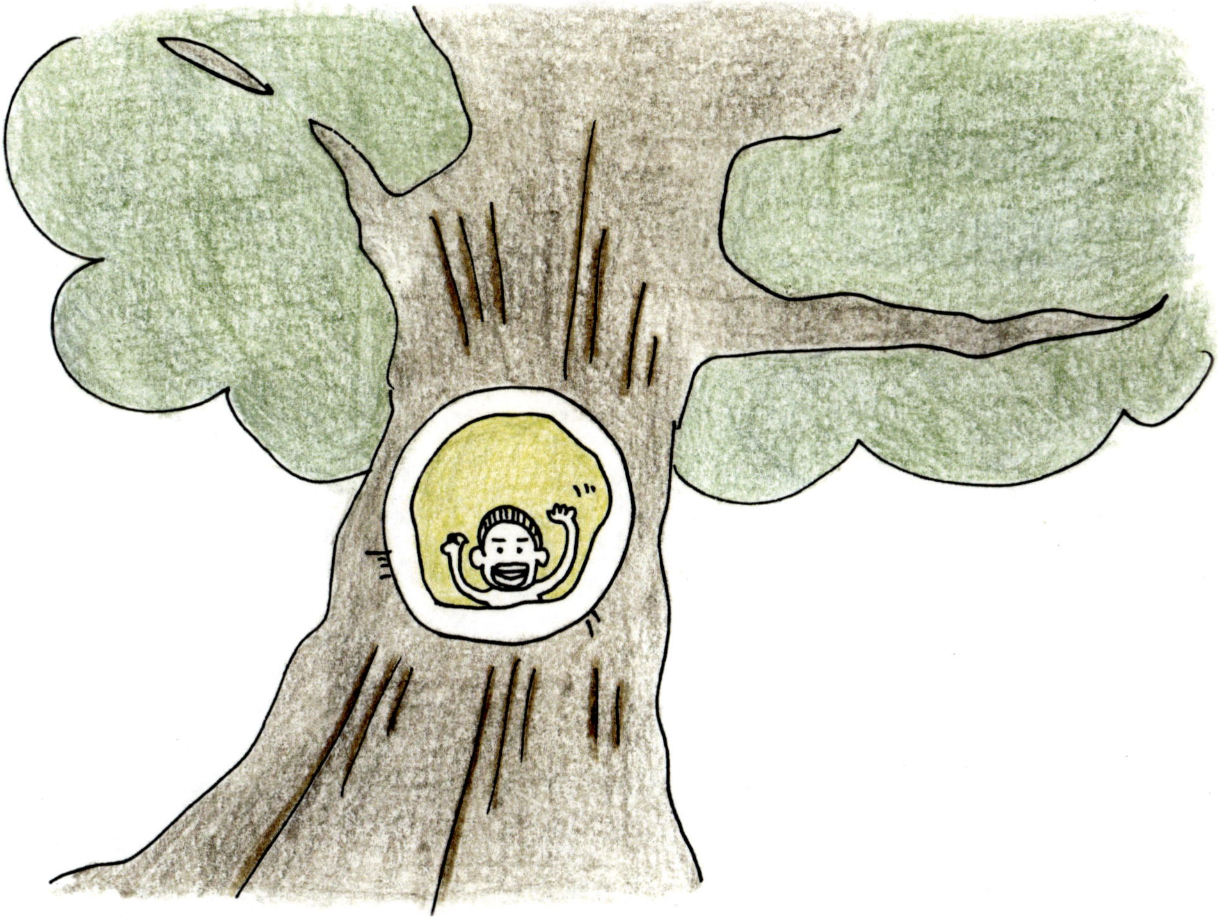

September 1

True value is beyond anything humanly imaginable.

Ever since humans first stood upright and walked out of the forests to the savannas, we have been going back to the forests for most of what we've needed to survive: water from springs and streams, fish, game animals, edible leaves, roots, fruits, fungi and nuts, building materials for our shelters, medicinal plants, and even feathers and dyes for dressing up. But that list doesn't even begin to measure the real value of forests to us. Forests not only create but also retain a great percentage of the fertile soils on earth, the material that provides us with our food base. They absorb water into the ground and protect and purify it in lakes and streams. We have learned the hard way, only after forests have gone, that transpiration from tree leaves as well as their ability to trap cloud and fog actually creates an area's rainfall. And of course, forests manufacture our atmosphere, absorbing the carbon dioxide that is poisonous to us in their tissues and exhaling the life-giving oxygen we need to survive. We have also recently learned that the presence of forests greatly softens climates—warming cold ones, cooling hot ones, mitigating wind and frost—to an extent not before realized until we began to lose them. All the elements necessary to the survival of the complex "higher" life forms—soil, water, atmosphere and a moderated climate—come from the collective life that makes up our planet's forests.

JR: If we were ever to do a real accounting of nature—economic as well as the life-giving aspects—and what she gives to us, we would come to see her as what she truly is—PRICELESS! We would finally come to understand that every act we perform which damages her is a crime that, in effect, hurts our present (and presence) and future potential far more than we ever thought. Considering a full accounting of all of nature's free gifts (tangible and intangible) and their importance to our livelihoods will surely move us to not only preserve her, but also work towards cultivating more of her bounty for the benefit of all.

PP: Contemplate the necessities of life which you use or consume today—food, drink, housing, clothing—and how most of these are, in essence, "gifts of nature."

September 2

Another of nature's never-ending magical displays

We should be clear about what happens when we destroy the living forms of this planet. The first consequence is that we destroy modes of divine presence. If we have a wonderful sense of the divine, it is because we live amid such awesome magnificence. If we have refinement of emotion and sensitivity, it is because of the delicacy, the fragrance, and indescribable beauty of song and music and rhythmic movement in the world about us. If we grow in our life vigor, it is because the earthly community challenges us, forces us to struggle to survive, but in the end reveals itself as a benign providence. But however benign, it must provide that absorbing drama of existence whereby we can experience the thrill of being alive in a fascinating and unending sequence of adventures.

If we have powers of imagination, they are activated by the magic display of color and sound, of form and movement.

JR: It is important to realize that nature is invaluable to us in order to live since she provides for our everyday needs. Correspondingly, seeing and feeling the magic and delight she brings to us fills us with the appreciation and love needed to make a commitment to preserve her. Feel the sun's warmth, experience a magical sunset, meditate in the mystical desert or dance in a lush forest—becoming aware of life's throbbing all about you and understanding that you are a part of this awesome life community. Herein lies the life source that forms the root of your own capabilities and power.

PP: Give yourself a gift today by spending a few minutes appreciating one aspect of nature and feeling your connection with it.

September 3

I'm always dressed up, showing respect to the divinity within and without.

So often in our homes we see a tiny ant that could never cause harm, and our first reaction is to kill it. Why? Do we actually feel threatened? In our minds we have formed the idea that the ant does not belong in the house. It is not convenient, so we kill it. This may seem like a small example, but the cumulative effects of such attitudes are crippling to humanity.

Respect for life must be developed at every level. Our inability to see life as being sacred has led us to apply the disposable attitude even to life.

JR: It is easy to feel so overwhelmed by the larger issues which invade your mental space from all sides—political, religious, and social—that you become "petrified into inaction." So focusing on simple actions which you have control of is one way to start taking control of your life. Finding ways of experiencing the sacred in your everyday life and demonstrating your love through kindness to all forms of life will bring you a sense of serenity and integration, which shall brighten and lighten up your whole being.

PP: In what way do you dishonor life? How can you mend this in order to move towards a more respectful disposition towards all life and creation?

September 4

Super cosy—living "in a planet" while on a planet

There was once a man who was busy building a home for himself. He wanted it to be the nicest, cosiest home in the world.

Someone came to him to ask for help because the world was on fire. But it was his home he was interested in, not the world.

When he finally finished his home, he found he did not have a planet to put it on.

JR: In an "Each man for himself" world, we tend to forget that survival is impossible without the cooperation of countless others and a natural environment which provides for our many needs. Only in mutual support for each other is long term survival for us, individually and as a species, made possible.

PP: You start caring for the world when you start caring for those around you. Whose needs have you been ignoring, and how can you start meeting them?

September 5

Forging a creative connection between the heavenly and the earthly

"By destroying our natural environment, we are destroying our creativeness/imaginations, for our imagination is directly proportional to the objects/experiences to which we are exposed. (As a result, those of us who come from areas which are naturally/culturally diverse tend to be more creative than those from deserts/homogenous areas.)"

JR: Pretty frightening to consider that our reckless destruction of the environment is simultaneously discreetly sabotaging our own creativity. However, viewed from the opposite perspective, when we build up our natural environment, making it more stable by increasing its diversity, we are feeding our own imaginations with nourishing stimuli, potentially moving us towards a more dynamic, awe-inspiring world.

PP: What can you do here and now to lend a hand to preserving and/or restoring the diversity of life (in your area or elsewhere)?

September 6

Tough feeling so worn down

There must be the direct and immediate experience of living itself: we must directly see, feel, touch, manipulate, sing, dance, communicate before we can extract from the machine any further sustenance for life. If we are empty to begin with, the machine will only leave us emptier; if we are passive and powerless to begin with, the machine will only leave us more feeble.

JR: Only life begets life. It is faulty thinking to believe that machines can give us life. This does not imply that machines are evil, but the concept does force us to question the foundation of our true sustenance. When we feel truly alive in our connections with other living beings, we deliberately choose the machines which further this aliveness, while understanding that other machines remove us from this life energy. Then, and only then, can we become capable of deciphering which machines truly serve life.

PP: Is there any machine that zaps you of life's energy, or gives you a temporary high but, in the end, leaves you feeling drained or powerless? Consider getting rid of it.

September 7

The counter-balance to excessive technology

There's no denying the benefits of the Internet. But electronic immersion, without a force to balance it, creates the hole in the boat—draining our ability to pay attention, to think clearly, to be productive and creative. The best antidote to negative electronic information immersion will be an increase in the amount of natural information we receive.

The more high-tech we become, the more nature we need.

JR: Many of our problems, personal as well as social, result from lack of balance within our multi-faceted lives. In today's society, our excessive involvement with electronic gadgets is stealing time and energy away from other needs—for love, for connection, for coming to understand, then create and live out, what we truly believe. Making space for these life-giving demands necessarily means withdrawing ourselves and our time away from deadening activities, some of which may well stem from our excessive use of today's technologies.

PP: What are the life-engendering parts of your life? How can you devote more time and energy to these empowering facets?

September 8

Find home wherever you can take root and settle down

Once upon a time there was a forest where the birds sang by day and the insects by night. Trees flourished, flowers bloomed, and all manner of creatures roamed about in freedom.

And all who entered there were led to Solitude, which is the home of God, who dwells in Nature's silence and Nature's beauty.

But then the Age of Unconsciousness arrived, when it became possible for people to construct buildings a thousand feet high and to destroy rivers and forests and mountains in a month. So houses of worship were built from the wood of the forest trees and from the stone under the forest soil. Pinnacle, spire, and minaret pointed toward the sky; the air was filled with the sound of bells, with prayer and chant and exhortation.

And God was suddenly without a home.

JR: It is easy to lose sight of those elements in our lives that feed our innermost desires. Advertising, the media, even our education systems do little to make us retrospect and search deep for our true needs, for, in so doing, we would come to learn the farce and worthlessness of much of what we are taught, told, and sold. Becoming conscious of our deepest longings would certainly steer us towards a more harmonious co-existence with other people at large and the rest of nature, bringing a life-engendering spirit back into our lives.

PP: What is something you want badly? Ask yourself "Why" and keep asking "Why?" for each answer you come up with in an effort to find the deeper desire lying beneath the surface.

September 9

Plants and air—the actual sustainers of animal life

Natural life is nurturing. The natural world also nurtures and sustains life and diversity without producing garbage, pollution or insensitive abusiveness. Nature is an unimaginable intelligence that we inherit but suppress.

Runaway stress, greed, violence, crime, diseases, and substance abuse continue to plague us. So do the costs to contain these problems. These evils have one thing in common. All of them are unknown in natural areas. Their root is not nature. Their root is our thinking's estrangement from nature's ways.

JR: Nature is full of lessons on how to live sustainably, for she has been doing so since the origin of the first earthly organisms. She continues to explore life in a multitude of new forms and finds countless ways to creatively deal with her wastes and excesses. She doesn't despair that some of her new experiments fail, but marches relentlessly on to seek out how best to create and maintain balance under ever-changing conditions.

PP: How much do you throw away every day? Think of some ways you can decrease this waste or, better yet, put it to good use.

September 10

Without good soil, this extensive life force is not possible.

We live from about eight inches of topsoil, containing earthworms, bacteria, fungi, and other microscopic forms of life, that provides us with vegetation, trees, insects, and animals. The only inexhaustible wealth is a fertile soil. Topsoil is the greatest natural resource of any nation; civilizations of the past have been destroyed when their fertile soils were lost.

JR: When we don't make a conscious effort to consider the many gifts of nature which make our lives possible, we end up taking them for granted, denying ourselves the blissful feeling of gratitude—especially the grimy, grubby soil so full of microscopic life, without which life would be but a dream. Thinking of the soil as a divine presence that makes all physical life a reality instills a sense of wonder and appreciation for this often-ignored miracle in our midst.

PP: Pick up some soil and imagine all of the microorganisms in it. Express appreciation for all life, which is made possible because of the soil.

September 11

Extraterrestrial terrestrials abound.

1) Perhaps plants are the true extraterrestrials, for they converted an early mineral world into a habitat suitable for man by processes that border on near-perfect magic.

2) "The Forest?

The highest-yielding, least labor-demanding production strategy known to Man."

JR: How can you not believe in miracles or magic whenever you consider the origin of life? For the believer in God and the non-believer alike, to contemplate how life arose from non-living material is mind-boggling and reeks of some kind of crafty wizardry. The only reason we aren't completely blown away by this mystery is because we don't take the time to deeply think about it.

PP: Look at a plant today and try to imagine how its distant ancestors first came into existence (eons ago) from the non-living mineral world. Contemplate this awe-inspiring mystery and feel how incredible it is.

September 12

Find your niche in a plant-dominated world

It depends on what "advances" you value. We value language, writing, all that. But plants evolved on Earth earlier than we did, and have adapted to more niches. In fact, you could argue that plants have domesticated us and not the other way around. For millennia humans have improved plant species by artificial selection. We also carry their genes farther distances than they could themselves, and we nourish them for their flowers and fruit and grains. In one sense, we're the plants' servants. We've functioned to help them reproduce, conquer disease, and multiply. We serve them.

In fact, if plants hadn't developed flowers, humans might not exist. The majority of large mammals could only occur after fruits and seeds concentrated and multiplied the world's supply of food energy. Without flowers, the world might still belong to reptiles. Flowers created us, and they developed shapes and scents pleasing to us, and we in turn serve them. They enslave us with beauty and sweetness, just like women.

JR: How easy it is to forget that we are completely dependent on plants for our survival, while plants can easily survive without the existence of humans. In destroying plant life and diversity, we are, in effect, destroying our own future prospects for survival. Developing greater appreciation and respect for our gentle and generous masters is necessary in order to halt our march towards environmental degradation.

PP: Take time to look at a piece of fruit, a seed, or a flower and realize its important contribution (pre-historically) in creating a planet hospitable to human habitation.

September 13

Bask in nature's nourishment and glory

A spider weaving its web, the perfect symmetry of a snowflake, the beauty and harmony of the lily, the cosmic quality of trees, the mysterious presence of the wind, the attraction of stillness, the radiance of light, the transparency of fragrances, the flow of water, the movement of leaves, the timeless feeling of some days and nights, the poetry of birds in flight, the transfiguring moments of dawn and sunset, the hypnotic rhythm of the tides—all speak to us of something beyond ourselves, something that transcends our understanding. All point to nature's ability to nourish us aesthetically and psychologically as well as materially.

JR: It's only a matter of time—that is, allowing yourself the time to fully experience these many blessings which nature bestows upon you. When you become completely wrapped up in the man-made, you miss out on the incredible wonders which the natural world has to offer free of charge. When you devote more time to experiencing them, you increasingly come to realize how little you need materially to feel a steady sense of peace and joy.

PP: Treat yourself to one of nature's wonders today—anything from the frantic darting about of an ant to the splendor of a tree's lush canopy providing shade, oxygen, wood, and our means of survival.

September 14

Nothing lacking here

Our estrangement from nature leaves us wanting, and when we want there is never enough. Our insatiable wanting is called greed. It is a major source of our destructive dependencies and violence. Rejoining with nature, people want less. They also get smarter about not letting themselves get hurt. Then problems dissolve. Communion with Earth sharpens the insight.

In nature, there is a definite perspective shift. It quickly downsizes your preoccupation with problems in your career or private world.

JR: Think of the many reasons why people visit psychologists—to lessen their worries and soothe their spirits. Cultivating a stronger connection to nature does the same, and it aids in a shift of your perspective which makes life freer and more inherently delightful, making nature the greatest psychologist that the Earth has ever known.

PP: How do you leave yourself wanting? In other words, what do you feel that you don't have enough of and need more? Try to get more exposure to nature, nesting in her mysteries, and see if it may help to alleviate that feeling.

September 15

Something's bugging me.

Charles Eisenstein notes that community is nearly impossible in a highly monetized society like our own. "There are many reasons—the layout of suburbia, the disappearance of public space, the automobile and the TV, the high mobility of people and jobs—and, if you trace the 'why's' a few levels down, they all implicate the money system." (Saint) Francis discovered this truth in his own time. Seeing how financial wealth can preclude the needs of others, he disowned his father's patrimony and gave all that he had to the poor. He made himself dependent on others.

JR: In a society where almost everything holds a monetary value, the compassionate and loving act of caring for others irrespective of financial reward becomes "devalued," meaning that it is seen as less important than going out and making money. We are not taught to question the role of money in society, or why we always want more. And, in many cases, contrary to freeing us, (our obsession with) money enslaves us and entices us away from the core loving relationships and meaningful values which we usually claim to be most important.

PP: What role does money play in your life? How can you make better use of money to bring more of those things that you consider most important?

September 16

Be purposeful—slow and deliberate

Satoyama is the traditional Japanese system of villages and the managed natural areas around them.

"The biodiversity in satoyama is significant because management has created a mosaic of forests, grasslands, fields, irrigation ponds and other elements, resulting in the diversity of ecosystems. These features cannot be found in intensive agricultural landscapes," says Takeuchi.

Cutting weeds is a constant refrain in the recollections of old folks in the area, and for good reason: That simple act is what stands between the village and the forest that presses relentlessly in on all sides. It is the cutting, harvesting, coppicing and weeding that have arrested for centuries the satoyama landscape in an intermediate stage of biological succession between open space and mature forest—allowing biodiversity to flourish.

JR: Humans are seen to have negatively impacted the natural world and, in many cases, we have. At the same time, insightful examples, like satoyama, signify the positive influence of humans in cultivating a richer, more diverse and sustainable natural environment. Finding ways to expand such efforts can make our species a benevolent power rather than a destructive cancer.

PP: What is one part of the natural environment in your area that needs "healing?" Can you do anything to be part of the healing process?

September 17

Are the patterns visible to you?

Creative genius is not the accumulation of knowledge; it is the ability to see patterns in the universe, to detect hidden links between what is and what could be. In 1977, the late Edith Cobb, a noted proponent of nature-based education, contended that geniuses share one trait: transcendent experience in nature in their early years. In 2006, a Danish study found that outdoor kindergartens were better than indoor schools at stimulating children's creativity. The researchers reported that 58% of children who were in close touch with nature often invented new games; just 16% of indoor kindergarten children did. One explanation, for adults as well as children, is suggested by the "loose parts theory" in education, which holds that the more loose parts there are in an environment, the more creative the play. A computer game has plenty of loose parts, but the number and the interaction of those parts is limited by the mind of the human who created the game. In a tree, a woods, a field, a mountain, a ravine, a vacant lot, the number of loose parts is unlimited. It's possible, then, that exposure to the loose but related parts of nature can encourage a greater sensitivity to patterns that underlie all experience, all matter, and all that matters.

JR: *By relying on given forms of passive entertainment, in the form of mindless TV shows or games which require no creative input on the part of the user, you are effectively immobilizing your own innate creative capacity. On the other hand, by providing a child with an enriching environment which requires her to discover autonomously ways of designing her own fun, you give nourishment to her imagination and encourage the genius within her. In so doing, she comes to be the master of her own destiny.*

PP: FEED YOUR CREATIVITY! *Go to a natural environment (if you have a child, take her there too) without any human-made gadgets and "create" a way of having fun.*

September 18

I don't mind having no mind—it makes life simple.

In 2012, the University of Kansas News Service reported: "Research conducted at the University of Kansas concludes that people from all walks of life show startling cognitive improvement—for instance, a 50% boost in creativity—after living for a few days steeped in nature. There's growing advantage over time to being in nature. We think that it peaks after about 3 days of really getting away, turning off the cell phone, not hauling the iPad and not looking for internet coverage. It's when you have an extended period of time surrounded by that softly fascinating environment that you start seeing all kinds of positive effects in how your mind works."

Researchers suggest exposure to the natural world restores the brain's ability to pay attention. It not only restores us, but excites us, by stimulating all of the senses.

As we spend more and more time in front of screens, we expend increased energy blocking out senses not required for visual learning. What are we not learning? What are we losing?

JR: Our increasingly shorter attention spans closely correspond to our decreasing mindfulness. Becoming overly busy and stimulated by our technologies necessitates that we no longer spend time focusing on the life-giving aspects of our lives. Thereby, we lose out in our relationships, in attaining a degree of spiritual serenity, and in our ability to think and act creatively. This awareness is key—with this realization, you can feel motivated to change these patterns and align them accordingly to your own benefit.

PP: If you are able, try to take off and go on a three-day nature retreat, without any gadgets. See how your senses reawaken and what effects this has on your mind.

September 19

Really a bummer to feel so disconnected

The problem is spiritual. We've lost a basic connection within ourselves. And, because of that, we cannot find our spiritual link to the natural world.

We who are alive today are the people who will determine the future of humanity. We are the ones who must goad the human race to squirm out of an obsolete cocoon of mindless consumerism and metamorphose into something more beautiful, and benign.

Spiritual balance is our natural state. Humans are capable of incredible beauty. We have the capacity to be the Earth's keepers, and to live together on this planet wisely, fairly, and with foresight.

JR: Unlike the other living organisms on Earth which are completely connected with their natural environment (except for those that have been domesticated or captured by humans), we have a choice to connect or disconnect. In choosing to increase our connection to nature, we establish a balance in our lives that "naturally" sets up limits to our desires and establishes a better-integrated spirit that becomes capable of living joyfully and sustainably with the rest of creation (rather than wantonly destroying it, which happens when we become separated).

PP: Make a conscious choice to connect more strongly with nature by developing a simple daily habit that brings you closer to nature.

September 20

Beauty inflames the spirit.

"We have no inner spiritual life if we don't have the outer experience of a beautiful world. The more we destroy the world, the less a sense of God is possible."

JR: Religion and spirituality are too often discussed without consideration of the natural setting that largely shapes them. When we come to understand nature's positive effects on the spirit, we are more likely to take care of her and feed our own souls in the process. The beauty of the flower comes to be reflected in the beauty of the soul and vice-versa in a never-ending cycle of benevolence.

PP: Imagine living in a world with no plants or other animals. How could your spirit flourish in such a dead and barren place?

September 21

Nature's shapes are a mystery.

1) "Our only true enemy is not people or institutions, but fear-laden thoughts that cling to our insides and sap us of our strength."

2) When you fail to bring awareness to the behaviors that have shaped you, you remain ignorant to all that you are and all that you can be. Where there is ignorance, there is intolerance; where there is intolerance, there is darkness; and where there is darkness, there is repetition.

JR: *Each of us is unique, having been shaped by the various influences of the past, the environment, his inborn character, and more. Many of our spiritual, social, and political ideologies state that all people should "act like this." It may well be true, but it is also totally useless, considering the great diversity of humankind. It is only through the effort of each person to better understand the reasons why he acts in a certain way that change for the better, for the individual and for society as a whole, becomes possible.*

PP: *What is one of your own behaviors that you dislike? Think of the reason (past experience, natural character, etc) you behave as such. Perhaps you will realize it is useful for you, or that it would benefit you to make an effort to change it.*

September 22

Beauty has its own radiance.

Sadness is a habit of processing the world from a perspective of lack by constantly thinking about not having enough of what you feel entitled to, such as money, health, love, friends, or even free time. On and on go the thoughts, which create a feeling of sadness.

Joy, on the other hand, is a way of processing the world from the perspective of what you have and what is right. Joyful people rejoice in their strengths, talents, and powers and do not compare themselves to anyone. They are not intimidated by the strengths, possessions and powers of anyone else. Joy comes from rejoicing in all that you are, all that you have, all that you can be and from knowing that you are divine, a piece of God.

Sadness derives from a scarcity consciousness that can be dissolved by tuning into the abundance that is yours for the taking.

JR: When you come to understand that much of your sadness and joy comes from your habits, it equips you with more control in steering your mental processing towards a more joyful perspective. Simply by focusing on what is good and right in your life rather than what you are missing, you cultivate a more jovial spirit. This can be challenging in a society which encourages comparison (especially with those who have more). It means that, in order to engender a more exultant perspective, you have a personal responsibility towards yourself to make the effort to concentrate on your good points and limit potential inputs which distract you from that focus.

PP: Give yourself a dose of delight by focusing on three good things about you.

September 23

Just BEE yourself, and be contented

1) "Often people attempt to live their lives backwards: they try to have more things, or more money, in order to do more of what they want so they will be happier. The way it actually works is the reverse. You must first be who you really are, then do what you love to do, in order to have what you want."

2) The formula for success is Be, Do, Have. If we seek abundance, we must be abundant in spirit. We can begin to cultivate spiritual wealth by opening our hearts in gratitude.

JR: "What do you want to have?" "What do you want to do?" These are the questions we hear most often from those around us. "What kind of person do you want to be?" It sounds kind of strange, doesn't it? And yet, without searching for the answer to this and moving towards it, your havings and doings may very well work against the deeper sense of who you wish to be, thereby leading to dissatisfaction and frustration.

PP: Ask yourself "What kind of person do I want to be?" and answer it with just one characteristic. What is one step you can take to move more towards your aspirational personality?

September 24

I can fill you with boundless wonder, but your real treasure lies within.

Discover the treasures inside

1) "Happiness cannot be traveled to, owned, earned, worn or consumed. Happiness is the spiritual experience of living every minute with love, grace, and gratitude."

2) Peace, joy, and well-being can only be found inside us. They exist within us now, waiting to be discovered. Yet we tend to look to the outside world to satisfy our needs and longings.

Our outer life reflects back to us the way we think, feel and behave. The outer world is all effects. Go to the source inside for all of life's treasures.

How are you searching for peace and contentment outside of yourself?

3) "The great Western disease is, 'I'll be happy when. When I get the money. When I get a BMW. When I get this job.' Well, the reality is, you never get to when. The only way to find happiness is to understand that happiness is not out there. It's in here. And happiness is not next week. It's now."

JR: Nothing outside of you, absolutely nothing, can give you happiness without your first cultivating an internal garden which is capable of graciously receiving the blessings bestowed from outside the physical body. For those who have largely experienced pain and despair in their youth, finding that treasure inside is much more challenging; however, because of the increased effort which is required of them, when it is eventually found, they are the ones who can become the brightest lights for those who are weary.

PP: What kind of meditation, reading, or activity gives you a holistic sense of peace and happiness? How can you incorporate this more into your life?

September 25

Looks can be deceiving.

"The essence of a Buddhist life lies in a person's own effort to purify the mind. By replacing its coarse, deluded states as anger, attachment and ignorance with their opposites: patience, equanimity and wisdom, a lasting internal happiness can be achieved, independent of external conditions."

JR: First impressions make a great impact on us. "She's so beautiful. He's so clumsy. She only sits around doing nothing. He has really made something of himself with his success." Being able to see beyond these initial judgements and into the heart of others becomes possible only when you have been able to do so with yourself, through the cultivation of a purity of mind.

PP: Think of a time when your first impression of someone was completely off the mark. Let this serve as an example to be wiser in seeing others.

September 26

Each river finds its own path.

Spiritual practice is revolutionary. It allows us to step outside our personal identity, culture, and religion to experience more directly the great mystery, the great music of life.

JR: Every system of thought—culture, religion, education—attempts to mold you in a particular way. While they are usually meant to steer us in a beneficial direction, our attempts to abide by them, even when we don't really feel as if they are right for us, can result in hostile obedience or deceptive resistance. True spirituality understands the uniqueness of each individual and her need to blaze her own path, with the use of the signposts provided by her environment (society, culture, nature) as needed. Spiritual practice involves taking radical responsibility for becoming who you truly are.

PP: How does your culture or your religion rub you the wrong way? How do your really feel about this issue, and how can you act according to what you believe deep inside rather than what you are told to believe/do?

September 27

Digging it by digging in—uncovering the real power

People who participate in the solution to problems don't seem to find themselves as depressed about those problems as do people standing on the sidelines doing nothing. Hope is born of participation in hopeful solutions. We are happy to the extent that we choose to notice and to create the reasons for happiness. Optimism and happiness are the results of spiritual work.

JR: *Talk about empowering—we are capable of creating our own happiness through spiritual work and taking corresponding action. Even when things may seem futile, reaching out and taking an active role to move towards even the faintest hope lessens the darkness by intensifying the core light within.*

PP: *What is one aspect of your life that burdens you or makes you despondent? Consider one thing which you can do, however small, which can shine a ray of hope onto the gloom and start bringing some warmth into the chilling feeling of despair?*

September 28

Revitalization—Let go and let it flow

Harboring resentments consumes a lot of energy. Why waste valuable energy on prolonged anger and guilt when you could use that energy for far greater things? When you let go of resentment, guilt, and anger, you become revitalized and create space in your soul for growth.

JR: There are two primary ways of invigorating yourself—nourishing yourself (spiritually and physically) from resources inside and outside of yourself and removing the blocks which are locking in negative energy. Resenting others, seeking revenge, and feeling guilty about the past only fruitlessly waste energy, entrap negativity, and prevent not only your growth, but your happiness as well. Removing these vitality zappers allows the life force to flow freely and be put to beneficial use.

PP: What resentment are you harboring? How can you start letting it go and using that previously pent-up energy for your own benefit?

September 29

Some spaces are conducive to remembrance and atonement.

1) "The stupid neither forgive nor forget: the naive forgive and forget: the wise forgive, but they do not forget."

2) "To forgive and forget means to throw away dearly bought experience."

3) Spiritual tradition sees it as a strange delusion that our problems have to be gotten rid of; instead, the sages and saints suggest, such difficulties are best put to use. The offense is precisely what must not be forgotten, since it is through the act of facing what has happened and fitting it into a whole by re-membering it that the possibility of atonement (making at-one) occurs and forgiveness comes to fruition.

4) "Salvation lies in remembrance."

JR: While it is important to let go of resentments in order to revitalize yourself, it is just as important not to forget the transgressions incurred against you, but rather to remember and learn from them. Building a spiritual practice that allows you to remember past hurts and wrongdoings, both those that were inflicted by you as well as those that were inflicted upon you, without harboring guilt or resentment, leads to a great wisdom necessary for living out a wholly integrated life.

PP: Is there a transgression you've tried to forget but which keeps stabbing at your heart? Can you find a way to remember it, inculcate its lesson to your benefit, and let it go?

September 30

Move on

Although forgiveness often looks like a generous gift we are giving to someone else, it is ultimately an act of self-love and a gift we give to ourselves. Only through forgiveness can we take back our power and move on with our lives. When we forgive, we break free from the bondage of our resentments and are released from the prison of our past. Forgiveness opens the door to greater intimacy, compassion for ourselves and others, and new hope for the future. It creates the space in our emotional world that is necessary for us to experience more love, joy, peace, and freedom. Forgiveness allows us to let go of the burdens of the past in favor of having full access to the magnificence of who we are now and who we can become.

JR: Forgiveness is mistakenly seen as something which you do for another when, actually, it is something which you do for yourself. When you don't forgive, you remain trapped in the past, bound by its chains and become an unsuspecting accomplice to the wounds which fester in your soul. In forgiveness, you become your own healer, thereby breaking the chains and tending to the injuries so that you can live your life anew with a renewed vigor.

PP: Who is someone who you haven't forgiven, but feel like you may be able to? Forgive him (in your heart or, better yet, telling him directly) and imagine a heavy burden being lifted from your shoulders.

OCTOBER

Envisioning & Faith

Having now cultivated a foundation firmly grounded in the first nine months' soulscapes, it is now time to move towards a more fulfilling implementation of them to build a caring, dynamic and fun-filled future. A primary ingredient towards building a better future is faith (and hope), strengthened with a sincere belief that such a future is possible. Such hope can be nurtured by moving towards a higher version of yourself by doing good works and being open to life in all its forms. Faith is cultivated through a consistent effort to move towards others striving to do the same, while being constantly on guard against ideas, people, and actions which destroy your faith. With faith firmly inculcated into your being, you become different and see others differently, for you are then securely grounded in a world of hope.

Accompanying this hope comes the realization that most of us (probably yourself included) are trapped by our culture's false stories, those very stories which destroy our environment and accelerate the injustices in our world. This awareness then becomes a seed for hope, not only for you to question these myths that you have been living by, but also to dare yourself to develop new paradigms and envision a sustainable future. You come to see the cynics' arguments for what they are—empty. For example, skeptics often use fear as a way of halting progressive ideas, like the idea that moving towards an environmentally harmonious lifestyle means depriving ourselves of the good things in life. But such arguments no longer carry any weight with you, for you clearly see that moving in that direction is far more spiritually and deeply fulfilling, while you also build on life's most precious gifts—light-heartedness, a sense of enchantment, security and freedom from fear (exactly those treasures which our current unsustainable lifestyles are stealing away from us). Envisioning a future that restores these gifts is the first step towards bringing them into reality.

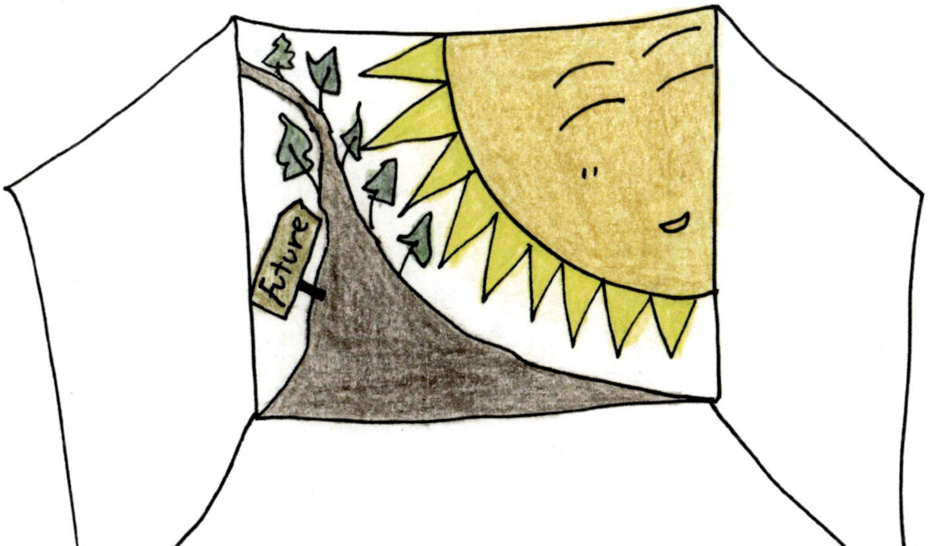
Future

October 1

Flowers have changed the world for the better and we can too.

1) Our greatest tool for changing the world is our capacity to change our mind about the world.

2) "Life isn't about waiting for the storm to pass.
It's about learning to dance in the rain."

JR: Talk about brain training! What does it mean to change your mind about the world? When you are able to re-perceive the world as a magical wonderland, similar to how it has been viewed throughout most of human existence, we will treat it with the care and love needed to restore the reciprocal relationship between humans and the rest of nature.

PP: Find a way to enjoy today's weather, whatever it is.

October 2

Inside each precious living thing lies a mystery to be uncovered.

1) "The voyage of discovery is not in seeking new landscapes but in having new eyes."
2) "Perception defines our reality."
3) "The eye sees only what the mind is prepared to comprehend."

JR: Being able to alter your perception blesses you with the ability to make new discoveries about anything. Developing new ways of seeing things introduces an element of fascination into any endeavor, even one that you practice regularly. In this sense, your increased capacity to perceive things from many angles serves as a natural stimulant in your life.

PP: Stretch your imagination. Touch or hold some living thing and imagine how it perceives you.

October 3

It just takes a little imagination.

If a culture lacks a positive vision of the future, its creative power begins to wither and the culture itself stagnates and eventually dies out. Negative images are even more destructive, leading to hopelessness, helplessness, and failure to provide for the future. The collective pessimism results in "endgame" behaviors, with people snatching and grabbing to secure something for themselves before everything falls apart. This behavior brings about the very collapse they fear.

Today as we are besieged by planetary problems, the risk is that we will deal with them in just this type of pessimistic and unproductive style. Transfixed by an image of our own future decline, we could actually bring it about. A positive vision of the future, according to writer and philosopher David Spangler, "challenges the culture to dare, to be open to change, and to accept a spirit of creativity that could alter its very structure."

JR: It is your choice—either to inundate your thoughts with pessimism and a feeling of hopelessness and, in so doing, become a conspirator, whether you are aware of it or not, in the destruction of the world. Or alternatively, you can choose to implant a vision, using your fathomless potential, for becoming an agent in the creation of a world that is filled with hope and caring. We, as a species, can go either way, and each individual's decision has an effect on the direction we will take.

PP: What do you choose? Yes, it is a choice. While you may "naturally" be more full of hope or less so, you choose which way to move towards based on what you feed your mind.

October 4

Another enticing display of planetary reality

The ecological crisis will not begin to turn around until we change at a very basic level how we feel about bodies and about the material creation in all its incredible variety and richness of forms. It is not enough to change our lifestyles; we must change what we value.

JR: How do you consciously change what you value? Surely it's easier said than done, but taking the time to consider what you wish to value and then seeing if the way you live truly reflects that is a good start. How much your desired value is reflected in how you live is one sign of how integrated your spirit and material life are. The key is to identify what you want to value, which may be different than what you value now.

PP: Imagine an outsider looking at your everyday life. What would she think you most value based on what she sees you doing? Is that what you want to value?

October 5

Something wonderful lies in the distance.

Our only hope for a more humane and environmentally sustainable future is changing dominator mindsets and the cultural values they reflect. As David Orr writes in Earth in Mind, the crisis in global ecology is first and foremost a crisis in values.

JR: As long as we live according to the dominator mindset, it is impossible to lead lives according to the values of love, caring and tolerance. In order to move towards a peaceful world which abides by such values, we must come to see the destructiveness of the dominator mindset for what it is and disempower it, while granting respect and power to those who can guide us to a more humane and sustainable world.

PP: What kind of power do you use or most respect, a domineering type or a loving type? How does this affect your life (for better or for worse)?

October 6

Feel instilled with life

This re-enchantment with the earth as a living reality is the condition for our rescue of the earth from the impending destruction that we are imposing upon it. To carry this out effectively, we must now, in a sense, reinvent the human as a species within the community of life species. Our sense of reality and of value must consciously shift from an anthropocentric to a biocentric norm of reference.

JR: Take a close look at the various living things around you, and immerse yourself in the mystery of the life force infused in all of us. In this sense, we are all one, and how we treat other life forms is how we treat their generous bestower.

PP: Bathe in the wonder of knowing that you share this gift of life with all living beings and that we are all in this together.

October 7

Keep an eye out on where to go from here

A vision without a task is a dream;
A task without a vision is drudgery;
A vision with a task is the hope of the world.

JR: How are we ever to get to where we want to go when we don't know where it is that we wish to go? And when we come to an understanding and feel a strong longing for where we wish to go, how can this vision not provide us with the fuel and the energy needed to start moving towards it? The task and the vision go hand in hand to create the hope our world so desperately needs.

PP: What is your vision of the future (it can be grand or something simple, but something which inspires you)? What task can you do now to move towards it?

October 8

You can become far-sighted wherever you live.

1) No matter where you live, the biggest defect we human beings have is our shortsightedness. We don't see what could be. We should be looking at our potential, stretching ourselves into everything we can become.

2) Potential donors want hope and optimism in their lives. They want to see solutions.

JR: We live in a society that encourages us to focus on the short-term life goals, making a lot of money now, this year's vacation, tonight's dinner. And in turn, it leads to the exclusion of searching out and moving towards what can fulfill us, as individuals and as a world community, long into the future. Many people in the world desire to offer their time and money to the gifted few who can both impart a long-term vision for the betterment of all and find constructive ways of moving towards it.

PP: Do you have the potential to offer a far-reaching vision for a sustainable future? If so, make a sincere effort to draw it up so it can inspire others. If not, try to find someone or some group that does so, and offer your support.

October 9
Filling the gaps to create a better tomorrow

"The spiritual nature of man abhors a vacuum, and if it finds nothing new with which to fill the vacuum, tomorrow it will fill it with religions that are less and less adapted to the present, and which, like Islam today, will [also] begin producing monsters.

The Koran itself declares that 'there is no compulsion in religion.' How can a civilization so betray its own sacred text?"

JR: As people focus more and more on satisfying (and over-fulfilling) their material needs, their spiritual needs are found starving and therefore seek out any kind of an outlet in order to be soothed. As the original messages of Islam, Christianity and other world religions come to be seen as too idealistic or impossible to follow in today's world, more people become attracted to their corrupt and bastardized forms which the founders would be unable to recognize as anything that could have arisen from what they had taught.

PP: How do you think your belief system has become corrupted? How can you move back towards its original teaching and intention?

October 10

Nature is forever designing new models.

1) "You never change things by fighting the existing reality. To change something, build a new model that makes the existing model obsolete."

2) The real job to be done is not to resolve the point of conflict but to change the paradigm that led to the conflict in the first place.

JR: While it is important to fight against the unjust practices in society, it is all the more important to provide alternatives—concrete new models and new paradigms—which reflect an enlightened way of thinking to honor all of life. Without showing a hopeful road to the future, and making efforts to put it into practice here and now, our efforts to resist and change the wrongful ways of today will simply lead to a sense of futility and burnout.

PP: There are numerous creative, new models of living sustainably and with hope. Find one that appeals to you and learn more about it.

October 11

New models can only come to life through hands-on work.

Sarvodaya celebrates the individual without celebrating individualism. Sarvodaya also celebrates community without celebrating communism. Individualism sacrifices the community, while communism sacrifices the individual. Sarvodaya perceives the relationship between the two. Sarvodaya also means the well-being of animals, plants, insects and all other forms of life.

Sarvodaya pursues decentralised and small-scale community politics, one which safeguards the interest of the collective as well as the individual. Moreover, sarvodaya embraces the well-being of the Earth... Capitalism and socialism are both anthropocentric, whereas sarvodaya cares for all, and it cares for the weak and poor first, because they need help the most. Neither any humans nor any part of the natural world fall outside the ambit of sarvodaya. Capitalism is self-centred, socialism is society-centred, and sarvodaya is life-centred.

JR: In our search for models, it is important to be mindful that their proposed paradigms demonstrate only a part of their potential effectiveness. The far more important factor in terms of their successful implementation lies in the people who are attempting to live out the ideals of the model. To have a paradigm leading to a kinder, more sustainable world is a good start. Cultivating people who can live out its vision is more time-consuming, as it involves much needed nitty-gritty work that can move the model closer to a living reality.

PP: How does Sarvodaya sound to you? If it appeals to you, learn about some of the communities seeking to live out its paradigm.

October 12

We spin our own web, and shape it as we choose.

Shape-shifting is an opportunity presented to us every day. Recently, I was sitting on the bench with another woman, who was reading a newspaper. A fourteen-year-old boy was buzzing by us on his skateboard. The third time, he came inadvertently too close, and knocked the newspaper out of the woman's hand.

Startled, she said, "Oh, why don't you grow up?" The boy skated off, down to the corner to talk to his buddy, and the two of them looked back at us. The woman then picked up her newspaper and walked to the middle of the block.

She called to him, "Could I talk to you for a moment?" Reluctantly, the boy came back, very slowly, on his skateboard. He stopped and said, "Yeah?" She said, "What I meant to say was that I was afraid that you might hurt me, and I apologize for saying what I did." He looked at her, his face lit up, and said, "How cool!" That moment is indelibly etched in my mind.

Within the space of minutes, a human being decided to shape-shift the experience and create what in Latin America is called a small miracle, a holy moment. This was an experience created between a boy and a woman, generations apart. We have the opportunity, as creative catalysts and healing agents, to become shape-shifters to create many holy moments.

JR: What an empowering concept shape-shifting is! Each one of us has the capacity to change a given situation with a few words or with the chosen reaction to a situation. You can blow someone's mind by returning someone's anger towards you with an act of kindness. Such a reaction can only leave him feeling bewildered (in a very positive way). Thus, the way you shape any situation is limited only by the confines of your imagination.

PP: What is one situation today which is quite stressful for you? How can you shift it into a "holy moment?

October 13

What's the buzz?

There are peaceful societies to which we can look for inspiration. The Zuni tribe of the American Southwest, the Arapesh of New Guinea, the Semai of Malaysia, the Xingo of Brazil, the Kogi tribe of Peru, and Buid of Mindoro—all are societies that accept the possibility of violence but stigmatize anger, violence, boasting, and arguing. They honor those who ascribe to generosity and gentleness. These are cultures that promote the importance of the individual to the greater good of all.

So, it can be done. It is a matter of culture. It is a matter of who and what we choose to be. It is matter of vision, of will, of heart.

JR: What's really happening in our world? If we let the mainstream media tell us about the happenings around us, it's easy to be convinced that most of our society and the world's people are killing each other, having affairs, or sinking into depression. The media acknowledges that bad news sells. Yet, without the people raising healthy families, working hard, and caring for others, there is no way that our society could be as law-abiding and safe as it has become (in most places). And in some societies, as mentioned in the passage, kindness and concern for the greater good is an intricate part of their culture. So the buzz is that culture is not a given—the kind of culture we cultivate is our choice.

PP: Choose one of the peaceful groups in the passage above, and find a video or article about them to learn how they are able to live more peacefully.

October 14

Let new possibilities enlighten your life

Algae are extraordinarily adaptable creatures. They can grow almost anywhere, including land utterly unsuited for agriculture. Since they don't have to compete against food crops for land, they avoid the problems this can cause: spiraling grain prices, food shortages, and conversion of tropical forests and wildlife habitat to plantations and cropland.

These single-celled wonders also have other notable virtues:
- Algae are stunningly productive—the fastest growing plants on Earth. They can double in mass in just a few hours, allowing daily harvest.
- Algae are oily and compact, producing 30 times more oil per acre than sunflowers or rapeseed.
- Algae don't need fresh water, and can thrive in water that's boiling, salty, frozen, or contaminated—even in sewage.
- Algae can eat pollution. They neutralize acids, split the nitrogen oxides that cause smog into harmless nitrogen and oxygen, and convert carbon dioxide (global warming pollution) into oxygen and biomass.

JR: *This is just one of countless possibilities that holds great promise of being employed for the betterment of humankind and the overall natural environment. Sounds too good to be true—perhaps it is. Sometimes we get so hooked on one idea that, even if it is debunked, we refuse to let it go. However, being open to new ideas and the evidence which both discredits and supports them, trying out the ones which electrify you, and discerning whether they are "right" for you or not brings an exciting, dynamic dimension to your life.*

PP: *What is an exciting development you've heard about recently which holds hope for helping us move towards a more sustainable world? Find out more about it.*

October 15

Trees continually clean the air and make our lives possible.

A typical future dense town has a radius of 800 meters (it's possible to walk across the city in about 20 minutes, is now 200 hectares in size, and totals 60,000 inhabitants). Trees and other vegetation are planted in a belt around the city and along existing roads (so they are easy to reach for horses and people) for biofuel, air cleaning, protection from winds, and growing fruits and vegetables.

Regional and local traffic systems rely mainly on railroads, canals, harbors by the sea, and lighter-than-air airships using city-center airship ports. Walking and biking are the normal ways of getting around. All locations are close to water and railroads and the region is approaching a self-supporting state that has little effect on the surrounding areas.

We studied one of Sweden's built ecovillages (Myrstacken, Malmo) and saw that the real costs of operation and maintenance were nine times lower than for a standard village.

JR: What are the best types of community to live in? Which kinds of community are ideologically sustainable for the world at large? If we stand any chance of living harmoniously with the natural environment while limiting and/or adapting to climate change, we must search for the answers to these questions. The concept of the ecovillage (like the one suggested in the passage) is today one of the best examples of a well-integrated, environmentally sustainable and economically feasible society.

PP: What is one good idea which you think could make your community a more sustainable and better place to live? How can you support the effort to implement this idea?

October 16

An example of true thriving

Are we doomed to tip? Vemeji sees opportunities to lessen the odds. He argues for targeted conservation strategies. Rather than trying to save every last tree frog or butterfly, conservation should emphasize the most important consumers and producers in ecosystems: forest trees and phytoplankton, reef-building corals and sponges, big mammals, and especially apex predators.

The guiding principle remains much the same: redefining what it means to thrive. We cannot continue to expand our economies, swell our population, and exploit the world's resources at present-day rates. "Our only hope is a change in values. Instead of wanting more material possessions, we need to find other ways of achieving happiness and satisfaction in life." The fossil record shows, over and over again, that "to cope with radically new situations, you have to change your criteria of what it means to be successful." We need to do that.

JR: The key question here is "What does it mean to thrive?" When we look at the subjects which are given the most time and attention in our schools, media and everyday lives, there is no question that "to thrive" has come to primarily refer to "succeed economically." News about the stock market, GDP growth, unemployment rates and other economic news far outweighs any other. As a result, we are destroying the long-term foundations (clean air and water, biodiversity, forests and so on) which make short-term economic growth possible, thereby sentencing our descendants to early deaths for our own immediate pleasures.

PP: For you, what does it mean to thrive? If your definition would be applied throughout society, who would suffer and who would benefit—a limited few or the greater part of society and nature?

October 17
Inspiring awe for free

A positive vision of "working less and living more," a vision that aims to create "an advanced lifestyle appropriate for a post-industrial era," is extremely important for green politics, which has suffered from the general impression that it involves an embrace of Malthusian austerity and dour asceticism.

JR: A lot in the natural world borders on the miraculous and can inspire a feeling of exaltation, particularly when we take the time to see and experience it. Our busy-ness and acquisition of more and more material goods prevent us from truly perceiving the wonders of the multitude of life forms around us. Contrary to common opinion, the busy, materialistic life is self-denying, preventing the innermost self from establishing and maintaining contact with its life source.

PP: How can you simplify your life or become less busy and move more towards fully appreciating the natural wonders around you?

October 18

Sensory contact with nature rejuvenates our energy.

The major challenge to education is for it to recognize and deal with the fact that we are emotionally bonded and addicted to our false stories. We need re-education, a process that will safely un-bond us from our present stories and re-bond us to living responsibly. I find that sensory contact with nature has the power to do this.

JR: The extraction of most of the contemporary energy sources, which power our industrial society, creates havoc in the natural environment and to the nearby human communities. We have come to feel dependent on fossil fuels, largely ignoring the abundant sources of energy in nature, both those which energize the spirit (through contact with nature) and those which can power the society in an environmentally friendly way. It is up to us whether or not to choose to develop and live in societies where such energies are fully and beneficially utilized.

PP: Personally, what endeavor makes you feel full of life and leaves you basking in its light afterward? How can you please yourself by doing this more often?

October 19

Healthy entertainment opportunities in nature—available for the taking

Our world has been turned inside-out by entertainment. Once it was built around work; now it's made up of thrills. In a Toys-R-Us world, we spend more and more to bring up kids who are less and less connected to what keeps them alive.

The obsession with technology has led us into increasing specialization. And that makes it harder for us to see the whole picture; we become more and more knowledgeable about less and less of the world. We can redesign education to bring up kids in physical contact with the physical world. Instead of teaching "subjects" (history, math, English), we can teach principles of learning that the kids can then use to bring meaning to those too often meaningless subjects.

It is a colossal foolishness, for example, to assume that what we need in order to fix our broken educational system is to put computers in all the schools. That's an extension of the same doctrine that was espoused by World Bank developers who decided decades ago that what would liberate the Third World was a proliferation of big power plants, highways, and office buildings. Many of those projects left only greater poverty. What children need now is not more extension of their already vastly extended corporeal powers, but more capability to make sense of the powers they have.

These are not policy steps. They're fundamental shifts, first in how we learn and then in how we perceive.

JR: We are most likely to comprehend those things that we frequently encounter. Is it any wonder why so few of us can understand even a small part of the natural world?

PP: What percentage of your waking time do you spend with technology, with people, with nature? Do you feel it's a good balance?

October 20

*Aspire to
greater heights*

A Brazilian theologian by the name of Ruben Alvez (who wrote "Tomorrow's Child") said:

What is hope? It is the pre-sentiment that imagination is more real, and reality less real than it looks. It is the suspicion that the overwhelming brutality of facts that oppress us and repress us is not the last word. It is the hunch that reality is more complex than the realists want us to believe. That the frontiers of the possible are not determined by the limits of the actual. And that in a miraculous and unexpected way, life is preparing the creative events which will open the way to freedom and to resurrection. But the two, suffering and hope, must live from each other. Suffering without hope produces resentment and despair. But hope without suffering creates illusions, naivete, and drunkenness. So let us plant dates, even though we who plant them will never eat them. We must live by the love of what we will never see. This is the secret of discipline. It is a refusal to let our creative act be dissolved away by our own need for immediate sense experience. And it's a stubborn commitment to the future of our grandchildren. Such disciplined love is what has given saints, revolutionaries, and martyrs the courage to die for the future they envisage. They make their own bodies the seed of their own highest hopes.

JR: In the absence of hope, we see despair and cynicism rule. Hope energizes us to envision a more enlightened future, and bear the sufferings which accompany the transition towards it. We are blessed to have so many guides throughout history who have balanced a hopeful perspective of a brighter future with the strong, committed discipline to live it out.

PP: Who is someone (in the present or in the past) who you feel has (had) such an inspiring balance? Learn more about that person's life.

October 21

Just imagine it—it's the first step

1) The opposite of faith is not doubt. Rather, the opposite of faith is nihilism, the inability to image any transcendent environment and despair about the possibility of even negative meaning.

2) The price of apathy towards public affairs is to be ruled by evil men.

JR: Life itself is a mystery and inherent in all mystery is an element of the unknown. By claiming to know, without a doubt, the meaning of life and what happens at the time of death, is to deny the mystery, which leads to a danger of extremism (believing that your belief is the only true one, all others be damned). Having a strong faith includes having doubt, but rising above it and allowing your faith to inspire a vision for a better future and provide fuel to act accordingly. Faith in action is the light of the world.

PP: What is the best way for you to put your faith into action, something that excites and uplifts you and others?

October 22

Great potential lies everywhere—waiting to be explored and pursued.

The anxious and depressed states people get into from watching the news—or various forms of "entertainment," that portray the same dismal picture of human nature—have a general impact: we start seeing everything more negatively.

Negative expectations mask from view our positive potentials, which are the very ones we need if we're going to avoid and resolve problems like violence.

JR: Some of us are drawn to the dismal, finding a perverse, temporary pleasure in bad news, but begetting more despair in the long term. Others focus on the positive and get a high from all of the good things happening in the world, and then are shocked or frozen into inaction when something horrifying occurs. Hope lies in gaining a clear sight of our positive potential and finding ways to put it into practice while acknowledging the negative as well.

PP: What negative expectations do you have? Are they preventing your positive potential from surfacing?

October 23

Seeking and identifying the ideal balance

For civilization as a whole, the faith that is so essential to restore the balance now missing in our relationship to the earth is the faith that we do have a future. We can believe in that future and work to achieve it and preserve it, or we can walk blindly on, behaving as if one day there will be no children to inherit our legacy. The choice is ours; the earth is in the balance.

JR: The demands made on our everyday lives make it difficult, if not impossible, to live a balanced life. The lack of balance in our personal lives (in the areas of work-play, material-spiritual, social time-personal reflection) is reflected in the imbalances around the world (concerning development vs. preservation, rich and poor, justice vs. compassion). Our inability to live in balance directly contributes to our world's crises. Thus, building hope in restoring the balance and finding ways to do so will greatly benefit our personal lives as well as the world at large.

PP: How is your life out of whack? What is one thing you can do now to bring it more into balance?

October 24

Hope combined with good works unleashes a dynamic force.

Hope is a state of mind, not of the world. It is an orientation of the spirit, an orientation of the heart; it transcends the world that is immediately experienced, and is anchored somewhere beyond its horizons. Hope, in this deep and powerful sense, is not the same as joy that things are going well, or willingness to invest in enterprises that are obviously heading for... success, but rather, an ability to work for something because it is good, not just because it stands a chance to succeed.

JR: The cynics claim that those who live in hope are impractical dreamers. But aren't the most unrealistic ones those who believe that we can continue along the path we are currently treading without suffering the inevitable, horrific consequences of the many injuries we inflict on other people and our living planet? The results of their beliefs are not so different from the cynics, trapped in hopelessness and remaining skeptical that any long-lasting good is possible, who abet in pushing the world to the brink through their accompanied inaction to heal the wounds. To build and maintain hope takes effort, but it can grow and become a dynamic force in the lives of even those living in dismal conditions (such as with Havel and Mandela, both who served long, punishing prison terms).

PP: What does a "spirit of hope" mean to you? What actions can you take to cultivate it?

October 25

Give yourself a treat

Many people are sure that living in a sustainable way must be about "giving up" things. It doesn't occur to them that living in an unsustainable way is also about giving up things, very precious things like security, hope, light-heartedness, and freedom from anxiety, fear, and guilt.

JR: When someone says "We must live sustainably," she is then put on the defensive, and is forced to explain that doing so really isn't so bad. Yet, those who claim (in action or in word) that "We can continue to live unsustainably" aren't questioned, for that is how the majority of us live, and we wish not to be burdened with the implications of continuing upon this path. We indeed give up many precious things because of the way we live. Living sustainably implies having more connection with others and the earth, more sharing, and once again enjoying the gifts of nature that we have grown oblivious to. In other words, it means living more joyfully.

PP: What activity do you do that is beneficial both for other people and for the earth? How about devoting more time and energy to it?

October 26

Creating a different way of being can bring in a lot of fun.

The usual reason why relationships fail is because there is too little love and mutual recognition, not because there is too little responsibility.

All too often, people have internalized the ethos of the marketplace, and view the other person primarily in terms of what one can get out of the exchange. In the ethos of the marketplace, every commitment is tentative, based on what is in one's own best short-term interest. If a better deal comes along, in this way of thinking, one naturally moves on.

To counter the marketplace consciousness, we need to foster a different way of being in the world, a way that emphasizes the primacy of love and mutual recognition, that encourages us to see other people as fundamentally deserving of respect and caring, and that repudiates instrumental ways of viewing the world and one another. Loving another person involves an ability to transcend ourselves and to see the other as a wonder, a miracle embodied, a manifestation of God's spirit, a being who moves us to care and who automatically evokes in us a concern for his or her well-being. This is a whole new way of seeing, often closely aligned to the insights of spiritual and religious traditions that validate joyful embracing of the other and invoke notions of loving our neighbor.

JR: Most of us don't realize how seduced we are with the market ideology. Even in our closest relationships, we calculate how we can benefit from them, or if we are giving too much. The world's main spiritual paths all emphasize the importance of love, caring, and respect, but this message is overshadowed by the market ethos controlling our lives. Yet, we can choose to live in a different way, a truly spiritual way, which breaks the chains of the market-ethos inflicted prison of self-absorption and creates a spirit-opening joy of mutual interdependence.

PP: When did you give something to someone with no expectation of anything in return? How did it make you feel?

October 27

The plant kingdom is no stranger to diversity.

The day you are different, others become different. And you will see them differently, too. Someone who seemed terrifying will now seem frightened. Someone who seemed rude will seem frightened. All of a sudden, no one has the power to hurt you anymore. No one has the power to put pressure on you. You become truly happy, the essence of spirituality. You can do this by putting this program into action, a thousand times: (a) identify the negative feelings in you; (b) understand that they are in you, not in the world, not in external reality; (c) do not see them as an essential part of 'I'; these things come and go; (d) understand that when you change, everything changes.

JR: Have you ever thought about how much of what you consider to be reality is not real at all? Most of your perceptions are shaded by the negative or positive undertone you hold. And it is within your power to change those connotations through meditation, experience, or the analysis of your ideas. You become different when you change your perceptions and, magically, the world around you also transforms.

PP: Carry out this four-step program with a negative feeling you now harbor.

October 28

Stay rooted

Optimism cannot be commanded, as Frankl observed, but hope can be nurtured by doing good work, being open to life, and rising above our lesser selves. Hope, real hope, comes from doing the things before us that need to be done in the spirit of thankfulness and celebration, without worrying about whether we will win or lose.

JR: It's impossible to maintain hope without acting on it. And taking action which is not rooted in hope can be potentially devastating if carried out with a sense of futility or, worse yet, to smash the hope of others. Such destructive deeds can be seen everywhere, especially by cynics whose worldview is threatened by those who bathe in good works filled with hope.

PP: Think of the work you must do today as a gift you are bestowing on others in the spirit of cheerfulness.

October 29

Who said trees can't dance?

The fact is, it's not a deception but rather a tribute to the amazing abilities of the human imagination. What enables banks—and the entire economy—to survive and flourish is our trust in the future. This trust is the sole backing for most of the money in the world.

Humankind was trapped in this predicament (not having money to borrow to progress) for thousands of years. As a result, economies remained frozen. The way out of the trap was discovered only in the modern era, with the appearance of a new system based on trust in the future. In it, people agreed to represent imaginary goods—goods that do not exist in the present—with a special kind of money they called 'credit.' Credit enables us to build the present at the expense of the future. It's founded on the assumption that our future resources are sure to be far more abundant than our present resources. A host of new and wonderful opportunities open up if we can build things in the present using future income.

JR: The human imagination may be the most powerful tool in the world, capable of reeking horrendous cruelties and of creating previously unimagined delights and fantasies. In our imagination, we can see dancing trees, UFOs, miracles, pink elephants, some of which may be real and some which aren't. And some we make real. When we see that our whole world of finance and credit is based on the imagination, on the belief in a better future, we come to understand the power of hope, which is what keeps the system going.

PP: Think about it—any credit you offer is made based on your belief in the future, and that it will somehow be more abundant than today.

October 30

Is it time to choose a new path?

In the hot and stormy future we have already made inevitable through our past emissions, an unshakable belief in the equal rights of all people and a capacity for deep compassion will be the only things standing between civilization and barbarism.

This is another lesson from the transformative movements of the past: all of them understood that the process of shifting cultural values—though somewhat ephemeral and difficult to quantify—was central to their work. And so they dreamed in public, showed humanity a better version of itself, modeled different values in their own behavior, and in the process liberated the political imagination and rapidly altered the sense of what was possible.

JR: In places where we witness societal chaos, inequality and lack of concern for others are found to be the general rule. It is in counteracting these privations that we ensure the foundation for a more ordered civilization. And in going beyond that, on to defining and living out the universal values which serve as the light posts for society's road into the future, we can blaze a trail towards a more peaceful co-existence, even under uncertain, ever-shifting circumstances.

PP: How can you better model your own life so that it reflects what you claim to believe in?

October 31

Soaring on the wings of hope and never looking back

Morton had a theory to explain the worldwide resonance of a day devoted to tree planting: "'Arbor Day' is not like other holidays. Each of those reposes upon the past, while Arbor Day proposes for the future. It contemplates, not the good and the beautiful of past generations, but it sketches, outlines, establishes the useful and the beautiful for the ages yet to come."

JR: Isn't it interesting how most national holidays throughout the world are based on past events, and few, if any, focus on our hopes for the future? What a revolutionary concept Arbor Day introduces—carrying out good work as a gift to future generations. Incorporating this kind of thinking into our holidays would be one way of focusing on what we can do now to move towards a better world far into the future.

PP: What would be one national holiday you'd like to propose for the benefit of the future?

NOVEMBER

Action & Leadership

You have now reached the point of bringing the paradigms you envisioned to life. When you take action, your hopes become embodied in physical reality. While fear has often bound you in the past, you now find that the best remedy to fear is to take action. There are bound to be failures along the way, yet each failure simply points to other ways that may bring success.

Once again, the kind of action you take depends on your character, environment, and, most important of all, what you have discovered about yourself through the many reflections (so far in this book) concerning the kinds of things which are fit for you. Never, ever base your major course of action only on what others tell you to do.

Actions can be taken by anyone; yet creating opportunities and spaces for concerned people to take action requires direction and leadership. In this sense of the word (rather than meaning to lead a group of followers), true leadership means listening closely to others to find the strengths they can use to build their self-esteem and forge important connections to enhance their sense of self-worth. By building up others, leaders diminish their own importance to the movement since others become capable of sustaining the initiative. Rather than making others dependent on her, a leader's true work lies in providing a vision of the good life which fills people with hope, keeping this hope alive, and making people believe in themselves sufficiently to carry it out. In this sense, leadership is multifaceted, and each person can enact some aspect thereof which is most suitable to her.

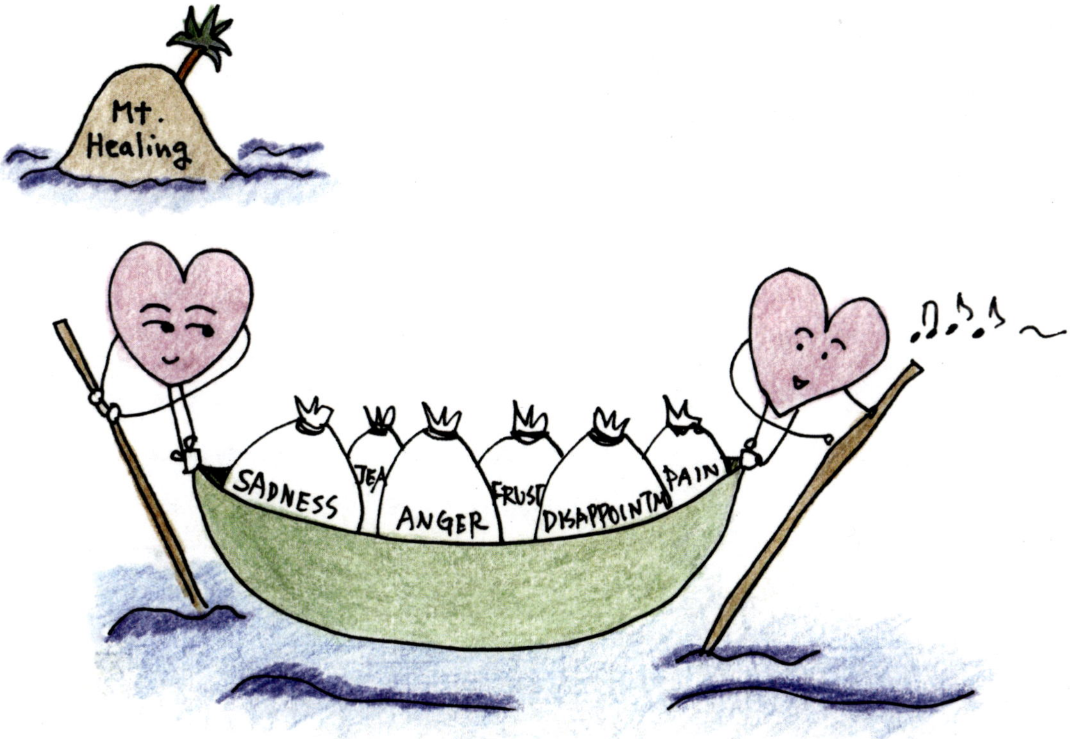
Mt.
Healing
SADNESS
ANGER
FRUST
DISAPPOINTM
PAIN

November 1

Make goodness reign

1) The best antidote to fear is action!
2) "The only thing necessary for the triumph of evil is for good men to do nothing."

JR: When we freeze up in fear, our whole being becomes paralyzed, and we are unable to move. The best antifreeze is for you to take action and, in doing so, weaken fear's grip. You probably will still be afraid, but your attempt to overcome the fear allows you to regain some control over it, and over your life.

PP: Think of a time when something was happening in your life that made you feel extremely afraid. What did you do to overcome the fear, or how did it come to pass?

November 2

With a grateful heart, participate in creating beauty

1) "Action is the antidote to despair."

2) "Sentiment without action is the ruin of the soul."

3) Most learning is not the result of instruction. It is rather the result of unhampered participation in a meaningful setting. I believe that a desirable future depends on our deliberately choosing a life of action over a life of consumption.

JR: Feelings are important message bearers. They are signposts to the things that are going well or going badly in our lives. When they serve as guides to our actions, our lives become more integrated and "effective." Simply allowing your feelings to control your life, without benefitting from what they are teaching you, makes you their victim and renders you powerless. Acting on their messages empowers you.

PP: What strong feeling have you had recently? What do you think it was teaching you?

November 3

Ringing in the new age

The task of redeeming the environment cannot succeed unless we redeem the idea of social change, and deliver the message that human beings can change themselves and the world for the better. Those advocating change have always fought the odds. Social change is never practical until it happens. Yet it has happened. We live in a world today that is probably more tolerant, humane, democratic and environmentally conscious than it has ever been. We can thank the activists of the world, past, present, and future for that.

An environmental movement that is apocalyptic will fail. Movements triumph on hope. Established regimes triumph on fatalism, resignation, and despair. Optimism, as anarchist writer David Graeber has said, is a moral necessity. It is also a political necessity. We are not going to make the needed changes by terrorizing people with visions of doom. We can make the needed changes if we speak to people with respect, inform them of the dangers we face and provide a compelling vision of a better life in an environmentally sane and socially just world. If we do our work, we will be amazed at the ingenuity people will apply to achieve that world. That world will be built with hope, not with despair.

JR: It is easy to look at the adverse happenings around the world and fall into despair. And it's just as easy to focus on the good things occurring all over the planet and get instilled with hope. The people throughout history who have preached and lived out hopeful messages of constructive change are those who have been instrumental in the creation of a better world. Each one of us has the power to be a part of sharing a better world in the way optimal to his or her unique character.

PP: What seed of hope can you plant in your own life to effect a constructive change on the people or the natural environment around you?

November 4

Consider the marvel which you are capable of becoming

1) "There is nothing with which every man is so afraid as getting to know how enormously much he is capable of doing and becoming."

2) "No punishment anyone might inflict on us could possibly be worse than the punishment we inflict on ourselves by conspiring in our own diminishment."

JR: How easy it is to claim ineptness and belittle yourself as an excuse for the inability to live out your full potential. Yet, in doing so, you are left wanting, having refused to water that unique seed inside of you. Thereby, you not only prevent the flowering of the seed from beautifying the world around you, but also deny yourself the feeling of fulfillment of becoming your grander self.

PP: What do you downplay about yourself—some potential that you have but refuse to fully make use of? How can you start putting it into practice for your own benefit and for the good of those around you?

November 5

Encounter
True Holiness

Rational thinking (attentive, intelligent, and reasonable) is not easily achieved, and never without authentic conversion first. Mature religion involves changing ourselves and letting ourselves be changed by a mysterious encounter with grace, mercy, and forgiveness. This is the truth that will set us free (John 8:32). Yet much of our history has involved trying to change other people—with our ideas. This has gotten us almost nowhere, and it allows us to remain untransformed and unconverted ourselves.

Remember, it is only transformed people who have the power to transform others, as if by osmosis. In the presence of whole people, or any encounter with Holiness Itself, we simply find that, after a while, we are different—and much better.

JR: Yet another cop-out practiced by most of us, in order to escape confronting our own personal weaknesses, is blaming and trying to change others. We ignore those things which we are most capable of changing (i.e. within ourselves) and the fact that self-change is the most effective way of changing others. Contrary to popular belief, attempting to change others actually breeds the power struggles, fighting, and war we claim to be trying to avert.

PP: Who is someone whose simple presence inspires in you a feeling of holiness? Research a bit about how she came to become such an inspiration.

November 6

Opening up lets in the light

1) Don't waste time with people who want to argue. They'll keep you immobilized forever. Look for people who are already open to something new.

2) It must be one way or the other. Either the day must come when joy prevails and all the makers of misery are no longer able to infect it: or else for ever and ever the makers of misery can destroy in others the happiness they reject for themselves. I know it has a grand sound to say ye'll accept no salvation which leaves even one creature in the dark outside. But watch that sophistry or ye'll make a Dog in a Manger the tyrant of the universe.

JR: It is a misconception to think that being open implies a complete acceptance of letting everyone in equally with no discernment. There are those who exploit such an idea by binding the agents of openness with their endless arguments that prevent any constructive progress or delighting in the infliction of despair, zapping the energy of those around them. A true opening for these people means showing them conceivable courses of action that are instilled with hope, and leaving it up to them to enter into the light to accept it or close the door and continue to dwell in the darkness.

PP: Who, or which of your own ideas, immobilizes you and zaps your energy? How can you shine a light on him/it?

November 7

*Set your own course
and venture on*

1) There are two types of people in this world—the proactive and the reactive—those who take responsibility for their lives and those who blame; those who make it happen and those who get happened to.

Proactive people make choices based on values. They think before they act. They recognize they can't control everything that happens to them, but they can control what they do about it. Unlike reactive people who are full of carbonation, proactive people are like water. Shake them up all you want, take off the lid, and nothing. No fizzing, no bubbling, no pressure. They are calm, cool, and in control.

2) Being proactive really means two things. First, you take responsibility for your life. Second, you have a "can-do" attitude.

JR: Developing a proactive attitude is not something that happens overnight. While some people may be so inclined naturally, for most of us it takes time and effort. As long as we search for problems "out there," that are beyond our control, we will forever feel victimized. It is only in taking responsibility for ourselves, the way we act and feel, that we stand any chance of reclaiming our lives through an earnest search for ways to act and feel better.

PP: What are you not taking responsibility for in your own life? What would happen if you did?

November 8

Looking outward can lift you upward

If you ever feel depressed, the best thing to do is to do something for someone else. Why? Because it gets you focused outward, not inward. It's hard to be depressed while serving someone else. Ironically, a by-product of helping others is feeling wonderful yourself.

JR: Self-reflection requires focusing within, and this is an important aspect of spiritual development. Like with everything else, a well-balanced approach brings about the greatest benefit, and that balance varies from one person to another. For a person who feels chronically disheartened, a greater effort may be required to reach out and help others, with personal gain resulting therefrom. Staying alone causes the despair to fester and grow, while reaching out, however difficult it may be, steals away the roost where the despondency is nurtured.

PP: When you feel depressed, what can you do, even something very simple, to be of service to others and instill your spirit with a ray of light and hope?

November 9

Each type flourishes under its own proper condition.

Exercise seems to work well for depression because it changes the physiological state the mood evokes: depression is a low-arousal state, and aerobics pitches the body into high arousal. By the same token, relaxation techniques, which put the body into a low-arousal state, work well for anxiety, a high-arousal state, but not so well for depression.

JR: One of the primary issues with many religions or spiritual systems of thought is that they attempt to adopt a "one pattern fits all" ideology. In a world made up of unique individuals with different backgrounds, cultures, characters—in other words, different conditions and conditionings—this is simply impossible. Each person must find his own best method, based on his own disposition, using his beliefs and universal values as guidelines.

PP: Is your natural temperament low-arousal or high-arousal? Based on this tendency, would it be more beneficial to do more exercise or more relaxation techniques?

November 10

Where is this ending up?

You may think that the world's evil is created by those you would term 'bad' people but, in fact, most of it depends upon the attitudes of ordinary people. The choices that each one of you make determine the direction of the world. No matter how many destructive people there are and no matter how much power those so-called evil people may have, they could not do anything if the majority of the people in the world consciously took responsibility for their own actions. So the majority of people are indirectly taking part in the evil. They are probably not doing it intentionally but ignorance is a sin, too. They have been living the way they were programmed by their society and have never questioned anything. And as a result, they have ended up having a hand in creating evil.

JR: It may be true that the majority of the world's people are kind-hearted; however, this will not contribute at all towards making a better world as long as we remain in the dark about the evil which is perpetrated due to our ignorance. Becoming conscious thereof, and moving towards consumption patterns and lifestyles which don't sustain exploitation or inflict pain on other living beings, but rather support a healthy and enjoyable life for others, is the way to expand our compassion and love beyond our immediate environment.

PP: What product or service that you use is embroiled in controversy? Check into it and decide whether to continue using it or find an alternative more in alignment with your values.

November 11

Show your true colors

"Nobody thinks anything of these (slave) traders! They are universally despised—never received into any decent society."

"But who, sir, makes the trader? Who is most to blame? The enlightened, cultivated, intelligent man, who supports the system of which the trader is the inevitable result, or the poor trader himself? You make the public sentiment that calls for this trade, that debauches and depraves him, till he feels no shame in it; and in what are you better than he? Are you educated and he ignorant, you high and he low, you refined and he coarse, you talented and he simple? In the day of a future Judgment, these very considerations may make it more tolerable for him than for you."

JR: Intelligence has frequently come to be considered as the ability to skirt around the issues and blame someone else or the circumstances and, in the process, justify our own inaction or lack of responsibility. When we learn to engage contemporary issues constructively, without energy-zapping condemnation or the infliction of guilt, the spark of hope is ignited.

PP: What is one profession that you despise? Consider why certain people choose to be employed in that line of work, seeking to understand rather than criticize.

November 12

Be a bridge to put an end to your isolation

The more we are caught in our isolation, in our lack of emotional response to the world, and at the same time the more unavoidable a catastrophic end seems to be, the more malignant becomes the new religion. We cease to be the masters of technique and become instead its slaves—and technique, once a vital element of creation, shows its other face as the goddess of destruction (like the Indian goddess Kali), to which men and women are willing to sacrifice themselves and their children. While consciously still hanging onto the hope for a better future, cybernetic humanity represses the fact that they have become worshipers of the goddess of destruction.

JR: Becoming isolated from others takes on many forms. Some are easy to perceive, like those who lock themselves in their rooms or get fixated on their games to the exclusion of all else. A far more dangerous type of isolation is to emotionally distance oneself from any and all of the problems of the outside world, and this has become a common and, worse yet, acceptable response to (not) dealing with the world's woes.

PP: What is a social/environmental problem of concern to you but that you've chosen to distance yourself from (emotionally)? Can you find a way to support efforts to constructively deal with the issue, feeling a joy in being part of the solution?

November 13

Only you can decide your true path.

There is a world of difference between calling something evil and calling someone evil. The first strategy mobilizes resources against the problem, the second only recycles the ultimate cause of the problem, which is ill-will, resentment, lack of empathy and eventually hatred.

JR: It is very important to notice the way in which you perceive problems. The information which floods our senses on an everyday basis define certain people, groups, and countries as wicked, thereby resulting in never-ending conflict and war. No matter how many of THEM we kill, the evil remains. By attacking the action, behavior, or belief which gives rise to the wrongdoing, we have a greater chance of nipping it in the bud, making it difficult for the evil to take root again.

PP: Who is someone you see as malicious? Is it the person's existence which is evil or what he does?

November 14

Shun obsession, not legitimate desire

When the great spiritual traditions speak about the evil of desire, they're speaking of obsession, of craving. But it has been misinterpreted in a deadly way, so that all desires are seen as bad, and that becomes anti-life hypocrisy. So the honest recognition of the legitimacy of desire is an interesting part of spiritual life and part of the money issue, too.

The answer to consumerism is that people are starved for real ideas. The materialism of the American soul is a disease of the mind starved for ideas and ideals. Putting real ideas back into the culture will chip away at the force of materialism.

Social justice is fine, but unless it's pointing to the soul in some way, it's going to be just a refined version of materialism.

JR: The most fanatical religions and cults preach the need for the greatest austerity among their followers. When people are forced to suppress their every desire (pure and impure alike), and bottle it up like a pressure cooker, the trapped energy explodes, often in violent ways like justifying genocide or violence against any outsider. Furthermore, becoming obsessed and entrapped by our cravings also breeds dangerous tendencies of acquiring that object in any possible way, no matter how sinister. Understand the cravings which can harm you and distance yourself from them. At the same time, have fun with your legitimate desires and enjoy them fully. This will help your inner light to shine on those around you.

PP: What desire do you have that you can delight in fully without harming yourself or others (or, better yet, one that helps yourself and others)? Engage in it to your heart's content.

November 15

Create space for goodness to happen

1) Faith that counts, then, is not the absence of doubt; it's the presence of action. It puts you into motion, propels you to action.

2) The positive and proactive forces in this universe will always defeat the dark and nihilistic ones. We simply must create the spaces in which concerned citizens are offered a way to take action.

JR: *"But what can I do?" This question is asked all over by good-hearted people with a desire to perform good acts, but are unable to find the "place" to carry out good deeds that fit their needs. Part of the problem is that our technologies, our architecture, and the widening wealth gap all conspire to thwart such spaces. Redesigning our communities and our lifestyles so that there are more opportunities for caring people to get involved is important to better mobilize the positive, constructive energy in society.*

PP: *Where is the "space" (organization, place, or people) that enables you to act on one of your primary concerns? Can you find a way to spend more time there?*

November 16

*The contrast creates
and enhances
the beauty.*

1) (Concerning social entrepreneurship) The job can be boiled down to one essential function: the social entrepreneur helps others to envision a new possibility, appreciate its meaning, and recognize how it can be broken down into doable steps that build momentum for change.

2) Resistance and alternatives are "the twin strands of the DNA" of social change. One without the other is useless.

JR: When we see a malicious action, we are inclined to fight against it in whatever way possible. However, without also developing a contrasting alternative to that act and holding out greater hope and possibility, few people will be moved to stay committed to the resistance.

PP: What is one wrongdoing in society that disgusts you? How can you fight against it while, concurrently, proposing a constructive alternative?

November 17

Feed the soul

You cannot imagine how important action is to the inner life. The interior joy we feel when we have done a good deed, when we feel we have been needed somewhere and have lent a helping hand, is the nourishment the soul requires. Without those times when man feels himself to be part of the spiritual world through his actions, his soul decays.

JR: Meditation and reflection on becoming a better person are food for your inner world—the soul. And the outside world provides the environment where the benefits attained from your reflections can be planted through action, thus according a concrete mechanism for the seeds of your meditation to grow and bear fruit. Without such action, the seeds remain fallow, and the acquired treasures remain hidden and of little value.

PP: What action would best embody the benefits you have gained through your personal reflections?

November 18

Get outside and energize yourself

One thing that leads to unhappiness is obsession with your own needs and interests.

Once you involve yourself actively in a greater cause, it makes your own problems pale in comparison.

When you touch others with love and caring and compassion, when you get outside yourself, that is when you can sometimes reach a state of spiritual transcendence.

JR: When feeling down and out, it becomes very difficult to get out, much less to move at all. However, in staying alone, you become fixated on your own needs and issues, driving you to greater despair. Getting out and compassionately connecting with another (for the more introverted, this can be with animals or plants as well) breaks the bind of the obsession on the self and enwraps you in a feeling of caring, sharing each other's warmth to the benefit of both of you. The tremendous effort it takes to get out is rewarded with an escape from your self-imposed dungeon.

PP: When you feel depressed, wallowing in your sorrows, what is one simple act of kindness you are capable of that can help loosen the grip of your misery?

November 19

Trees—the gift of life

In one village in the foothills of the Himalayas, a single villager, Vishweshwar Dutt Saklani, has planted more the 20,000 trees—all native species—creating a little oasis of forest in an area that has been devastated by timber cutting. Streams have begun to flow again, birds and other animals have returned in large numbers, and the hillside is no longer eroding.

JR: It is often claimed that venturing out and doing good works befits only the extroverted, but what about the withdrawn and the timid? Nature, being non-judgmental and sharing her gifts with all, ensures the perfect environment for them. Whatever humanity does to her, she will invariably find ways to survive as she always has since time immemorial. Through inflicting damage on her, and being an accomplice to the extinction of countless species, humanity concurrently moves towards her own extinction as well, at which time nature will heal her wounds and renew her growth. Or, anyone who is of service to nature, finding ways to assist her and promote her protection and growth, is also serving humankind, thus becoming a co-creator of a world where people and the rest of nature interact to each others' benefit.

PP: What is one constructive project for the natural environment you'd like to see? Check if it is already being done in some way and give your support.

November 20

Rocky places hold treasures too.

Indian Environmentalist Abdul Kareem has spent the last 24 years of his life assembling a lush 30-acre woodland expanse that is now a haven for nature lovers and those in search of peace. Starting with a rocky five-acre patch of wasteland in Puliamkulam, Kareem dug a well and began to plough his savings from a job as an airlines ticketing agent into his dream project. The forest is now home to 1,500 medicinal plants, 2,000 varieties of trees, rare birds, animals and insects. Kareem refuses to sell even the leaf litter for money and has declined several lucrative offers to turn the reserve into a resort.

JR: One person's waste can be another's treasure! The beauty of being human is that our imaginations can function as the seeds for growing value from that which was previously considered worthless. Sometimes it takes only one person to dream and water that dream for it to sprout up into a reality of her choosing.

PP: Do you have a dream, something (perhaps a bit off the wall but which fills you with energy just thinking about it) which you'd love to make real? What steps can you take now to move towards doing so?

November 21

Transformation through integrating the differences

If the fire of the mystic's passion for God could be married to the activist's passion to enact change, then a new kind of human being would be born. The human being would be grounded in universal, all-embracing, mystical truth and would be acting for justice in a local context with a global consciousness, beyond national or tribal or religious boundaries. This is the key to preparing and transforming the human race.

JR: The social and environmental problems seen in today's world are but a reflection of the internal struggles which are more difficult to decipher. A strong faith in something good which lies beyond is attacked by the cynics and those who have come to feel hopeless. Our energy to take constructive action is zapped if we constantly feed ourselves with valueless entertainment and time-wasting games which require no creative input on the part of the user. However, it is within the power of each of us to reclaim our lives, and develop spiritual practices to instill hope and actively engage the imagination towards constructive action.

PP: How can your desire for goodness and your innate or learned capabilities be matched to marry your faith with action?

On a train in Tokyo, a big drunk man came in screaming obscenities. He aimed a wobbling kick at an old lady. "You old whore!" he bellowed. I stood up. I was young then, and had trained 3 years in Aikido. We had studied how to resolve conflict, not how to start it. But this drunk was a menace and I looked at him in disgust. He gathered himself for a rush at me, but then someone shouted "Hey!" It came from a little old man in a kimono. He looked at the drunk man and said "What'cha been drinking?"

"I been drinking sake," the laborer bellowed back.

"Oh, that's wonderful. Every night, me and my wife warm up a little bottle of sake and take it out to our persimmon tree."

"I love persimmons, too…" the laborer mellowed.

"Yes, and I'm sure you have a wonderful wife."

"No, my wife... she died last year." The suddenly changed drunk hung his head in heavy sorrow and began to sob. "I don't got no wife. I don't got no home any more. I lost my job."

When the train arrived at my stop, I saw the ragged laborer sprawled on the seat with his head on the man's lap. What I had wanted to do with muscle and meanness had been deftly accomplished with but a few kind words. What I had just witnessed was true Aikido in combat.

JR: Simple acts of love and kindness have a far greater potential of creating deep and long-lasting transformation than any form of coercion or violence.

PP: Think of a time when you used violence to get what you wanted. Did it lead to any kind of long-lasting change, or was it simply an immediate band-aid, only covering a wound which continued to fester underneath?

November 23

Build on your faith, whatever it may be

Negative synergy works like this. First, I dehumanize you and set you up as my enemy. You hit me, I hit you back. Things will get better if I can hit you hard enough and knock you out of the picture. War is the ultimate expression of the zero-sum mentality.

By contrast, positive synergy is the opposite of war. It's proactive, not reactive. It's abundant, not scarce. It means deliberately going for the 3rd Alternative: The maintenance of peace requires an aggressive commitment to imaginative diplomacy.

One of the most imaginative strokes of diplomacy in history was the Marshall Plan, truly a 3rd Alternative to ongoing European war. The Marshall Plan was the abundance mentality in action, the mind-set that says I can help my enemy, I can share, we can build together a plentiful future. The resulting revival broke the cycle of centuries of violence in Europe.

JR: The realization that we are all in this together, and that, in the long run, what I do to you is what I do to myself, makes us perceive violence and war as counterproductive acts that lead to more resultant fighting which we claim to be trying to stop. War and violence often arise due to mental laziness. Rather than relying on our mental capabilities to bring about imaginative solutions which bring people together, we too often depend on physical or military strength to force the other into submission, tearing people apart and feeding a repressed anger ready to flare up at the slightest provocation. Only in working together, seeking out ways where both sides benefit, can we move towards the peaceful and bountiful future which is ours for the taking.

PP: Recall a past war that you are familiar with. Stretch your creative powers, and imagine what could have been done beforehand to prevent the war and bring the two sides together.

November 24

Enlightened spirituality made real

In a seminal work, *The Great Transformation*, Karen Armstrong details the origins of our religious traditions during what is called the Axial Age, a 700-year period dating from 900 to 200 BCE, during which much of the world turned away from violence, cruelty, and barbarity. The upwelling of philosophy, insight, and intellect from that era lives today in the works of Socrates, Plato, Lao-tzu, Confucius, Mencius, Buddha, Jeremiah, Rabbi Hillel, and others. Rather than establishing doctrinaire religious institutions, these teachers created social movements that addressed human suffering.

The early expressions of religiosity during the Axial Age were not theocratic systems requiring belief, but instructional practices requiring action. The arthritic catechisms and rituals that we now accept as religion had no place in the precepts of these sages, prophets, and mystics. Their goal was to foster a compassionate society, and the question of whether there was an omnipotent God was irrelevant to how one might lead a moral life. They asked their students to question and challenge and, as opposed to modern religion, to take nothing on faith. They did not proselytize, sell, urge people to succeed, give motivational sermons, or harangue sinners. They urged their followers to change how they behaved in the world. All relied on a common principle, the Golden Rule: Never do to anyone what you would not have done to yourself.

JR: Warmongers and critics of human goodness often claim that humans have a natural tendency towards aggression and fighting. There are times in history and numerous examples of various human societies which prove them wrong. We are capable of both great cruelty as well as boundless love and compassion. We choose our direction through the faith traditions and lifestyles that we live and embody.

PP: What do your beliefs and lifestyle say about how you feel towards living compassionately? How could you alter them to put your love more into action?

November 25

Reconciling nature and humanity

Do not utter words that can create discord and cause the community to break. Make every effort to reconcile and resolve all conflicts, however small. In order to help reconcile a conflict, we have to be in touch with both sides. We must transcend the conflict; if we are still in the conflict, it is difficult to reconcile. We have to have a non-dualistic viewpoint in order to listen to both sides and understand. The world needs persons like this for the work of reconciliation, persons with the capacity of understanding and compassion.

JR: Reconciliation between two opposing sides is difficult, even when an effort is made to understand each other. It becomes impossible when they refuse any contact with each other, or only have contact when fighting. Seeking out people from both sides or third parties outside of the conflict, who understand and explain possible non-violent solutions which go beyond the current state of conflict, can begin to pry open the combatants' hearts enough for they themselves to engage in a mutual search for a way that benefits both.

PP: What is an "irreconcilable" conflict that you are in? Try to think of (or talk with the other about) an alternative that may be acceptable to both of you.

November 26

Rising above the fray

How does a person change his or her attitude? It takes practice—thinking and doing together.

Be a good listener. Show understanding. Make people feel important. Be tolerant. Handle resistance with patience, harmony, and reason. Let others be themselves. Give of yourself.

The best way to favorably impress others is to let them impress you!

You can only give away what you have. That's especially true with your inner characteristics such as love and understanding. Those are thoughts and feelings nourished and grown in your own heart and mind, aren't they?

One way of growing them is by giving them. Because then they come back to you in ever increasing abundance.

JR: There are many people who have low self-esteem and feel little sense of personal worth, having been abused, belittled, or ignored by significant others. For these people, it is hardest to change and adopt these good practices but, if they are able to do so, they will notice others treating them in the same way. In the process, they overcome their inferiority complex, becoming heroic figures—having overcome the hardships of their youths—for others who loathe themselves to emulate.

PP: When you come across a loved one who is expressing and showing resistance, try to "listen" to what she is feeling and battling inside more than her words.

November 27

Essential beauty is impossible to ignore.

If you and your colleagues ignore someone, that person's disengagement goes up to about 45%. If you don't ignore them but criticize them, it falls to 20% because people would rather be criticized than ignored. If you notice their strengths and put them in the right place where they can use their strengths, disengagement falls to less than 1%. So the bottom line is totally dependent on how engaged people are.

You engage workers by finding out their strengths and using them, by enhancing their self-esteem and by building careful, caring, compassionate relationships, including personal friendships. People want their leaders to offer them hope, trust and stability but also to maximize their own strengths.

JR: How does it feel to be ignored by those around you, being treated as if you don't exist? Contemplating this provides you with a small insight into how most of the homeless and others who are spurned by society constantly feel. Is it any wonder that they become disengaged and feel no sense of hope? Paying attention to them, engaging them in conversation and making them visible is the only way they will come to eventually re-engage and potentially become constructive members of society.

PP: Who is someone you deliberately ignore? Why do you do so? Can you think of a way to engage him so both of you are empowered?

November 28

Water—such a soft but powerful force

Sooner or later, all leaders find themselves trying to build confidence. This requires a positive attitude about the future and what individuals can accomplish. Confidence has a subtle but powerful effect in shaping the future of a nation. The settlement of the West, for example, was marked by a positive belief in the future. Settlers felt they were a part of an immensely exciting drama about to unfold.

JR: Soft power has far more potential of creating sustainable change than coercive force. Most often, people universally used as our role models are those who have influenced the masses through their unbounded love, spiritual strength, and belief in humankind's capacity for goodness.

PP: What kind of soft power do you (or can you) yield in your everyday affairs? How can you use it more often?

375

November 29

C'mon—take the leap

MLK (Martin Luther King) said "First, teach them to believe in themselves." The first and last task of a leader is to keep hope alive. Leaders should also seek to correct the circumstances producing negative attitudes. In the transition to a sustainable state, that means working diligently to confront the root causes of human unsustainability and finding ways to alter individual, corporate, and government behavior so that it complies with the biological principles of sustainability.

JR: Although life transitions are nerve-wracking, they are necessary components of growth. As our unsustainable ways dig a deep hole from which it gets increasingly difficult to emerge, we become forced to make a greater leap (of faith and of lifestyle) if we are to live in a world where we can not only survive, but also thrive.

PP: Find a person or group who has made a leap to a much more sustainable lifestyle (by changing energy sources, eating habits, or something else of significance). What can you learn (and implement) from that example?

November 30

OOPS! Forgot what I was looking for

Whoever has the power to project a vision of the good life and make it prevail has the most decisive power of all. American business, after 1890, acquired such power and, in league with key institutions, began the transformation of American society into a society preoccupied with consumption, with comfort and bodily well-being, with luxury, spending, and acquisition, with more goods this year than last, more next year than this.

JR: As a society, we have a severe case of amnesia. We have forgotten those aspects of life which give us deep-down contentment and joy. We have allowed others' versions of "the good life" (made to benefit them, not us) to become our own. It has become so bad that, when asked what the ideal kind of society we aspire is, most of us are rendered speechless, having no clue as to a good answer. How can we move towards something when we don't even know what it is that we wish to move towards?

PP: How about you—what do you think are three characteristics of an ideal society you hope we can move towards? What small part can you play to help move us in that direction?

DECEMBER

Empowerment & Creating

One of the primary aims of going through the soulscapes of the previous eleven months is to build a strong spiritual foundation, which is a source of inspiration to others in the present and also a guiding light to a more enlightened future. When you become confident that you can bring your deep-down desires to life, your whole being shines bright and beckons others to do the same. Having empowered yourself, it is now time to assist others in self-empowerment, the most blessed gift of all. And in doing so, you are engendering a world where the "common man" becomes his own creator.

It is then, too, that you have become a creator, but it doesn't stop there. No longer dependent on the outside world to determine your destiny, now you have developed the capacity to choose your own fortune and are able to mobilize yourself towards living it out. Through the process of going through these soulscapes again and again—for you are forever discovering new aspects of yourself and how to better fulfill your future—you finally have the power to break free of the personal and cultural stories which have kept you chained down, while building on those that harmonize with your own deepest beliefs.

The act of creation could mean:
- establishing a do-good organization that helps the poor
- building a caring, loving home for family
- bringing nature back to an environmentally devastated area
- choosing from a boundless list of other pursuits limited only by the imagination

Armed with self-knowledge, you can create your own story and blaze an exciting future for yourself and for nature/society as a whole. Though invariably there will always be obstacles, struggles and pains along the way, the process of discovery, setting a vision which truly inspires you, and moving towards creating it will bring far more enchantment and uplifting fulfillment than you ever thought possible. Time for some seriously fun trail-blazing. TREASURE THE TRIP!

379

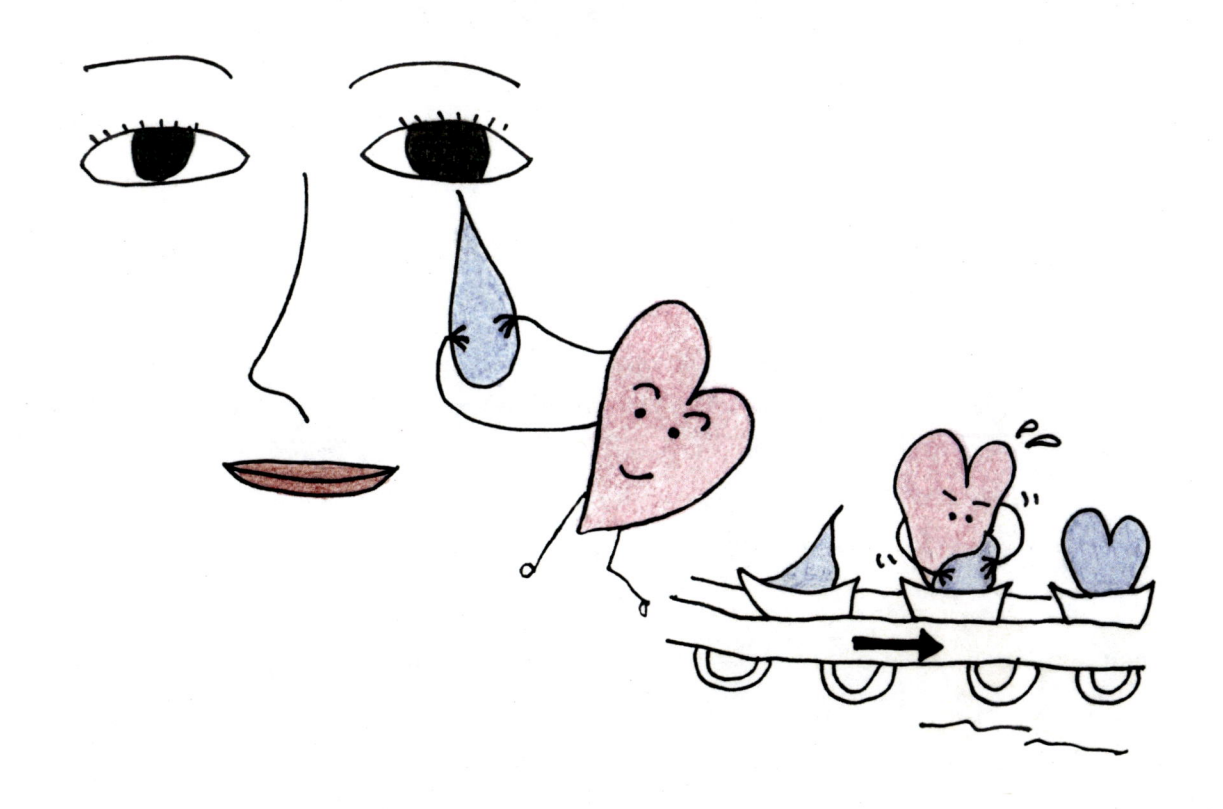

December 1

The miracle of shape-shifting

1) "Life does not happen to us, it happens from us."

2) There's a saying in the East: "Reality is an act of perception." When we become mindful of that perception, we gain control of our reality. The ability to steer our own perception—or point of view—is the art of shape-shifting, a core quality of superheroes, but also something we are all equipped to do.

JR: Becoming the creator of your own reality—sounds enticing, doesn't it? And to some extent, we all do. While you may think that you perceive an objective reality, the toxic stew of preconceptions, connotations, and beliefs which you bring to any experience colors your reality. Becoming aware of those and getting a handle on them (by eliminating the ones not to your benefit and adjusting them as you see fit) give you more mastery in what and how you perceive things.

PP: Take control of an important aspect of your life (a thought, a behavior, or an action) which you had, until now, let outside forces control you. See what happens.

December 2

Great care makes anyplace special.

1) The only deserts are deserts of the imagination. Gaviotas is an oasis of imagination.

2) Most every place can be special when we care for it and make it so.

JR: *Some people go in search of places where they can feel intense spiritual energy, without realizing that they are instrumental in creating (or detracting from) such energy pockets wherever they are. Our very existence—this mystery called life—is spiritual energy in physical form, so we cannot help but to instill energy into every place we go. Through our actions and our attitudes, we help to determine what kind of place it becomes.*

PP: How can you make the place where you spend most of your time feel more special? Do it.

December 3

Stretch your limits

1) "Is there anything worse than blindness? Yes! Eyesight ... but no vision!"

2) What would a green society look like—a vision of a positive environmental future? When the Turner Foundation put out a call to fund a novel based on such a vision, it was unable to award the grant because of the lack of a winning entry. This disturbing absence of vision underscores the dilemma that it's hard to get somewhere if you don't know where you want to go.

JR: Envisioning the kind of world we want to live in requires an investment of time and effort. There are so many conflicting desires, often at battle amongst themselves, that we give up the effort, become lethargic, and move aimlessly into the future. Furthermore, we have the audacity to criticize and blame others for where we are headed. By not envisioning where we want to go, and failing to take steps to move in that direction, we become a part of the problem.

PP: What are some of the characteristics of a truly enlightened, sustainable society? Find and support a group that is moving in that direction.

December 4

Refresh and heal yourself with nature's blessings

The aimlessness of everyday life experienced by millions in modern society has deep roots in the individual's alienation from nature, from work, and from other human beings. What's needed more than anything else is an energetic program of technological detoxification. We must admit that we are intoxicated with our science and technology and that we are deeply committed to a Faustian bargain that is rapidly killing us spiritually and may eventually kill us all physically.

JR: People who condemn our excessive use of technology, and claim that it leads to many personal and societal ills, are often labeled as "anti-technology." On the contrary, far from being so, they are usually pro-technology, understanding the benefits of technology when used in balance and in support of the life systems on which our existence depends. Rather, they see the problem of the obsession with technology, to the point of ignoring or destroying the foundation of our lives, which can only be cured by healthy doses of direct experience with nature, the cradle of life.

PP: How often do you get out into nature and take the time to soak in its life-inspiring energies? Can you give yourself this healing experience more often?

December 5

Bridging the gap

Three urgent changes are needed for survival. The first, from anthropocentrism to life-centrism, would bring traditional Christian thinking into greater harmony with that of many Asian and indigenous peoples, for whom the earth is the source of life and nature is sacred.

The second change, from the habit of dualism to the habit of interconnection, might be intuited from the Asian concept of energy, Ki (or Chi), the breath of life, thriving in the harmonious interconnections among the sky, earth, and people.

The third change would be from the patriarchal culture of death to the culture of life. Women's powerful tears have been the redemptive energy. Only when we have an ability to suffer with others can we transform the culture of death to one of life.

JR: Many of our current ways of thinking and acting move us in the direction of destructive tendencies that we blindly condone. Rather, we need to make bridges connecting us to means that not only make human life sustainable, but also season our lives with more gratitude, joy, and fun in this temporal abode.

PP: Choose one of the three changes suggested in the passage and consider a practical way in which you can move to start bridging that gap in your everyday life.

December 6

Harmonious diversity indicates true health.

Healthy societies depend on healthy, empowered local communities that build caring relationships among people and help us connect to a particular piece of the living earth with which our lives are intertwined. Such societies must be built through local-level action, household by household and community by community. Yet we have created an institutional and cultural context that disempowers the local and makes such action difficult, if not impossible.

JR: People who have inhabited a place the longest have the highest stakes in what happens to it. When outside influences come in and take control, to ravage it to their benefit and move on, the local people are the ones who suffer. Keeping the local stakeholders empowered is the best way to keep their community environment healthy.

PP: What is one of the healthiest (in terms of the integration of society and nature) parts of your city or region? What makes it that way?

December 7

*Show off your
true abundance*

Humans are complex creatures. We have a demonstrated capacity for hatred, violence, competition, and greed. We have as well a demonstrated capacity for love, tenderness, cooperation, and compassion. Healthy societies nurture the latter and in so doing create an abundance of those things that are most important to the quality of our living. Dysfunctional societies nurture the former and in so doing create scarcity and deprivation. A healthy society makes it easy to live in balance with the environment, whereas a dysfunctional society makes it nearly impossible.

JR: The word "abundance" has come to mean materialistic abundance, and "showing it off" conjures up the image of a proud man flaunting his private luxuries and instilling envy in others. However, attaining and the subsequent positive "showing off" of spiritual abundance can be likened to the farmer, who patiently fertilises the ground and spreads out the seed in the fruitful endeavor of creating ever more plenitude.

PP: How do you nurture compassion and cooperation in your own life and pass it on to others? Be proud of yourself for spreading such invaluable wealth.

December 8

The combination is what does it.

King said "Power without love is reckless and abusive, and love without power is sentimental and anemic." He went on to say, "This collision of immoral power with powerless morality constitutes the major crisis of our time."

JR: The mistaken perception that power and love are opposed to each other directly results in coercive power taking the reins and love being pushed to the back seat, or being forced to hide in the shadows. When the majority of people come to see that the combination of power and love is the only way to create a world that most people aspire towards, we will give it our full support, to reignite the embers of hope.

PP: Where can you see the effective combination of power and love? What is the result?

December 9

Choose life

The demand for circuses, and when the milder spectacles are still insufficiently life-arousing, the demand for sadistic exploits and finally for blood is characteristic of civilizations that are losing their grip: Rome under the Caesars, Mexico at the time of Montezuma, Germany under the Nazis. These forms of surrogate manliness and bravado are the surest signs of a collective impotence and a pervasive death wish. The dangerous symptoms of ultimate decay one finds everywhere today in machine civilization under the guise of mass-sport.

In the latest forms of mass-sport, like air races and motor races, the thrill of the spectacle is intensified by the promise of immediate death or fatal injury.

JR: Even the good people of this world often take delight, albeit hidden, at the misery and sufferings of certain people. We like to watch this melancholy on the news, or in dramas soaked in violence and full of love affairs. However, when we become over-exposed and seek out increasing pain and violence in our spectator sports, feeding the blood-thirsty side of ourselves, where does that leave the caring and nurturing part of our being room to grow?

PP: What kind of things (sports, dramas, etc) do you like to watch? How do they affect your perception and attitude towards humanity as a whole?

December 10

Look far and deep for what you wish to want

1) Since we might soon be able to engineer our desires too, the real question facing us is not 'What do we want to become?', but 'What do we want to want?'

We are wreaking havoc on our fellow animals and on the surrounding ecosystem, seeking little more than our own comfort and amusement, yet never finding satisfaction.

Is there anything more dangerous than dissatisfied and irresponsible gods who don't know what they want?

2) Buddhism focuses on the three unwholesome roots of evil, also known as the three poisons: greed, ill will, and delusion. In place of the struggle between good and evil, Buddhism emphasizes ignorance and enlightenment. The basic problem is one of self-knowledge: do we really understand what motivates us?

JR: "What do I want?" The answer to this question may appear fairly simple—a new car, a good job, a fulfilling relationship. But on introspecting further, and asking "Why do I want it?" some surprising answers may appear. The deeper you dig, the more you come to understand yourself, and what really motivates you.

PP: If you could consciously choose what you wish for, what would it be? This throws another light onto the issue of your desires.

December 11

Keeping the flow keeps us alive.

1) Positive actions rewire your brain no matter what you think while doing these actions.

2) "A very common thing with depression or pessimism is that people really find it difficult to motivate themselves to do anything. But invariably if they do force themselves to do something, they generally do actually enjoy it. If you do that on a regular basis, it becomes a kind of habit. It's about shifting the habits of the mind. It's really important to break up the normal way of doing things."

JR: Developing positive habits, both in mind and in action, is key to leading a spiritually fulfilling life. Inevitably, there are times when you don't feel like doing something good or reaching out to others. But at these junctures in life, it is most important to do so, because it confirms you're committed to taking action to feel good about yourself, even when you may not think that way at the moment. Carrying out positive actions consistently will effect an alteration in your thinking for the better.

PP: Which positive habits do you now practice? Remember to exercise them even (and especially) when you're feeling down and out.

December 12

Create a life-giving space

Once, long ago, rulers in India kept monks close to their courts. They knew the ascetics' daily meditations had a calming effect on the populace. The kings took care of the monks so they could care for society. Even in medieval Europe, villages felt protected against robbers in the presence of a nearby monastery.

There was a study of the impact of meditation in places where at least 1% of the population was practicing Transcendental Meditation (TM). In "TM towns" where communities of meditators had sprung up, the crime rates had fallen 8% since residents had begun meditating—and according to FBI statistics, crime rates had risen 8% in the same time frame within towns of similar makeup.

A groundbreaking experiment was held in Washington DC in the summer of 1993. At the time, the District of Columbia was seen as "the murder capital of the world." Meditation sessions were held in locations around the city, and gradually, the number of participants swelled. When the group reached between 2,500 and 4,000 meditators, crime rates began to fall. In the end, the study showed a 23% reduction in homicide, rape and assault.

This is a radically different, effective and cheap way to bring violence down. It creates self sufficiency, self governance, and leads to less government. But first, it has to find acceptance.

JR: We easily believe in the effective power of a group towards making a successful physical effort because the result is easily visible. Mental energy is simply another form of power, so why do we suspect the power of larger groups which get together to exert mental energy for the good of society, even when the evidence stares us in the face?

PP: What do you think? Can a large group of people exert a combined mental force to influence others' behaviors? If you think so, how can you somehow incorporate this idea into your life?

December 13

Growing in even the most challenging places

I saw a moving documentary of a young man by the name of Bill. He was born without legs, feet, arms, or hands, and had appendages on his shoulders that looked somewhat like small fins, but the most striking thing about him was the wonderful radiating presence he exuded.

Bill's mission was to help emotionally troubled and disabled youths to have a more positive outlook on life. This program showed Bill working with one boy in particular. The boy told a dark, angry story about just how unlucky and disabled he was. Several times Bill tried to say something positive and the boy interrupted him saying, "What you say is just bullshit!"

Finally, Bill looked at the angry boy and calmly yet fiercely said: "Do you know what's different about you and me? Anyone that looked us would say that I am much more disabled than you."

For the first time, the boy did not respond. "And do you know one more important difference? I don't feel sorry for myself and you do. No one escapes life without hardships. We can appreciate the gifts and talents we do have, or spend our life complaining about what we don't have. I've chosen happiness. What path will you choose from here on out?"

The young boy began to cry. Bill stooped over and said, "If I had arms I would pick you up and hold you right now. Please know that I do love you and care about you."

JR: Often, even those with the most severe disabilities can find opportunities for growth in their own way. And where they can't, they provide opportunities for those around them to grow in the most important aspects of life to cultivate more love, compassion, tolerance and caring.

PP: What do you consider your greatest struggle, the greatest challenge you have? Try looking at it from a different angle, perceiving how it blesses your life.

December 14

Heightened awareness brings out nature's revelation.

The 2 best things you can do for your life are aerobic exercise and meditation.

The documented physical and mental benefits of aerobic exercise are legion. What exercise doesn't do, however, is restructure cognition. But meditation can change our brains. Meditation helps keep us moving moment to moment all day with increased resilience, flexibility, detachment, awareness, engagement in the flow and the ability to deal with whatever comes up while remaining relaxed and at ease.

Meditation changes things remarkably—and quickly. Within weeks, practitioners can have an increased sense of focus, better moods and a heightened state of compassionate, loving kindness. With sustained practice, the effects of 20-30 minutes of meditation in the morning should last all day.

Paying attention to our sensory and emotional experiences may not always be pleasurable, and is sometimes uncomfortable, boring or even frightening. But is it worth it? Studies suggest so. King cites one study of mindfulness meditation on depression in which the rate of relapse over the subsequent 18 months was cut by 50%, an effect that rivals medication.

JR: Our search for healing most often begins with the search for doctors and other health practitioners. Few people realize the tremendous healing capabilities that lie within. Taking responsibility for our mental and physical health, through doing practices like appropriate exercise and regular meditation, is the best thing you can do to live in a "heightened state" more consistently.

PP: Do you practice regular (preferably daily) exercise and meditation? Try to do so for one month and see the beneficial effect.

December 15

Blessed are those who shape their own paths.

Only one serious difference does exist from city to suburb, and at times (within one city) from one district to the next: The children of those who are already literate, enfranchised, and empowered learn the exercise of power. The children of those who are not literate, who have been disenfranchised and remain excluded from the exercise of power, learn to accommodate themselves to impotence and to capitulation. Those who are privileged achieve the competence with which to shape the future. Those who are not acquire an attitude of civilized accommodation which will allow them to fit into slots that are provided for them in that future—or else to remain excluded from the future altogether.

JR: Imagine if you couldn't read. You could enjoy the pictures and drawings of this book but that's about it. Your whole life would be limited and you would be faced with far fewer job possibilities, driving restrictions, failure to understand the instructions to your new gadgets, and so on. How could you help but to feel separated from society and disempowered. If empowerment is the way towards providing hope, literacy is a necessary part of the process.

PP: Could you offer your time to teach an illiterate person or group of people? If you can't, or don't know any such individual personally, how about supporting organizations that are empowering people through teaching literacy?

December 16

Empowerment through the art of creation

1) The greatest gift you can give anyone is a gift of empowerment and love. What could be more loving than helping people you care about get free from their limiting beliefs and ignorance about success, and empowering them to create the life that they truly want from the depths of their soul?

2) "You will get all you want in life, if you help enough other people get what they want."

JR: All of us are brought up with certain beliefs which prevent us from achieving our full potential. It is important to discover these limiting beliefs within yourself, see them for what they are, and discard the ones which disempower you so that you can then build and enable your hidden gifts. Only in so doing can you help others to do the same.

PP: Think of how liberating it was when you saw the falsity of a limiting belief you once held and became more fulfilled as a result. Want to feel that way again? Find another belief that is holding you back now and do the same.

December 17

Going beyond and further into the unknown

Creativity is anything that takes you out of the zone of the known and into the zone of wonder. In order to bring vitality to relationships, people need to spend a little time, preferably every day, in a state of wonder and invention. Whatever it takes to do that is your best form of creativity.

By this definition, practically anything can be creative.

Wonder and invention are sure cures for boredom and dissatisfaction. Staying within the zone of the known drains energy and saps satisfaction.

One of the greatest sources of pain in the world is unfulfilled creative potential.

JR: How uncomfortable it can be to go outside of your knowledge zone! It feels so cozy and secure there…..and deadening as well if you never leave. The seed of creativity lies within each of us. However, it will stay dormant without the nourishment of inspiration which is brought about by a sense of awe and wonder within the beholder, in turn leading to her efforts to invent something based on this pure delight. When she comes to be able to be her own source of enchantment through her creation, without concern of how good or how right it is, she is a creator indeed (of both feeling and object).

PP: What engenders a sense of delightful wonder in you? What does this tell you about your domain of creative potential?

December 18

A living example of constant transformation

Creativity requires constant transformation, experimentation, flexibility. Cynicism, a chronic state of distrust, is antithetical to the openness necessary for a creative society. To the cynic, experiments are futile. All conclusions are foregone. Cynics know the answers without having penetrated deeply enough to know the questions.

JR: Concealed within the meaning of the word "creativity" is the desire and effort to try new things and be open to different ways, as well as holding the belief that change is possible. The unwillingness to experiment and the belief that we can't change are the assassins of the creative, thus resulting in a hollowed out shell with decay fermenting therein.

PP: Experiment with something new in your life, something that takes you out of your zone of knowing and instills a sense of fun and excitement.

December 19

*Beautiful or ugly—
depends on how you
look at it*

Blame consumes the very energy that could be used for creativity. The moment they commit to ending blame, they feel the possibility of a fresh new wave of creativity in themselves.

Blame and creativity are closely tied to each other. In a relationship, both partners will engage in blame to the extent that they are not fulfilling their own creative urges.

JR: *How do you perceive your life—mainly as a victim or as a creator? This perception will greatly influence what you become and how you use (or don't use) your potential. Blaming others justifies your doing little or nothing since your bad situation is then most often seen as being somebody else's fault. Accepting that there is nobody to blame places the sole responsibility on your shoulders, empowering you to develop and use your talents to create new possibilities that open the doors of abundance.*

PP: *When have you blamed another for your problem(s)? How could you have become the creator of a better solution by refusing to blame and owning responsibility for it?*

December 20

It's difficult to explore your creativity when you're fenced in.

1) "Life isn't about finding yourself; it's about creating yourself."
2) "I am not what has happened to me. I am what I choose to become."

JR: People are partially entrapped by their beliefs, their obsessions about the past, their fears and their grudges. Fortunately, the majority of us are not completely fenced in, but retain some degree of freedom to create ourselves. There are certain things which are helpful to find out about yourself, especially those things that prevent personal constructive progress, in order to realize what you wish to be and how to move towards that.

PP: What kind of person do you want to become? What is preventing you from moving towards that?

December 21

The never-ending miracle of photosynthesis

Photosynthesis is one such moment of grace. About 3.9 billion years ago, the planet faced a crisis when the early Earth's generation of chemically rich compounds was slowing just at a time when the population of prokaryotic cells (bacteria and blue-green algae, for example) feeding off the compounds was expanding exponentially. Instead of a major die-off from starvation, some prokaryotes learned to capture photons hurtling at the speed of light from the sun and convert them to food. The result, photosynthesis, was a creative act of elegance born out of crisis.

JR: *An inspiring creative act has the power to transform the world, and has often done so, in nature (like in the development of photosynthesis) and with humanity (in our multitude of inventions, with the historically recent development of the computer completely transforming society). The creative acts of nature occurring through evolution are nothing short of miracles in action. We, too, as creators, can perform mini-miracles when our faith combines with a radically new, constructive, creative act to explode into physical form.*

PP: *Ponder upon the miracle of photosynthesis, and imagine what the world would be like in the absence of this "invention."*

December 22

Some things can't come back, but you can.

1) "Don't ask what the world needs. Ask what makes you come alive and go out and do it. Because what the world needs is people who have come alive."

2) "The creation of a thousand forests is in one acorn."

JR: IT'S NEVER TOO LATE! At whichever juncture you are in your life, you can seek and find what truly makes you come alive and implement ways of doing it. So many good-intentioned people go out and help others, but feel little upliftment in doing so, largely because they are trying to help others while ignoring what it is that makes they themselves feel alive. When you find that, and devote time and energy to do it, you become a source of inspiration to others while basking in your own light.

PP: When is a time in your life that you felt most alive? What was it that made you feel that way? Can you find ways to do that more often in your life now?

December 23

Look at the creation outside and add to it in your own way

Buddha was once threatened with death by a bandit.

"Then be good enough to fulfill my dying wish," said Buddha. "Cut off the branch of that tree."

One slash of the sword, and it was done!

"What now?" asked the bandit.

"Put it back again," said Buddha.

The bandit laughed. "You must be crazy to think that anyone can do that."

"On the contrary, it is you who are crazy to think that you are mighty because you can wound and destroy. That is the task of children. The mighty know how to create and heal."

JR: The world can be a scary place, especially when we believe that the strong are those who have (and often use) power to wreak havoc. With this thinking, those needing to feed their egos through the acquisition of power spend inordinate amounts of energy becoming forces of destruction. When we come to realize, and have faith, that true strength lies in creating and healing, the ego-full and ego-less alike will move towards the betterment of the world.

PP: Contemplate the message of this eye-opening story—how destruction requires little effort or thought while creation necessitates both.

December 24

We were once just the figment of someone's imagination.

1) Believe You Are A Creator

We hold the power to create whatever we desire. Our ability to manifest the changes we desire depends on the depth and passion of our beliefs and on the focus of our attention.

With this understanding, we, as individuals and as a society, can design a whole new future for ourselves. Our challenge is to break free of society's world view, to truly empower our imaginations to create brand new realities. It brings a whole new meaning to 'vision.'

What do you passionately desire for your own life? For the planet?

2) "By believing passionately in something that still does not exist, we create it. The non-existent is whatever we have not sufficiently desired."

JR: Humanity has moved through unimaginable futures throughout its history—from hunter-gatherer tribes to agricultural communities to current industrial societies. And spirituality and religion have exerted their influences from the relatively peaceful Axial Age through the violent Dark Ages to the multi-faith conundrum of today. These changes could not be accurately predicted, similar to the situation today where we know not what new inventions lie ahead and how they will effect human society. However, the creations and faith systems we choose to live by will serve as our future's compass.

PP: What historical heyday do you find most nostalgic? What creations and beliefs made that period possible?

December 25

All life, and truth, progresses through stages.

All truth passes through 3 stages: First, it is ridiculed. Second, it is violently opposed. Third, it is accepted as being self-evident.

JR: What makes becoming a creator most difficult is the ridicule and possible (violent) resistance which follows in the creation's wake, especially when it comes to new ideas and concepts. Simply knowing that this is a part of the process, as well as having a strong belief in your creation and the support of other believers, will support you in getting through the initial fallout.

PP: What belief system do you adhere to? Reflect back (or research, if you don't know) on its origins, and the opposition it confronted.

December 26

Create and foster beauty within—then it will accompany you wherever you go

You can never end the loneliness in your life until you end the loneliness within your life. If you feel alone within, if you feel incomplete inside yourself, you will search outside yourself for the rest of your life to find that which cannot be found. And, after experiencing this over and over, you could wind up with a series of relationships that do not last.

The relationships don't last because you do not understand what you are doing there. You are trying to find fulfillment rather than create fulfillment. You are trying to find joy rather than create joy. You are trying to find completion rather than create completion. You believe that relationship is a process of discovery, and it is not. It is a process of creation. The same thing can be said about "Life."

"But I have tried to "create" joy, happiness, and completion in relationship, and sometimes the other person has still left. So what is true about that?"

"Did that take the joy, happiness, and completion out of your life?"

"Of course"

"Then you didn't have it there to begin with. Nobody can take with them what is in you."

JR: Everyday, we are bombarded daily with messages, straightforward as well as subliminally, from the media, advertising, love songs, and so on, which tell us to find our happiness somewhere "out there." And that's why many of us become miserable—because that is impossible. The only real, long-lasting, and steady sense of joy comes from within. When you create it from within, the ever-changing external conditions exert less and less effect on your internal condition.

PP: What "makes you happy?" Could you be happy without it? If not, why are you giving it the power to determine your happiness?

December 27

Living in moderation in the midst of nature

The great British historian, Arnold Toynbee, studied the rise and fall of 22 different civilizations and summarized everything he knew about the growth of human civilizations in one law called the "law of progressive simplification." This law states that the measure of a civilization's growth is its ability to shift energy and attention from the material side to the spiritual and aesthetic and cultural and artistic side.

Essentially, they (states that have made this shift) learned how to meet the most needs with the least amount of resources and effort—developing an ethic that supported and ritualized this approach. They implemented policies that valued cultural traditions; they took care of nature with terraces that minimized erosion from hillside farms; and they minimized conflict with other cultures. Cultures based on moderation and meeting needs precisely are Costa Rica, Denmark, Kerala (in India), Cuba, and Switzerland—enclaves of cultural pride, relative peacefulness, and social satisfaction.

JR: Living beings in nature are forced to live moderately, or they die out. When a species either takes too little or starves (due to adverse environmental conditions) or when it takes too much (more than the land can sustainably provide), its numbers dwindle. This phenomenon is analogous with the human species as well. However, we have the twin benefits of being able to willingly work to enhance nature and to add value to our lives through various forms of non-material (spirituality, art, etc.) growth.

PP: How can you shift your own growth patterns increasingly away from the material to the non-material?

December 28

Gaining clarity requires distance from obstructions.

In order to become a master of creativity, understand and activate the following principles:

1.) Determine what to get rid of. What in your life detracts from its quality and is unnecessary?

2.) Practice clarity of vision. What do you want to create? Ask yourself what you really want, why you really want it, and if manifesting it will serve a higher purpose for humanity.

JR: It becomes increasingly difficult to maintain a clear vision and focus on moving towards clarity in a life cluttered with innumerable things (an overload of possessions and entertainment, for example) which divert your attention and limit you from developing such an insight. One of the best things you can do to gain clarity and stay focused is to get rid of as much counter-productive clutter as you possibly can from your life.

PP: Make a list of the things which prevent you from setting and centering on a future of your dreams. Try to discard (or, at least, decrease) as many of these as you can.

December 29

What a dream-like experience!

1) "Be the change you want to see in the world."

2) We might describe the challenge before us by the following sentence. The historical mission of our times is to reinvent the human—at the species level, with critical reflection, within the community of life-systems, in a time-developmental context, by means of story and shared dream experience.

I say reinvent the human because humans, more than any other living form, invent themselves.

JR: The fact that we can change, and have changed throughout history, completely discredits the idea that we are fated to be as we are, and that there is no hope to escape from our self-induced disarray. We have the capacity to envision a different future, and to mold ourselves as we have many times before, to adapt to the world of our dreams. The ride thereto will be as smooth or as rough as the degree of willingness of society, as a whole, to transition. And it is in the making of an appealing story—one that shows the need, the possibility, and the ultimate joy (personally and socially) of making such a change, as well as outlines the way of carrying it out—that the majority of people can be effectively enticed to make the effort to do so.

PP: What change would you like to see in the world? How can you modify yourself (or your life) in order to be a change agent, however small, of transformation thereto?

December 30

Co-creators in the making of paradise

To create a world of delight—WHAT A JOY!

In today's world, being in a hurry shows one's sense of importance but, in a deeper sense, it can also be a form of mental laziness. When we are too busy, we don't have time to nurture our relationships. We passively accept that causing animals to suffer in order to provide our meat, or people to suffer in order to provide us with cheap goods, is inevitable in the modern world. And yet, all of this is UP TO US!

Our laziness permits these evils to persist. How much easier it is to cut down a tree (destroy) than to plant a tree and nurture it (create). But how much more beautiful a forest full of different kinds of trees and animals is than a lifeless landscape. Creating takes time and effort, and the fruits therefrom can create a world where all good people benefit. To do so, we must redefine our idea of progress—from one of simply "advancing economically" (even to the point of encouraging destructive practices) to one of creating a "culture of good," one that harmoniously pleases mind, spirit, and body and respects all life. When we take steps in this direction, we become co-conspirators in moving towards heaven on earth.

JR: Nature provides us with a plethora of sensory experiences—some bordering on the heavenly and others that could aptly be defined as onslaughts of torment. Both extremes, and everything in between, are acts of nature, containing no will of doing good or evil. Humanity is a part of nature and is also blessed with the capacity to insert its will into its creation. Collectively, our laziness results in more evil than that carried out by the worst of men, and in becoming aware of this and deciding to consciously live and create for the good of the earth (including us), we have the power to instigate a more delightful and enchanting world.

PP: What is one way your laziness and ignorance may be contributing towards an "evil" you see in the world? How can you become more aware and stop being an unwilling accomplice?

December 31

The end of another year—What will next year bring, and what will I bring to it?

1) "Whatever you can do, or dream you can, begin it. Boldness has genius, power, and magic in it."

2) "The best way to predict the future is to CREATE it!"

JR: Rather than asking what tomorrow will bring, you can ask "What will I bring to tomorrow?" Instead of asking what will happen in the future, you could ask "What will I make happen in the future?" Some things are bound to happen despite our greatest efforts to alter them. But the nature of our species gives us good reason for hope, with the most significant one being that we can envision a future of our dreams, and move towards it by modifying ourselves so that we find our own appropriate fit into this more sustainable, enchanting, and fun-filled world of our choosing. The puzzle is now being put together, piece by piece, and each of us can play a part in designing a beautifully integrated work of art.

PP: Create a future of your dreams on paper. Think of ways you can translate your dreams into reality.

Where Do We Go From Here?

WHAT A TRIP THAT WAS! But now what—where is the landing pad? What good was all of that soul-searching and discovery if there's nowhere to go with it and take it forward? It's kind of like preparing a feast and finding out that everyone who comes is fasting—the ultimate cruelty.

And herein lies the bad news—there is no physical place to land. Just like the soulscapes, the landing pad first exists in you. On the other hand, this may be considered great news, for it is now up to you to design a physical reality based on the soulscapes through which you've journeyed. Even though there may not yet be a physical plane where people who have taken this trip can work together to put their learning into practice, that is our next step. The task that lies ahead of us is to build a landing pad where people who want to integrate these ideas and move towards actively living them out in their everyday lives can feel at home—a place where we become each other's teachers and discover, with other like-minded individuals, new thoughts and tools for mastering and implementing these ideas more fully. If you can find people around you to further the discussion, discovering ways to integrate these soulscapes and implement them at the local level, you become, in essence, a (physically real) foundation builder.

Then, hopefully in the near future, we can find ways of bringing together these leaders—these foundation builders—periodically as a way of encouraging and empowering each other. And beyond that, we can come to establish a living/learning center where people who are dedicated to this work can build a solid, physical community based on these principles and teach others how to do the same. This community can serve as a beacon that provides the light of hope, fun and creativity for all life forms on this beautiful planet.

To begin with, the Jambo Blogs (https://www.jambo.ngo/david-howenstein-blog and https://jambointernational.org/en/blog/) will have periodic commentaries related to this book's messages. Feel free to sign on as a subscriber. You may also contact david@jambointernational.org with your comments.

With people committed to this process, it will surely come into reality. It's up to us!

About The Pictures

Contrary to popular opinion, the area in and around Tokyo has an abundance of natural features, which include the diverse terrains of rocky coasts, beautiful beaches, low hills, and high mountains. For the reader's convenience, the pictures for each month proceed in the following order (Tokyo pictures are followed by pictures from Chiba, and then Chichibu, etc.), and the date numbers are followed by the letter code (corresponding to the respective area) in the Picture Bibliography (the following section). For example, the picture from Tokyo on January 1 is labeled under January as 1A:

Tokyo City (A) – Tokyo is known for its many Japanese gardens and some of the most beautifully landscaped canals in the world.

Chiba (B) – Lying east/southeast of Tokyo, Chiba Prefecture has beautiful beaches on the Pacific Coast (with good waves for surfing) and on the inner Bousou Peninsula, lying on the gentler waters of Tokyo Bay.

Chichibu (C) – The low mountains of Chichibu are northwest of Tokyo, and have an extensive network of hiking trails.

Okutama/Tama (D) – Officially still part of the Tokyo Metropolitan Area, Okutama is west-northwest of the city and is defined by the scenic Tama River valley. It has both low and high mountains for the avid outdoorsman.

Chuo Line (E) – The Chuo Line runs west of Tokyo and is dotted with scenic rivers and lakes, as well as hiking possibilities at every station between Takao (in west Tokyo) and Otsuki (another hour beyond Takao by train).

Tanzawa/Hakone (F) – The mountains of Tanzawa and the renowned mountain scenery and hot springs of Hakone lie to the southwest of Tokyo, providing opportunities for both the rugged trekker as well as for the more relaxed traveler who wishes to sightsee from outdoor hot springs or cable cars and ropeways.

Pacific Coast/Miura Peninsula (G) – The Miura Peninsula lies to the south of Tokyo. With its diversified forests and scenic coastline, Miura is a place where one can enjoy both the mountains and the ocean in one shot. The historic city of Kamakura and coastal haven of Zushi, both favorites among tourists, are north of the peninsula and mark the beginning of the westward extension of the Pacific Coast, dotted with beaches and more tamed hiking courses.

Other (H) – The other areas where these pictures were taken generally are over two hours from Tokyo and, while it may be possible to cover them in a day trip, overnights are recommended.

In the (following) Picture Bibliography, the following information is provided for each photo:

1) Place (where the picture was taken from)

In Parentheses after "Place"

    1.) Nearest train station (or bus stop, which is clearly indicated)

    2.) Train line name (in parentheses)

    3.) Time to walk there (from the nearest stop or station)

    4.) Year when the picture was taken

For example, looking at January 1st:

Wakasu Peninsula (in Koutou Ward) overlooking part of Toukyou Bay to the East (Shin-Kiba (Yuurakuchou), 1 hour, 2013)

Place – Wakasu Peninsula (in Koutou Ward) overlooking part of Toukyou Bay to the East

Nearest train station – Shin-kiba

Train line name – Yuurakuchou

Time to walk there (from Shin-kiba station) – 1 hour

Year when the picture was taken – 2013

What is with the bizarre spelling?

The Japanese language has many long vowel sounds, and when written in roman characters (to be transcribed into Kanji characters), they are written with two vowels. For example,

    Oonara

    Oume (usually long "o" sounds are written as "ou")

    Odakyuu

    Keiou (usually long "e" sounds are written as "ei")

    Toukyou (In Japanese, both "o" sounds for Tokyo are long – therefore, this spelling)

Why bother with such funky spelling?

For two reasons:

1) For those wishing to find places or train schedules using a Japanese system, the words must be typed in with roman characters using the short vowel or long vowel (as written in the description), which are then transcribed to Japanese characters. For those looking for information on sites only in English, it may be necessary to drop long vowels (for example, instead of "Toukyou," type in "Tokyo").

2) There are many cases of two separate Japanese words that are only different because one has a short vowel and the other a long one.

Where do the pictures come from?

All of the pictures have been shot by the author (except October 31, courtesy of Eichi Sakakibara). Nearly all of the pictures come from JAMBO International (Japan) hikes from 2001 to 2015, and each picture is reflective of the scenery for the respective month.

For more information about JAMBO, please look at *"About Jambo."*

Picture Bibliography

JANUARY

1A) Wakasu Peninsula (in Koutou Ward) overlooking part of Toukyou Bay to the East (Shin-Kiba (Yuurakuchou), 1 hour, 2013)

2A) Wakasu Peninsula (in Koutou Ward) overlooking part of Toukyou Bay to the East (Shin-Kiba (Yuurakuchou), 1 hour, 2013)

3B) Nokogiriyama Hiking Course (Hamakanaya (Uchibou), 1 hour, 2009)

4B) Nokogiriyama (Hamakanaya (Uchibou), 2 hours, 2009)

5C) FudouTaki Waterfall (Nishi Agano (Seibu Chichibu), 2 hours, 2010)

6C) Road to Myuuzu Park (Kagmori (Chichibu Tetsudou), 30 minutes, 2010)

7C) Katsuragi Kannon (Ogose (Toubu Ogose), 2 hours, 2011)

8D) Oonara Hiking Course (Kori (Oume), 1 hour, 2009)

9D) Oonara Pass Hiking Course (Kori (Oume), 2 hours, 2009)

10D) Mt. Sekirou Hiking Course (Sagamiko (Chuuou, 1.5 hours, 2011)

11D) Takamizu Hiking Course (Ikusabata (Oume), 2 hours, 2008)

12D) Mitsukama Waterfalls (Kori (Oume), 3 hours, 2011)

13D) Mt. Shiroyama (Takaosanguchi (Keio), 2.5 hours, 2012)

14D) Tama River (Fuchuu (Keio), 1.5 hours, 2014)

15E) Sagami Lake (Sagamiko (Chuuou), 15 minutes, 2011)

16E) Shiroyama Hiking Course (Sagamiko (Chuuou), 1.5 hours, 2011)

17E) Takarayama Hiking Course (Fujino (Chuo), 45 minutes, 2012)

18E) Mt. Takagawa (Hatsukari (Chuuou), 2 hours, 2013)

19F) Mt. Kintoki Hiking Course (Ashigara (Gotemba), 1 hour, 2003)

20F) Shibusawa Hills Course (Shibusawa (Odakyuu), 1.5 hours, 2006)

21F) Shibusawa Hills Course (Shibusawa (Odakyuu), 2 hours, 2010)

22F) Gokoku Pass Agricultural Path (Shimo Soga (Gotemba), 2 hours, 2013)

23F) Gokoku Pass Agricultural Path (Shimo Soga (Gotemba), 2 hours, 2013)

24F) Shibusawa Hills Course (Shibusawa (Odakyuu), 1.5 hours, 2015)

25F) Shibusawa Hills Course (Shibusawa (Odakyuu), 2 hours, 2015)

26F) Shibusawa Hills Course (Shibusawa (Odakyuu), 2.5 hours, 2015)

27F) Kuri no Ki Dou Hiking Course (Ookura bus stop (30 minutes by bus from Shibusawa (Odakyuu), 2.5 hours, 2014)

28G) Enoshima Bridge (KataseEnoshima (Odakyuu), 10 minutes, 2008)

29G) Enoshima Bridge (KataseEnoshima (Odakyuu), 10 minutes, 2008)

30H) Urami no taki Waterfall (Uraminotaki Iriguchi bus stop (15 minutes by bus from Nikko (JR Nikko), 45 minutes, 2013)

31H) Urami no taki Waterfall (Uraminotaki Iriguchi bus stop (15 minutes by bus from Nikko (JR Nikko), 45 minutes, 2013)

FEBRUARY

1A) Yushima Shrine (Yushima (Chiyoda), 5 minutes, 2014)

2A) Harima Slope (Myougadani (Marunouchi), 10 minutes, 2014)

3B) 21st Century Forest (Yabashira (Musashino), 20 minutes, 2014)

4B) 21st Century Forest (Yabashira (Musashino), 20 minutes, 2014)

5C) Shiroyasawa River Trail (From Sawarabi no Yu bus stop (45 minutes by bus from Hanno Station (Seibu-Ikebukuro), 2 hours, 2008)

6C) Mt. Ootakatori Hiking Course (Ogose (ToubuOgose), 1 hour, 2013)

7C) Tennou Marsh (Toubu Takezawa (Toubu Toujou), 2.5 hours, 2009)

8C) Mt Futago Hiking Course (Ashigakubo (Seibu Chichibu), 30 minutes, 2014)

9C) Mt Futago Hiking Course (Ashigakubo (Seibu Chichibu), 30 minutes, 2014)

10C) Mt Futago (Ashigakubo (Seibu Chichibu), 2.5 hours, 2014)

11D) Higashitakane Park (Mukougaoka Yuuen (Odakyuu Line), 45 minutes, 2008)

12D) Yoshino Baigou (Plum Park) (Hinatawada (Oume Line), 30 minutes, 2008)

13D) Todoroki Gorge (Todoroki (Toukyuu Oimachi), 20 minutes, 2009)

14D) Japan Old House Park (Nihon Minkaen) (Mukougaoka Yuuen (Odakyuu), 30 minutes, 2011)

15D) Japan Old House Park (Nihon Minkaen) (Mukougaoka Yuuen (Odakyuu), 30 minutes, 2011)

16D) Ikuta Green Area (Mukougaoka Yuuen (Odakyuu), 1 hour, 2011)

17E) Mt. Takara Hiking Course (Fujino (Chuuou), 40 minutes, 2014)

18E) Mt. Takara Hiking Course (Fujino (Chuuou), 1 hour, 2014)

19E) Mt. Takakura Hiking Course (Fujino (Chuuou), 1 hour, 2014)

20F) Mt. Oono Hiking Course (Yamakita (Gotemba), 2.5 hours, 2012)

21F) Shasui Waterfall (Yamakita (Gotemba), 30 minutes, 2012)

22F) Mt Ooyama (Yabitsu Touge Bus Stop (35 minutes by bus from Hadano Station (Odakyuu), 1.5 hours, 2012)

23G) Mt. Futago Hiking course (ShinZushi (Keikyuu ShinZushi), 40 minutes, 2015)

24G) Mt. Futago Hiking course (ShinZushi (Keikyuu ShinZushi), 1.5 hours, 2015)

25G) Taura Bairin (Plum Park) (Taura (Yokosuka), 1 hour, 2015)

26H) Mt. Nakimushi Hiking Course (Nikko (JR Nikko), 1 hour, 2010)

27H) Mt. Nakimushi Hiking Course (Nikko (JR Nikko), 1.5 hours, 2010)

28H) Mt. Nakimushi Hiking Course (Nikko (JR Nikko), 2 hours, 2010)

29H) Toushouguu Pagoda (Shinkyou bus stop (10 minutes by bus from Nikko (JR Nikko), 15 minutes, 2010)

MARCH

1A) ShinjukuGyoen (Shinjuku Gyoen (Marunouchi), 10 minutes, 2010)

2A) ShinjukuGyoen (Shinjuku Gyoen (Marunouchi), 10 minutes, 2010)

3A) ShinjukuGyoen (Shinjuku Gyoen (Marunouchi), 10 minutes, 2010)

4A) Koishikawa Shokubutsuen (Botanical Garden) (Myougadani (Marunouchi), 30 minutes, 2014)

5A) Koishikawa Shokubutsuen (Botanical Garden) (Myougadani (Marunouchi), 30 minutes, 2014)

6A) Rikugien Japanese Garden (Komagome (Nanboku), 30 minutes, 2014)

7B) Mt. Nokogiri Hiking Course (Hamakanaya (Uchibou), 40 minutes, 2012)

8B) Mt. Nokogiri Hiking Course (Hamakanaya (Uchibou), 2 hours, 2012)

9C) Mt. Kinshou Course (Toubu Takezawa (Toubu Toujou), 30 minutes, 2013)

10) Mt. Honida Hiking Course (Okutama (Oume), 20 minutes, 2010)

11D) Kyoudo no Mori Park (FuchuuHonmachi (Musashino), 45 minutes, 2012)

12D) Sasaragi Green Area (Karakida (Odakyuu), 1.5 hours, 2012)

13D) Mogusaen (Mogusaen (Keiou), 40 minutes, 20015)

14D) Mogusaen (Mogusaen (Keiou), 40 minutes, 20015)

15D) Ikuta Green Area (Mukougaoka Yuuen (Odakyuu), 1 hour, 2014)

16D) Shukugawara (Noborito (Odakyuu), 40 minutes, 2014)

17F) Begoniaen (Hakone Yumoto (Hakone Tetsudou), 40 minutes, 2009)

18F) Mt. Sengen Hiking Course (Miyanoshita (Hakone Tozan), 1 hour, 2009)

19F) Mt. Koubou Hiking Course (Hadano (Odakyuu), 1.5 hours, 2015)

20F) Soga Plum Park (Shimo Soga (Gotemba), 1.5 hours, 2009)

21F) Odawara Flower Park (Iidaoka (IzuHakoneTetsudouDaiyuuzan), 20 minutes, 2015)

22F) Sengen One Hiking Course (Sengen One Tozan Guchi Bus Stop (50 minutes by bus from MusashiItsukaichi (MusashiItsukaichi), 2 hours, 2014)

23F) Hossawa Waterfall (Hossawa no Taki Bus Stop (20 minutes by bus from MusashiItsukaichi (MusashiItsukaichi), 20 minutes, 2014)

24F) West Hills Hiking Course (Odawara (Odakyuu), 2 hours, 2015)

25G) Atami Plum Park (Atami (Toukaidou), 1 hour, 2008)

26G) Atami City (Atami (Toukaidou), 20 minutes, 2008)

27G) Tsuruoka Shrine (Kamakura (Yokosuka), 25 minutes, 2010)

28G) Mt. Oogusu (Anjintsuka (Keihin Kyuukou), 2.5 hours, 2011)

29G) Mt. Oogusu (Anjintsuka (Keihin Kyuukou), 2 hours, 2011)

30H) Kinugawa River (KawajiOnsen (Noiwa Tetsudou AizuKinugawa)1 hour, 2008)

31H) Kinugawa River (KawajiOnsen (Noiwa Tetsudou AizuKinugawa)1 hour, 2008)

APRIL

1A) Ooyokogawa Canal (Monzennakachou (Tozai), 15 minutes, 2015)

2A) Sendaiborigawa Park (Toyocho (Tozai), 30 minutes, 2015)

3A) Kiba Park (Kiba (Tozai), 10 minutes, 2013)

4A) Sendaiborigawa Park (Kiba (Tozai), 40 minutes, 2013)

5A) Shinjuku Gyoen (Shinjuku Gyoen (Marunouchi), 25 minutes, 2004)

6A) Shinjuku Gyoen (Shinjuku Gyoen (Marunouchi), 15 minutes, 2006)

7C) Taishou Pond Hiking Course (Yorii (Toubu Toujou), 1 hour, 2012)

8C) Taishou Pond Hiking Course (Yorii (Toubu Toujou), 2 hours, 2012)

9C) Seiunji Temple (BushuuNakagawa (Chichibu Tetsudou), 30 minutes, 2014)

10C) Hitsujiyama Park Hiking Course (Kagemori (Chichibu Tetsudou), 1 hour, 2014)

11C) Gokoku Goddess of Mercy (BushuuNakagawa (Chichibu Tetsudou), 1.5 hours, 2014)

12C) Mt. Azalea Hiking Course (NishiAgano (Seibu Chichibu), 3 hours, 2014)

13C) Minoyama Park Hiking Course (Wadoukuroya (Chichibu Tetsudou), 1 hour, 2015)

14C) Minoyama Park (Wadoukuroya (Chichibu Tetsudou), 2 hours, 2015)

15C) Totoro no Mori Course (SeibuKyuujoMae (Seibu Ikebukuro), 30 minutes, 2015)

16C) Taishou Pond (Yorii (Toubu Toujou), 45 minutes, 2012)

17C) Sayama Fudouson Pagoda (SeibuKyuujoMae (Seibu Ikebukuro), 30 minutes, 2015)

18D) Tama River (Fussa (Oume), 1 hour, 2014)

19D) Komine Park Hiking Course (MusashiItsukaichi (MusashiItsukaichi), 3 hours, 2013)

20D) Koutokuji Temple (MusashiItsukaichi (MusashiItsukaichi), 1.5 hours, 2013)

21D) Okutama Mountains (Kawai (Oume), 15 minutes, 2007)

22F) Cherry Tree Tunnel at station (Yaga (Gotemba), 5 minutes, 2010)

23G) Toukeiji Temple (KitaKamakura (Yokosuka), 30 minutes, 2014)

24G) Itachi River (Hongoudai (Keihin Tohoku), 1 hour, 2008)

25G) Toukouji Temple (KeikyuuNagasawa (Keihin Kyuukou), 30 minutes, 2009)

26G) Kamakura (Kamakura (Yokosuka), 2 hours, 2014)

27G) Kamakura (Kamakura (Yokosuka), 1 hour, 2014)

28G) Kamakura (Kamakura (Yokosuka), 1 hour, 2014)

29G) Meigetsuin (KitaKamakura (Yokosuka), 30 minutes, 2014)

30G) Meigetsuin (KitaKamakura (Yokosuka), 30 minutes, 2014)

MAY

1A) Kameido Shrine (Kameido (Soubu), 20 minutes, 2010)

2A) Family Sports Plaza (Kasai (Tozai), 30 minutes, 2011)

3A) Sakaigawa Shinsui Park (Funabori (Toei Shinjuku), 30 minutes, 2014)

4B) Sakura Furusato Hiroba (Keisei Usui (Keisei Honsen), 1 hour, 2008)

5B) Sakura Furusato Hiroba (Keisei Usui (Keisei Honsen), 1 hour, 2008)

6C) Yugate (HigashiAgano (Seibu Chichibu), 1.5 hours, 2006)

7C) Godaison(Ogose (ToubuOgose), 45 minutes, 2013)

8C) Hitsujiyama Park (Seibu Chichibu (Seibu Chichibu), 30 minutes, 2011)

9C) MeriBazaka Pass Hiking Course (NishiAgano (Seibu Ikebukuro), 2 hours, 2014)

10D) Shiofune Goddess of Mercy (Oume (Oume), 1 hour, 2010)

11D) Nishizawa Azalea Garden (ChitoseKarasuyama (Keiou), 30 minutes, 2011)

12D) Nagaramimae Mizuta (Hamura (Oume), 20 minutes, 2012)

13D) Ikuta Ryokuchi Baraen (Rose Park) (MukougaokaYuuen (Odakyuu), 1 hour, 2012)

14D) Baji Park (Youga (Tokyuu Denen Toshi), 40 minutes, 2013)

15D) Nogawa River (Mitaka (Chuuou), 30 minutes (by bicycle), 2015)

16D) Tama Zoo Woods (TamaDoubutsuKouen (KeiouDoubutsukouen), 20 minutes, 2014)

17D) South Takao Ridge Hiking Course (Takao (Keiou), 3 hours, 2014)

18D) Along the Nogawa River (Kitami (Odakyuu), 1 hour, 2015)

19G) Temple in Kamakura (Kamakura (Yokosuka), 1 hour, 2013)

20G) Arasaki (Arasaki bus stop (20 minutes from Misakiguchi (Keihin Kyuukou)), 20 minutes, 2013)

21G) Arasaki (Arasaki bus stop (20 minutes from Misakiguchi (Keihin Kyuukou)), 1 hour, 2013)

22H) Tenjinja Hiking Course (Kawaguchiko (Fuji Kyuukou), 3 hours, 2007)

23H) Kawaguchiko Lake (Kawaguchiko (Fuji Kyuukou), 2 hours, 2007)

24) Jukai Forest (Kouyoudai Bus Stop (30 minutes by bus from Kawaguchiko (Fuji Kyuukou), 30 minutes, 2009)

25H) Solar Cafe (Kouyoudai Bus Stop (30 minutes by bus from Kawaguchiko (Fuji Kyuukou), 10 minutes, 2009)

26H) Mt. Tsukuba Hiking Course (Tsutsujigaoka Bus Stop (40 minutes from Tsukuba (Tsukuba Express)), 20 minutes, 2009)

27H) Mt. Tsukuba Shrine (TsukubasanjinjaIriguchi bus stop (35 minutes from Tsukuba (Tsukuba Express)), 10 minutes, 2013)

28H) Mt. Tsukuba Hiking Course (TsukubasanjinjaIriguchi bus stop (35 minutes from Tsukuba (Tsukuba Express)), 30 minutes, 2013)

29H) Mt. Tsukuba mountain top area (TsukubasanjinjaIriguchi bus stop (35 minutes from Tsukuba (Tsukuba Express)), 2 hours, 2013)

30H) Mt. Tsukuba mountain top area (TsukubasanjinjaIriguchi bus stop (35 minutes from Tsukuba (Tsukuba Express)), 2 hours, 2013)

31H) Mt. Tsukuba Hiking Course (Tsutsujigaoka Bus Stop (40 minutes from Tsukuba (Tsukuba Express)), 20 minutes, 2013)

JUNE

1A) Shoubunuma Park (KitaAyase (Chiyoda), 15 minutes, 2014)

2A) Shoubunuma Park (KitaAyase (Chiyoda), 15 minutes, 2014)

3A) Mejiro Japanese Garden (Mejiro (Yamanote), 10 minutes, 2007)

4A) Gyousen Park (Japanese Garden) (NishiKasai (Tozai), 30 minutes, 2011)

5C) Maruyama Hiking Course (Ashigakubo (Seibu Chichibu), 2 hours, 2010)

6C) Taki no Iri Rose Garden (HigashiMoro (Toubu Ogose), 1.5 hours, 2011)

7C) Fudoutaki Waterfall (NishiAgano (Seibu Ikebukuro), 2.5 hours, 2012)

8C)   Sayama Park (MusashiYamato (Seibu Shinjuku), 1 hour, 2014)

9C)   BentenIke Park (HigashiMurayama (Seibu Shinjuku), 30 minutes, 2014)

10C) Chichibu Shrine (SeibuChichibu (SeibuChichibu), 30 minutes, 2015)

11D) Tama River (Kori (Oume), 15 minutes, 2011)

12D) Old Therapy Road Hiking Course (Okutama (Oume), 2 hours, 2012)

13D) Mitsukama no taki Waterfall (Kori (Oume), 3 hours, 2012)

14D) Old Zelkova Tree (a Natural Treasure) (Mitake (Oume), 2 hours, 2013)

15D) Tamagawadaishigyokushinin Temple (Futagotamagawa (Tokyuu Denen Toshi), 40 minutes, 2015)

16D) Tamagawadaishigyokushinin Temple (Futagotamagawa (Tokyuu Denen Toshi), 40 minutes, 2015)

17E) Mt. Takao (TakaoSanguchi (Keiou), 1 hour, 2006)

18E) Takao Nature Restoration Area (TakaoSanguchi (Keiou), 30 minutes, 2009)

19E) Katsuragawa River (Fujino (Chuuou), 1 hour, 2010)

20F) Mt. Matsuda Herb Garden (ShinMatsuda (Odakyuu), 45 minutes, 2008)

21F) Kaisei Hiking Course (ShinMatsuda (Odakyuu), 45 minutes, 2015)

22F) History and Culture Walking Course (Odawara (Odakyuu), 2 hours, 2014)

23F) History and Culture Walking Course (Odawara (Odakyuu), 2.5 hours, 2014)

24F) Saimyouji Shiseki Park Hiking Course (ShinMatsuda (Odakyuu), 3 hours, 2015)

25F) Kaisei Hydrangea Village (ShinMatsuda (Odakyuu), 1 hour, 2015)

26)   The Great Buddha Statue (Hase (Enoshima Dentetsu), 10 minutes, 2001)

27G) GenjiYama Park (KitaKamakura (Yokosuka), 1 hour, 2013)

28G) Enoshima Island (KataseEnoshima (Odakyuu), 1 hour, 2015)

29G) Enoshima Island (KataseEnoshima (Odakyuu), 1 hour, 2015)

30G) Enoshima Island (KataseEnoshima (Odakyuu), 1.5 hours, 2015)

JULY

1A)   Otomeyama Park (Takadanobaba (Tozai), 15 minutes, 2007)

2A)   Otomeyama Park (Takadanobaba (Tozai), 15 minutes, 2007)

3B)   TadaraKitahamaKaigan (Tomiura (Uchibou), 30 minutes,2015)

4B)   TadaraKitahamaKaigan (Tomiura (Uchibou), 30 minutes,2015)

5B)   Daibusamisaki Point (Tomiura (Uchibou), 2.5 hours, 2015)

6C)   Hydrangea Mountain Park (Ogose (Tobu Ogose), 3 hours, 2012)

7C) Hydrangea Mountain Park (Ogose (Tobu Ogose), 3 hours, 2012)

8C) Gojou no Taki Waterfall (MusashiYokote (Seibu Chichibu), 40 minutes, 2014)

9C) Mt. Hiwada (Koma (Seibu Chichibu), 1.5 hours, 2014)

10C) Mt. Hiwada (Koma (Seibu Chichibu), 1.5 hours, 2014)

11D) Tama Zoo Butterfly House (TamaDoubutsuKouen (TamaDoubutsuKouen), 15 minutes, 2004)

12D) Oonara Ridge (Hatonosu (Oume), 2 hours, 2008)

13E) Takao Environmental Restoration Area (Takao (Chuuou), 30 minutes, 2012)

14E) Takao Environmental Restoration Area (Takao (Chuuou), 30 minutes, 2012)

15E) Sagamigawa River (Fujino (Chuuou), 30 minutes, 2009)

16E) IpponMatsuYama Hiking Course (Fujino (Chuuou), 1.5 hours, 2009)

17E) IpponMatsuYama Hiking Course (Fujino (Chuuou), 2 hours, 2009)

18E) Sasago Ganharasuriyama Hiking Course (Sasago (Chuuou), 2 hours, 2011)

19E) Sasago Ganharasuriyama Hiking Course (Sasago (Chuuou), 3 hours, 2011)

20E) Takao Station Platform (Takao (Chuuou), On Platform, 2011)

21F) Mt. Matsuda Herb Garden (ShinMatsuda (Odakyuu), 45 minutes, 2008)

22F) Mt. Matsuda Herb Garden (ShinMatsuda (Odakyuu), 45 minutes, 2008)

23F) Mt. Matsuda Herb Garden (ShinMatsuda (Odakyuu), 45 minutes, 2008)

24G) Arasaki (Arasaki bus stop (20 minutes from Misakiguchi (Keihin Kyuukou)), 15 minutes, 2008)

25G) Arasaki (Arasaki bus stop (20 minutes from Misakiguchi (Keihin Kyuukou)), 15 minutes, 2008)

26G) Arasaki (Arasaki bus stop (20 minutes from Misakiguchi (Keihin Kyuukou)), 20 minutes, 2008)

27G) Arasaki (Arasaki bus stop (20 minutes from Misakiguchi (Keihin Kyuukou)), 2 hours, 2008)

28G) Manazuru Peninsula (Manazuru (Toukaidou), 2 hours, 2009)

29G) Arasaki (Arasaki bus stop (20 minutes from Misakiguchi (Keihin Kyuukou)), 20 minutes, 2011)

30G) Arasaki (Arasaki bus stop (20 minutes from Misakiguchi (Keihin Kyuukou)), 20 minutes, 2013)

31G)Arasaki (Arasaki bus stop (10 minutes from Misakiguchi (Keihin Kyuukou)), 20 minutes, 2013)

AUGUST

1B) YatsuHigata Wetlands (MinamiFunabashi (JR Keiyou), 20 minutes, 2008)

2B) KaihinMakuhari Park (KaihinMakuhari (JR Keiyou), 20 minutes, 2014)

3B) KaihinMakuhari Park (KaihinMakuhari (JR Keiyou), 20 minutes, 2014)

4B) Daibusamisaki Point Walking Course (Tomiura (Uchibou), 1.5 hours, 2012)

5B) Tomiura Station (Tomiura (Uchibou), 1 minute, 2012)

6C) Yoshimi Hyakketsu (HigashiMatsuyama (Toubu Toujou), 40 minutes, 2011)

7D) Tama River Walk (Sawai (Oume), 30 minutes, 2001)

8D) Takahatafudouson Pagoda (Takahatafudou (Keiou), 5 minutes, 2007)

9D) Sagamiko Lake (Sagamiko (Chuuou), 40 minutes, 2014)

10D) Environmental Restoration Project (Friends of the Earth) (Utsugidai Bus Stop 20 minutes from Hino (Chuuou), 15 minutes, 2014)

11D) KomatsuUchiura Park (TamaSakai (Keiou), 1 hour, 2014)

12D) KomatsuUchiura Park (TamaSakai (Keiou), 1 hour, 2014)

13D) Akigawa Hills Course (Akigawa (Musashiltsukaichi), 2 hours, 2014)

14D) Akigawa River (Musashiltsukaichi (Musashiitsukaichi), 1 hour, 2014)

15E) Yanagawa Pyramid & landscape (Yanagawa (Chuo), 10 minutes, 2007)

16E) Katsuragawa River (Yanagawa (Chuo), 30 minutes, 2007)

17E) Katsuragawa River (Yanagawa (Chuo), 30 minutes, 2008)

18E) Katsuragawa River (Yanagawa (Chuuou), 30 minutes, 2012)

19E) ShinOochiTouge Hiking Course (Shiotsu (Chuuou), 2 hours, 2015)

20E) ShinOochiTouge Hiking Course (Shiotsu (Chuuou), 1 hour, 2015)

21E) ShinOochiTouge Hiking Course (Shiotsu (Chuuou), 2 hours, 2015)

22G) Tenen Hiking Course (Kamakura (Yokosuka), 1.5 hours, 2007)

23G) Tsuruoka Hachimangu Pond (Kamakura (Yokosuka), 20 minutes, 2007)

24G) Tsuruoka Hachimangu Pond (Kamakura (Yokosuka), 20 minutes, 2007)

25G) Tsujidou Seaside Park (Chigasaki (Toukaido), 2 hours, 2008)

26G) Enoshima Bridge (Mt. Fuji) (KataseEnoshima (Odakyuu), 10 minutes, 2010)

27G) Enoshima Island (KataseEnoshima (Odakyuu), 30 minutes, 2014)

28G) Kannonzaki Point (Uraga (KeihinKyuukou), 1.5 hours, 2014)

29G) Kannonzaki Point (Uraga (KeihinKyuukou), 1.5 hours, 2014)

30G) Seaside Promenade (Mabori (Keihin Kyuukou), 30 minutes, 2014)

31H) Sumatakyou Gorge (SamatakyouOnsen (40 minutes by bus from Senzu (Ooikawa Testsudo), 1.5 hours, 2012)

SEPTEMBER

1B) Onjuku Coast Area (Onjuku (Sotobou), 30 minutes, 2007)
2B) Osenkorogashi Hiking Course (NamegawaAirando (Sotobou), 2 hours, 2009)
3B) Osenkorogashi Hiking Course (NamegawaAirando (Sotobou), 1 hour, 2009)
4B) Daibusamisaki Point Walking Course (Tomiura (Uchibou), 2 hours, 2009)
5B) IinumaKannon Pagoda (Choushi (Soubu), 20 minutes, 2010)
6C) Takayama Fudouson Hiking Couse (Agano (Seibu Chichibu), 2 hours, 2007)
7C) Kinchakuda (Koma (Seibu Chichibu), 30 minutes, 2012)
8C) Kinchakuda (Koma (Seibu Chichibu), 30 minutes, 2012)
9C) Mt. Tounosuyama Hiking Course (Hannou (Seibu Ikebukuro), 2 hours, 2013)
10C) Toki River (MusashiRanzan (Toubu Toujou), 1 hour, 2014)
11C) Toki River (MusashiRanzan (Toubu Toujou), 1 hour, 2014)
12D) Mt. Takao Hiking Course (TakaoSanGuchi (Keiou), 2 hours, 2006)
13D) South Takao Ridge Hiking Course (Takaosanguchi (Chuuou), 2 hours, 2006)
14D) Mt. Sengen Hiking Course (Sengen One Tozan Guchi bus stop (50 minutes from MusashiItsukaichi (MusashiItsukaichi), 2 hours, 2009)
15D) Oume Ridge Hiking Course (Miyanohira (Oume), 1 hour, 2009)
16D) Tama Riverside (Hamura (Oume), 20 minutes, 2012)
17D) Okutama Lake (Okutamako Bus Stop (20 minutes from Okutama (Oume), 5 minutes, 2014)
18D) Okutama Lake (Okutamako Bus Stop (20 minutes from Okutama (Oume), 5 minutes, 2014)
19D) Environmental Restoration Project (Friends of the Earth) (Utsugidai Bus Stop 20 minutes from Hino (Chuuou), 15 minutes, 2014)
20D) KasumiKyuuryou Nature Park (Oume (Oume), 2 hours, 2015)
21D) KasumiKyuuryou Nature Park (Oume (Oume), 2 hours, 2015)
22E) Sagamiko Lake Area (Sagamiko (Chuuou), 30 minutes, 2007)
23E) Kirigamine (Kirigamine bus stop (1.5 hours by bus from Chino (Chuuou), 1 hour, 2009)
24E) Kirigamine (Kirigamine bus stop (1.5 hours by bus from Chino (Chuuou), 2 hours, 2009)
25E) Kirigamine (Kirigamine bus stop (1.5 hours by bus from Chino (Chuuou), 1 hour, 2009)
26E) Katsuragawa River (Yanagawa (Chuuou), 5 minutes, 2014)
27E) Mt. Kuratake Hiking Course (Yanagawa (Chuuou), 2 hours, 2014)

28E) Katsuragawa River (Yanagawa (Chuo), 10 minutes, 2007)

29G) Shrine near Nagahama Beach (Misakiguchi (Keihin Kyuukou), 1.5 hours, 2013)

30H) Nasu Highlands Boardwalk (Nasu Highlands Bus Stop (30 minutes by bus from Kuroiso (Tohoku Honsen), 2011)

OCTOBER

1A) Yoyogi Park (MeijiJinguMae (Chiyoda), 15 minutes, 2010)

2B) KaihinMakuhari Park (KaihinMakuhari (JR Keiyou), 20 minutes, 2009)

3B) KaihinMakuhari Park (KaihinMakuhari (JR Keiyou), 20 minutes, 2009)

4C) Kinchakuda (Koma (Seibu Chichibu), 30 minutes, 2007)

5C) Kaburi Pass (Agano (Seibu Ikebukuro), 3 hours, 2009)

6C) Kusumi Slope (MusashiYokote (Seibu Chichibu), 2 hours, 2009)

7C) Mt Hinata Hiking Course (Ashigakubo (Seibu Chichibu), 5 minutes, 2010)

8C) Meribazaka Pass (Shoumaru (Seibu Chichibu), 2 hours, 2011)

9C) Meribazaka Pass (Shoumaru (Seibu Chichibu), 2.5 hours, 2011)

10D) Shouwa Park (NishiTachikawa (Oume), 30 minutes, 2010)

11D) Takao Work Project (Takao (Keiou), 30 minutes, 2012)

12D) Toukouin Temple Hiking Course (Akikawa (MusashiItuskaichi), 1 hour, 2011)

13D) Ikuta Ryokuchi Baraen (Rose Park) (MukougaokaYuuen (Odakyuu), 1 hour, 2013)

14D) Mt. Takamizu Hiking Course (Kawai (Oume), 1 hour, 2013)

15D) Mt. Takamizu Hiking Course (Kawai (Oume), 2 hours, 2013)

16D) River near Sagami Lake (Sagamiko (Chuuou), 1.5 hours, 2012)

17E) Chigootoshi Cliffs (Ootsuki (Chuuou), 2.5 hours, 2010)

18E) Sagami River (Sagamiko (Chuuou), 1.5 hours, 2012)

19E) Sagami Lake (Sagamiko (Chuuou), 15 minutes, 2012)

20F) Mt. Kintoki Hiking Course (Asagara (Gotemba), 1 hour, 2007)

21F) Mt. Kintoki Hiking Course (Asagara (Gotemba), 1 hour, 2007)

22F) Myoujougatake Hiking Course (Goura (Hakone Tozan Tetsudo), 2.5 hours, 2011)

23F) Sengokuhara (Sengokuhara bus stop (30 minutes by bus from Goura (Hakone Tozan Tetsudou), 2011)

24F) Yuujo no taki Waterfall (Surugaoyama (Gotemba), 1 hour, 2009)

25G) Morito Beach (Zushi (Yokosuka), 1 hour, 2009)

26G) Mt Rokkokumi (Kitakamakura (Yokosuka), 1.5 hours, 2011)

27G) Oofuna Flower Center (Oofuna (Toukaidou), 45 minutes, 2011)

28G) Kannonzaki Point (Uraga (Keihin Kyuukou), 2 hours, 2012)

29G) Tenen Hiking Course (Kanazawa Hakkei (Keihin Kyuukou), 2 hours, 2014)

30G) Kanazawa Shizen Kouen (Kanazawa Bunko (Keihin Kyuukou), 1.5 hours, 2014)

31H) Somewhere in Tohoku after the big March Earthquake (2011)
(Photo taken by Eiichi Sakakibara (A1))

NOVEMBER

1A) Arakawa River (NishiKasai (Tozai), 1 hour, 2012)

2C) Kuroyama Santaki (Agano (Seibu Ikebukuro), 3 hours, 2013)

3C) Katsuragi Kannon (Ogose (Toubu Ogose), 2 hours, 2013)

4C) Ranzan Gorge (MusashiRanzan (Toubu Toujou), 2 hours, 2014)

5C) Ranzan Gorge (MusashiRanzan (Toubu Toujou), 2 hours, 2014)

6D) Tama River (Mitake (Oume), 30 minutes, 2009)

7D) Okutama Therapy Road (Okutama (Oume), 2.5 hours, 2010)

8D) Mt. Takamizu Hiking Course (Kawai (Oume), 30 minutes, 2011)

9D) Mt. Takamizu Hiking Course (Kawai (Oume), 2 hours, 2011)

10D) Tama River (Mitake (Oume), 30 minutes, 2011)

11D) Tama River (Mitake (Oume), 10 minutes, 2011)

12D) Sarubashi Bridge (Sarubashi (Chuuou), 30 minutes, 2009)

13D) Katsuragawa River (Sarubashi (Chuuou), 30 minutes, 2009)

14D) Yakuouin Temple (TakaoSanGuchi (Keiou), 2 hours, 2010)

15D) Ginkgo Lined Street (Takao (Keiou), 20 minutes, 2010)

16D) Satoyama Nature Course (KeiouKatakura (Keiou), 2 hours, 2015)

17E) Shousenkyou Gorge (Shousenkyouguchi bus stop (30 minutes by bus from Koufu (Chuuou), 45 minutes, 2011)

18E) Shousenkyou Gorge (Shousenkyouguchi bus stop (30 minutes by bus from Koufu (Chuuou), 1.5 hours, 2011)

19E) Nishizawa Gorge (Nishizawa keikoku iriguchi bus stop (1 hour from Enzan (Chuuou) 1 hour, 2014)

20E) Nanatsugamagodan no taki Waterfall (Nishizawa keikoku iriguchi bus stop (1 hour from Enzan (Chuuou), 2 hours, 2014)

21E) Near bus stop (Nishizawa keikoku iriguchi bus stop (1 hour from Enzan (Chuuou), 10 minutes, 2014)

22E) Mt Takao Peak (TakaoSanGuchi (Keiou), 1.5 hours, 2014)

23E) Yakuouin Torii Gate (TakaoSanGuchi (Keiou), 1.5 hours, 2014)

24F) Saijouji Temple (Douryouson bus stop (10 minutes by bus from Daiyuuzan (Daiyuuzan), 15 minutes, 2008)

25F) Saijouji Temple (Douryouson bus stop (10 minutes by bus from Daiyuuzan (Daiyuuzan),15 minutes, 2015)

26F) Saijouji Temple (Douryouson bus stop (10 minutes by bus from Daiyuuzan (Daiyuuzan), 15 minutes, 2015)

27F) Myojingatake Hiking Course (Douryouson bus stop (10 minutes by bus from Daiyuuzan (Daiyuuzan), 1 hour, 2015)

28F) Hiryuu no taki Waterfall (Hatajuku bus stop (20 minutes from HakoneYumoto (Hakone Tozan), 1 hour, 2012)

29G) Itachi River (Hongoudai (Keihin Tohoku), 1 hour, 2011)

30G) Itachi River (Hongoudai (Keihin Tohoku), 1 hour, 2011)

DECEMBER

1A) Gyousen Park (NishiKasai (Tozai), 25 minutes, 2015)

2A) Mejiro Japanese Garden (Mejiro (Yamanote), 10 minutes, 2010)

3A) Zenyouji Temple (Koiwa (Soubu), 30 minutes, 2012)

4B) Keikoku Bridge (Youroukeikoku (Kominato Testsudou), 20 minutes, 2007)

5B) Yourou Keikoku Hiking Course (Youroukeikoku (Kominato Testsudou), 40 minutes, 2007)

6B) Yourou Keikoku Gorge (Youroukeikoku (Kominato Testsudou), 45 minutes, 2013)

7B) Yourou Keikoku Gorge (Youroukeikoku (Kominato Testsudou), 1.5 hours, 2013)

8B) Yourou Keikoku Gorge (Youroukeikoku (Kominato Testsudou), 1 hour, 2013)

9B) Yourou Keikoku Station (Youroukeikoku (Kominato Testsudou), 5 minutes, 2013)

10C) Mt. Ootakayama Hiking Course (Agano (Seibu Chichibu), 1 hour, 2007)

11C) Kuroyama Santaki (Agano (Seibu Chichibu), 3 hours, 2010)

12C) Old Shoumaru Pass (Shoumaru (Seibu Chichibu), 2 hours, 2014)

13C) Nagaiwa Pass (Shoumaru (Seibu Chichibu), 1.5 hours, 2014)

14D) Atagoyama Green Area (Tama Center (Odakyuu), 1 hour, 2013)

15D) Tama River (Hinatawada (Oume), 15 minutes, 2014)

16D) Tama Central Park (Tama Center (KeiouSagamihara), 15 minutes, 2011)

17D) Atago Shrine (Ikusabata (Oume), 45 minutes, 2014)

18D) Environmental Restoration Project (Friends of the Earth) (Utsugidai Bus Stop (20 minutes from Hino (Chuuou), 15 minutes, 2014)

19D) Tama YomiuriLand Course (Mukougaokayuuen (Odakyuu), 2 hours, 2014)

20D) Yakushidou Park Area (Keiou Inadatsutsumi (Keiou), 1 hour, 2014)

21D) Jufukuji Temple (Mukougaokayuuen (Odakyuu), 2 hours, 2014)

22E) Near Fuefukigawa Fruits Park (YamanashiShi (Chuuou), 1.5 hours, 2012)

23E) Hottarakashi Hot Springs (YamanashiShi (Chuuou), 2 hours, 2012)

24F) Mt. Koubou (Hadano (Odakyuu), 2 hours, 2007)

25F) Mt Ooyama Hiking Course (Yabitsu Touge Bus Stop (35 minutes by bus from Hadano Station (Odakyuu Line), 1.5 hours, 2012)

26F) Ooyamadera Temple (Yabitsu Touge Bus Stop (35 minutes by bus from Hadano Station (Odakyuu Line), 3 hours, 2012)

27F) Ooyamadera Temple (Yabitsu Touge Bus Stop (35 minutes by bus from Hadano Station (Odakyuu Line), 3 hours, 2012)

28F) Mt Sengen Hiking Course (Miyanoshita (Hakone Tetsudo), 2 hours, 2014)

29G) Sankeien Garden (Yamate (Negishi), 40 minutes, 2006)

30G) Sankeien Garden (Yamate (Negishi), 40 minutes, 2006)

31G) Morito Beach (Zushi (Yokosuka), 1 hour, 2011)

References

JANUARY

1) Anthony De Mello, and J. Francis Stroud, Awareness: A De Mello Spirituality Conference in His Own Words (New York: Image Books/Doubleday, 1992 (Reprint Edition), 37-8.

2) "DailyGuru.com," DailyGurucom RSS, Meditations from Conscious One Daily Guru, accessed June 9, 2014, http://www.dailyguru.com/.

3) Carlos Valles, Unencumbered by Baggage(Gujarat, INDIA: Gujarat Sahitya Prakash, 2003 (Reprinted Edition)), 114.

4) Leo F. Buscallia, and Steven Short, LIVING, LOVING & LEARNING (New York: Fawcett Columbine,1983 (Reissue Edition)), 70.

5) Brian Weiss, Messages from the Masters (New York: Warner Books, 2000), 127

6) "DailyGuru.com," DailyGurucom RSS, Meditations from Conscious One Daily Guru, accessed March 5, 2005, http://www.dailyguru.com/.

7) Larry Rosenberg, and David Guy, Breath by Breath: The Liberating Practice of Insight Meditation (Boston, MA: Shambhala, 1998), 108.

8) Bstan-'dzin-rgya-mtsho (Dalai Lama), and Jeffrey Hopkins, How to See Yourself as You Really Are (New York: Atria Books, 2006), 218-9.

9) Jeremy Naydler, "Perennial Wisdom – Making time to reconnect with our spiritual roots," Resurgence & Ecologist (Digital Edition), No. 279. July/August 2013: 47.

10) "Nails In The Fence," Inspiration Peak, accessed September 03, 2016, http://www.inspirationpeak.com/cgi-bin/stories.cgi?record=50.

11) Karen Armstrong, Twelve Steps to a Compassionate Life (New York: Alfred A. Knopf, 2011 (Kindle Edition)), 186.

12) Marianne Williamson, Everyday Grace: Having Hope, Finding Forgiveness, and Making Miracles (New York: Riverhead Books, 2002), 13.

13) Weiss, Messages from the Masters, 90-1.

14) Cherie Carter-Scott, If Life Is a Game, These Are the Rules: Ten Rules for Being Human, as Introduced in Chicken Soup for the Soul, (New York: Broadway Books, 1998 (Kindle Edition), 82.

15) Valerue Austin, Self-hypnosis: The Key to Success and Happiness, (London: Thorsons, 1994), 98-9.

16) Jurriaan Kamp, "The Honeymoon Effect," ODE Magazine, May-June 2012, 40.

17) Marianne Williamson, A Return to Love: Reflections on the Principles of a Course in Miracles (New York, NY: HarperCollins, 1992), 131.

18) Duane Elgin, Voluntary Simplicity(New York: HarperCollins, 1981), 159-60

19) Colin Wilson, Mysteries (New York: Putnam, 1978), 589-90.

20) 1.) Rhys Alywn, qtd. in Brower, David R. Forward. Green Plans: Greenprint for Sustainability. By Huey D. Johnson (Lincoln: U of Nebraska, 1995).
    2.) Lewis Mumford, Technics and Civilisation (New York: Harcourt, Brace and, 1934), 282.

21) Derrick Jensen, "You Choose" in Moral Ground: Ethical Action for a Planet in Peril, ed. Kathleen Dean Moore and Michael P. Nelson (San Antonio, TX: Trinity University Press, 2010), 61.

22) Jacob Needleman, Money and the Meaning of Life (New York: Doubleday/Currency, 1991), 113.

23) Lester W. Milbrath, Envisioning a Sustainable Society: Learning Our Way out (Albany: State University of New York Press, 1989), 225-226

24) Austin, Self-Hypnosis, 90.

25) Eric Fromm, To Have or to Be? (New York: Harper & Row, 1976), 77.

26) John de Graaf, David Wann, and Thomas H. Naylor, Affluenza: The All Consuming Epidemic (San Francisco, CA: Berrett-Koehler Publishers, 2001), 50.

27) E. F. Schumacher, Small Is Beautiful; Economics as If People Mattered (New York: Harper & Row, 1973), 31-2.

28) Carolyn Mackler, 250 Ways to Make America Better (New York: Villard, 1999), 20-1.

29) 1.) ""When We Dead Awaken: Writing as Re-Vision," by Adrienne Rich," Cest La Vie, 2011,accessed September 06, 2016, https://emeire.wordpress.com/2011/01/28/when-we dead-awaken-writing-as-re-vision-by-adrienne-rich/
    2.) H.G. Wells Quote.

30) 1.) William Butler Yeats Quote
    2.) Sydney J. Harris Quote.

31) David Howenstein, "A World Without JAMBO?" Jambo International, April 2015, http://jambointernational.org/en/category/writing/page/3/.

FEBRUARY

1) 1.) Thomas R. Dunlap, Faith in Nature: Environmentalism as Religious Quest. (Seattle: University of Washington Press, 2004), 112
   2.) J. Krishnamurti, Think on These Things (New York: Harper & Row, 1964), 82.

2) Bob Burg, "Gratitude — Your Gateway to Success: A Special Report," (page 5), 2004, accessed September 4, 2015, http://www.burg.com/wp-content/uploads/2009/12/BurgGratitude.pdf.

3) David Howenstein, "Seeing the Miracles," Jambo International, April 2013, http://jambointernational.org/en/2013/04/10/3593/.

4) Buscaglia, LIVING, LOVING & LEARNING, 76-7.

5) Thomas Berry, The Dream of the Earth (Berkeley, CA: Counterpoint, 1988), 10.

6) "DailyGuru.com." DailyGurucom RSS. Meditations from Conscious One Daily Guru, accessed March 5, 2004, http://www.dailyguru.com/.

7) Anthony De Mello, Taking Flight: A Book of Story Meditations (New York: Doubleday, 1988), 30-1 (Abridged).

8) Sakyong Mipham, Ruling Your World: Ancient Strategies for Modern Life (New York: Morgan Road Books, 2005), 70-1.

9) Stephen Covey, and Breck England, The 3rd Alternative: Solving Life's Most Difficult Problems (New York: Free Press, 2011 (Kindle Edition)), 402.

10) Jeff Kottler, Change: What Really Leads to Lasting Personal Transformation, 2013 (Kindle Edition)), location 4345.

11) "The Seven Wonders of the World." Reconnections, accessed August 19, 2016, http://www.reconnections.net/seven_wonders.htm.

12) Leszek Rybicki, "Enjoy Life," Jambo International, March 2011, http://jambointernational.org/en/2011/03/09/1643/.

13) 1.) Sigmund Freud Quote.
    2.) "DailyGuru.com." DailyGurucom RSS, Meditations from Conscious One Daily Guru, accessed June 27, 2005, http://www.dailyguru.com/.
    3.) Joseph Campbell Quote.

14) "Nonviolent Communication." NVC Extracts From Marshall Rosenberg Books, 41, accessed September 04, 2016, http://www.ayahuasca-wasi.com/english/articles/NVC.pdf.

15) Nicole Washburn, "A Challenge to the letters on Population," From Readers, Letter to the Editor, WorldWatch Magazine, JANUARY/FEBRUARY 2004, 6-7.

16) Buscaglia, LIVING, LOVING & LEARNING, 81.

17) Wilson, MYSTERIES, 495.

18) 1.) Charles Eisenstein, The More Beautiful World Our Hearts Know Is Possible (Berkeley, CA: North Atlantic Books, 2013 (Kindle Edition)), 230.
    2.) Thomas Moore, The Soul of Sex: Cultivating Life as an Act of Love (New York: HarperCollins, 1998), 176.

19) 1.) Brian D. McLaren, The Secret Message of Jesus: Uncovering the Truth That Could Change Everything (Nashville: W Pub., 2006 (Kindle Edition)), location 1886.
    2.) Carter-Scott, If Life is a Game, These are the Rules, 29.

20) Eckhart Tolle, A New Earth: Awakening to Your Life's Purpose (New York: Plume, 2006), 190.

21) Henry David Thoreau Quote.

22) 1.) Abraham Joshua Heschel, Between God and Man; an Interpretation of Judaism, from the Writings of Abraham J. Heschel (New York: Harper, 1959), 53.
    2.) Anonymous.

23) 1.) Thomas Moore Quote.
    2.) Andrew Schneider Quote.
    3.) Albert Einstein Quote.

24) Dan Clark, "Never Too Old To Live Your Dream," in Chicken Soup for the College Soul: Inspiring and Humorous Stories About College, (Cos Cob, CT: Chicken Soup for the Soul Publishing LLC, 1999), 286-290 (Abridged).

25) Corinne McLaughlin, and Gordon Davidson, Spiritual Politics: Changing the World from the inside out (New York: Ballantine Books, 1994), 357.

26) David Wann, Simple Prosperity: Finding Real Wealth in a Sustainable Lifestyle (New York: St. Martin's Griffin, 2007), 126.

27) David Howenstein, "The Importance of Having Fun," Jambo International, October 2013, http://jambointernational.org/en/2013/10/08/3919/.

28) Wann, Simple Prosperity, 127.

29) Margaret J. Wheatley, and Deborah Frieze, Walk Out, Walk On: A Learning Journey into Communities Daring to Live the Future Now (San Francisco: Berrett-Koehler, 2011), 64.

MARCH

1) Neale Donald Walsh, Conversations with God Bulletin, December 1998, 11-12, Print.

2) 1.) Krishnamurti, Think on These Things, 82.
   2.) Krishnamurti, Think on These Things, 205.

3) 1.) Williamson, Everyday Grace, 15.
   2.) Dam Helder Camara Quote.

4) Ilia Dello, Compassion: Living in the Spirit of St. Francis (Cincinnati, OH: St. Anthony Messenger Press, 2011), 71-2.

5) Martin Luther King Quote.

6) "Help Us Remember." beliefnet.com, accessed September 4, 2016, http://www.beliefnet.com/prayers/protestant/compassion/help-us-remember.aspx.

7) Howard John Clinebell, Ecotherapy: Healing Ourselves, Healing the Earth (New York: Haworth Press, 1996), 181.

8) Erich Fromm, and Ruth Nanda Anshen, The Art of Loving (New York: Harper & Row, 1956), 3. The Objects of Love.

9) David Howenstein, "Our Greatest Challenge," Jambo International, June, 2010, http://jambointernational.org/en/2010/06/10/899/.

10) Williamson, A Return to Love, 89.

11) A Course in Miracles (Tiburon, CA: Foundation for Inner Peace, 1985), 338.

12) Amy McCready, "Can I Borrow $25? – Positive Parenting Solutions." Positive Parenting Solutions, accessed September 04, 2016(ABRIDGED), http://www.positiveparentingsolutions.com/parenting/can-i-borrow-25.

13) Sam Keen, The Passionate Life: Stages of Loving (San Francisco: Harper & Row, 1983), 191.

14) Nina Simons, "Learning Love Through Limbic Liaisons," Nina Simon's Blog, September 26, 2013, http://www.ninasimons.com/#!Learning-Love-Through-Limbic-Liaisons/cd23/D6E07CC1-85AA-4532-945B-68E8E9BE90A0.

15) David Howenstein, "Grow the Love," Jambo International, August, 2010, http://jambointernational.org/en/2010/08/11/1057/.

16) Keen, The Passionate Life, 221.

17) Richie Chevat, and Michael Pollan, The Omnivore's Dilemma: The Secrets behind What You Eat (New York: Dial Books, 2009), 172-3.

18) Ibid, 318.

19) Neale Donald Walsch, "Happy New Year," Conversations with God Bulletin, December 31, 2005. Print.

20) 1) Neale Donald Walsch, "The Killing of Osama Bin Laden," Conversations with God Bulletin, May 6, 2011. Print.
    2) Neale Donald Walsch, "Happy New Year," Conversations with God Bulletin, December 31, 2005. Print.

21) Don Mackenzie, Ted Falcon, and Jamal Rahman, Getting to the Heart of Interfaith: The Eye-opening, Hope-filled Friendship of a Pastor, a Rabbi & a Sheikh (Woodstock, VT: SkyLight Paths Pub., 2009 (Kindle Edition), 133.

22) Michael N. Nagler, Is There No Other Way?: The Search for a Nonviolent Future (Berkeley, CA: Berkeley Hills Books, 2001), 55.

23) 1) Stone, Difficult Conversations: How to Discuss What Matters Most, location 807.
    2) Ibid, location 2377.

24) Paul H.Ray, and Sherry Ruth Anderson, The Cultural Creatives: How 50 Million People Are Changing the World (New York: Harmony Books, 2000), 314

25) Krishnamurti, Think on These Things, 204.

26) Albert Einstein Quote.

27) Jack Kornfield, A Path With Heart:A Guide Through the Perils and Promises of Spiritual Life (New York, NY: Bantam Books 1993), 295.

28) Joel C. Hunter, "Civility is Only a Beginning," Sojourners Magazine, March 2011, 39.

29) Gandhi, and Louis Fischer, The Essential Gandhi: His Life, Work, and Ideas: An Anthology, (New York: Vintage Books, 1983), 186-7.

30) Marilyn Turkovich, "The Charter for Compassion," Charter for Compassion, accessed September 09, 2016, http://www.charterforcompassion.org/index.php/charter.

31) Shantideva (Buddhist mystic) Quote.

APRIL

1) Thomas Merton Quote.

2) Renard, Gary R. Renard, The Disappearance of the Universe: Straight Talk about Illusions, past Lives, Religion, Sex, Politics, and the Miracles of Forgiveness (Carlsbad, CA: Hay House, 2004), 397.

3) Mahatma Gandhi Quote.

4) Donna Corso, When the Wind Chimes Chime, (Bloomington, IN: Xlibris Publishing, 2013 (Kindle Edition), 129.

5) Charlene Spretnak, States of Grace: The Recovery of Meaning in the Postmodern Age, (San Francisco, CA: HarperSanFrancisco, 1991), 61.

6) Hermann Hesse Quote.

7) 1.) Armstrong, Twelve Steps to a Compassionate Life, 18.6
   2.) Stephen Biko Quote.

8) Elizabeth Harris, Violence and Disruption in Society: A Study of the Early Buddhist Texts (Sri Lanka: Buddhist Publication Society, 1994), 19-20

9) Fromm, To Have or To Be, 100-1.

10) Nagler, Is There No Other Way? The Search for a Nonviolent Future, 257.

11) 1.) Nagler, Is There No Other Way? The Search for a Nonviolent Future, 56.
    2.) Nagler, Is There No Other Way? The Search for a Nonviolent Future, 301.

12) Nagler, Is There No Other Way? The Search for a Nonviolent Future, 285.

13) Joshua Wolf Shenk, Lincoln's Melancholy (Boston: Houghton Mifflin, 2005 (Kindle Edition), location 3694-3702.

14) Jeannie Choi and Bernard Lafayette, "Freedom Fighter," Sojourners Magazine, May 2011, 25-6.

15) Nagler, Is There No Other Way, 249-50.

16) Gregg Braden, The Isaiah Effect: Decoding the Lost Science of Prayer and Prophecy (New York: Harmony Books, 2000), 236-7.

17) 1.) Mary McCarthy Quote.
    2.) "DailyGuru.com." DailyGurucom RSS. Meditations from Conscious One Daily Guru, accessed April 24, 2006, http://www.dailyguru.com/.

18) Maulana Wahiduddin Khan Quotes (Satish Kumar, You Are Therefore I Am (Foxhole, Dartington: Green Books Ltd, 2010f (Kindle Edition), location 2189).

19) Graaf, Affluenza, 43.

20) Dan Ariely, Predictably Irrational (New York, NY: HarperCollins Publishers, 2010), 138.

21) Wilson, MYSTERIES, 588.

22) Woody Tasch, Slow Money (White River Junction, VT: Chelsea Green Publishing Company, 2010 (Kindle Edition), 184.

23) Courtney Carver, "The Story of the Mexican Fisherman," (ABRIDGED), Be More With Less, May 24, 2010, http://bemorewithless.com/the-story-of-the-mexican-fisherman/.

24) 1.) Yuval Noah Harari, Sapiens: A Brief History of Humankind (New York, NY: HarperCollins Publishers, 2015 (Kindle Edition), 382.
2.) Ibid, 384.

25) David Howenstein, "Bicycle Benefits" (My Writings – ESSAYS, 2015).

26) Mello, Awareness, 166.

27) Fromm, To Have or To Be, xxix.

28) Ernest Kurtz, and Katherine Ketcham, The Spirituality of Imperfection: Storytelling and the Journey to Wholeness (New York: Bantam, 1994), 36.

29) Gary Gardner, "The Virtue of Restraint," World Watch, 1 Mar. 2001, Print, 14-18.

30) 1.) Elgin, Voluntary Simplicity, 137.
2.) Ibid, 139.

MAY

1) Thomas Lickona, Educating for Character: How Our Schools Can Teach Respect and Responsibility (New York, NY: Bantam, 1991), 38.

2) McLaughlin, Spiritual Politics: Changing the World from the inside out, 15.

3) Samuel P. Huntington, The Clash of Civilizations: And the Remaking of World Order (London: Simon & Schuster, 2002), 320.

4) Rohr, The Naked Now, 94.

5) Madeleine Bunting, "Comment: Intolerant Liberalism," The Guardian, 2001, accessed September 12, 2016, https://www.theguardian.com/world/2001/oct/08/afghanistan.politics1.

6) Nagler, Is There No Other Way, 291.

7) Mathew Kelly, Rediscover Catholicism: A Spiritual Guide to Living with Passion & Purpose (Place of Publication Not Identified: Beacon Pub., 2010), 32-5.

8) "Two Wolves," Virtues for Life, accessed September 12, 2016, http://www.virtuesforlife.com/two-wolves/.

9) Neale Donald Walsch, Tomorrow's God: Our Greatest Spiritual Challenge (New York: Atria Books, 2004), 302.

10) Mackler, 250 Ways to Make America Better, 212.

11) Jim Wallis, "A Global Call for a New Social Covenant," Sojourners Vol. 42, No. 5 (May, 2013): 7.

12) Harari, Sapiens: A Brief History of Humankind, 164.

13) Thomas L. Friedman, "Who We Really Are," in Moral Ground: Ethical Action for a Planet in Peril, ed. Kathleen Moore and Michael Nelson (San Antonio, TX: Trinity University Press, 2010 (Kindle Edition)), 192.

14) Jacob Needleman, The American Soul: Rediscovering the Wisdom of the Founders (New York: J.P. Tarcher/Putnam, 2002), 10.

15) Marianne Williamson, "Our Greatest Fear," Our Greatest Fear Marianne Williamson, accessed September 12, 2016, http://explorersfoundation.org/glyphery/122.html.

16) Fromm, To Have or To Be?, 110.

17) Thea Alexander, 2150 A.D. (New York: Warner, 1976), 317-8.

18) Matt Ridley, The Origins of Virtue: Human Instincts and the Evolution of Cooperation (New York: Viking, 1997), 38.

19) 1.) Alan Storey, "For the Healing of the Nation," Sojourners, May 2011: 30.
    2.) Harari, Sapiens: A Brief History of Humankind, 180.
    3.) Ibid, 186.

20) Richard Louv, The Nature Principle: Reconnecting with Life in a Virtual Age, (Chapel Hill, NC: Algonquin Books of Chapel Hill, 2012 (Kindle Edition)), 75-6.

21) Sarah Van Gelder, Sustainable Happiness: Live Simply, Live Well, Make a Difference, (Oakland, CA: Berrett-Koehler Publishers, 2015 (Kindle Edition)), location 359.

22) Armstrong, Twelve Steps to a Compassionate Life, 39-40.

23) Erich Fromm, The Heart of Man: Its Genius for Good and Evil (New York: Harper & Row, 1964), 108.

24) 1.) Paul Ferrini Quote.
    2.) "DailyGuru.com." DailyGurucom RSS. Meditations from Conscious One Daily Guru, accessed April 29, 2005, http://www.dailyguru.com/.
    3.) Wayne Dyer Quote.

25) David Howenstein, "Jambo Message Activities," Jambo International, August 2010, http://jambointernational.com.

26) Susan Howrath, Scandalous Risks: A Novel (New York: Knopf, 1990), 457.

27) Joan Borysenko, Guilt Is the Teacher, Love Is the Lesson (New York, NY: Warner Books, 1990), 5.

28) Ken Wilber, No Boundary: Eastern and Western Approaches to Personal Growth (Boulder, CO: Shambhala, 1981) 3.

29) 1.) Alexander Smith Quote.
    2.) Nelson Mandela Quote.

30) Covey, The 3rd Alternative, 181.

31) Charles Eisenstein, Sacred Economics: Money, Gift, & Society in the Age of Transition (Berkeley, CA: Evolver Editions, 2011 (Kindle Edition)), 152.

JUNE

1) 1.) Wayne Dyer Quote.
   2.) Harvey Mackay Quote.

2) Rebecca Solnit, A Paradise Built in Hell: The Extraordinary Communities That Arise in Disasters (New York: Viking, 2009 (Kindle Edition)), 306.

3) Tom Hayden, The Lost Gospel of the Earth: A Call for Renewing Nature, Spirit and Politics (San Francisco: Sierra Club Books, 1996) 149.

4) Lerner, The Politics of Meaning, 70-1.

5) Ibid, 5.

6) Thomas Merton, New Seeds of Contemplation (New York, NY: New Directions, 1972), 110.

7) 1.) Nagler, Is There No Other Way? The Search for a Nonviolent Future, 169.
2.) McLennan, Jason F. McLennan, Transformational Thought (Portland, OR: Ecotone Pub., 2012 (Kindle Edition)), location 681.

8) Ken Robinson, Out of Our Minds: Learning to Be Creative, (Oxford: Capstone, 2011 (Kindle Edition)), 173.

9) Schumacher, Small is Beautiful, 9.

10) M. Scott Peck, Further along the Road Less Travelled: Wisdom for the Journey towards Spiritual Growth (London: Pocket, 2010), 67-8.

11) Frances Moore Lappé, Rediscovering America's Values (New York: Ballantine Books, 1989), 265.

12) 1.) Jim Rohn Quote.
2.) Jim Rohn Quote.

13) Fred Eppsteiner, The Path of Compassion: Writing on Socially Engaged Buddhism (Berkeley, CA: Parallax Press, 1988), 86.

14) Andrew Harvey, The Hope: A Guide to Sacred Activism (Carlsbad, CA: Hay House, 2009 (Kindle Edition)), location 238 – 257.

15) David Howenstein, "Volunteering your Way to JOY," Jambo International, June 2011, http://jambointernational.org/en/2011/06/20/1911/.

16) Wilson, Mysteries, 265-6.

17) Robert Costanza, "Sustainable Wellbeing," Resurgence & Ecologist (Digital Edition), No. 279, July/August 2013: 39-40.

18) James Gustave Speth, Red Sky at Morning: America and the Crisis of the Global Environment (New Haven: Yale University Press, 2004), 192.

19) Lerner, The Politics of Meaning, 251.

20) Ed Ayres, "Let Them Eat "Cakewalk,"" World Watch, November 1, 2003, 4.

21) Alexander Fraser Tytler, The Decline and Fall of the Athenian Republic, quoted in John and Janice Corson, "The Rise And Fall Of Great Civilizations: From Apathy to Dependence to Slavery," Sociological Issues, September 1, 2009, accessed August 08, 2016, http://www.corson.org/archives/sociological/S27_090109.htm.

22) Anders Hayden, Sharing the Work, Sparing the Planet (London: Zed Books, 1999), 100-1.

23) 1.) Gay Hendricks, and Kate Ludeman, The Corporate Mystic: A Guidebook for Visionaries with Their Feet on the Ground (New York: Bantam Books, 1996), 168-9.
2.) Albert Einstein Quote.

24) Covey, The 3rd Alternative, 403-6.

25) Robert Thurman (Professor/Author), in 250 Ways to Make America Better. Ed Carolyn Mackler (New York: Villard, 1999), 80-1.

26) 1) Leo Tolstoy Quote.
    2) Helen Keller Quote.

27) Weiss, Messages from the Masters, 89.

28) Po Bronson, What Should I Do with My Life?: The True Story of People Who Answered the Ultimate Question (New York, NY: Ballantine Books, 2003) 47-8.

29) Nathaniel Branden Quote.

30) Jack Canfield, and Janet Switzer, The Success Principles: How to Get from Where You Are to Where You Want to Be (New York: Harper Resource Book, 2005 (Kindle Edition)), 433.

JULY

1) Frances Moore Lappé, EcoMind: Changing the Way We Think, to Create the World We Want (New York: Nation Books, 2011), 170.

2) Lerner, The Politics of Meaning (Also in "The Politics of Meaning Intro Letter, 1997).

3) Parker J. Palmer, Healing the Heart of Democracy: The Courage to Create a Politics Worthy of the Human Spirit (San Francisco, CA: Jossey-Bass, 2011), 4-5.

4) Eboo Patel, Sacred Ground: Pluralism, Prejudice, and the Promise of America (Boston: Beacon Press, 2012 (Kindle Edition)), xv.

5) Richard Stearns, The Hole in Our Gospel (Nashville, TN: Thomas Nelson, 2009), 119.

6) Harry Palmer, Living Deliberately: The Discovery and Development of Avatar (Altamonte Springs, FL: Star's Edge International, 1994), 86.

7) Ken Ausubel, Restoring the Earth: Visionary Solutions from the Bioneers (Tiburon, CA: H J Kramer, 1997), 153.

8) 1.) Ford, Debbie Ford, Why Good People Do Bad Things: How to Stop Being Your Own Worst Enemy (New York: HarperOne, 2008), 188.
   2.) Eisenstein, The More Beautiful World Our Hearts Know Is Possible, 172.

9) 1.) Francis, Church of Mercy (Chicago, IL: Loyola Press, 2014, (Kindle Edition)), location 789.
   2.) "EVANGELII GAUDIUM – Page 46," EVANGELII GAUDIUM, accessed September 13, 2016, http://www.vatican.va/evangelii-gaudium/en/files/assets/basic-html/page46.html.

10) Alexander Sutherland Neill, Albert Lamb, and Alexander Sutherland Neill, Summerhill School: A New View of Childhood, (New York: St. Martin's Press, 1993), 48.

11) Covey, The 3rd Alternative, 318.

12) Hayden, The Lost Gospel of the Earth, 242.

13) Mitch Albom, Tuesdays with Morrie: An Old Man, a Young Man, and Life's Greatest Lesson (New York: Doubleday, 1997), 154.

14) Ibid, 35-6.

15) Chuck Colson, published: November 29, 1996, by Eric Metaxas, and by John Stonestreet. "Tough Love With A Vengeance," Tough Love With A Vengeance, accessed September 13, 2016, http://www.breakpoint.org/bpcommentaries/entry/13/11919.

16) Nagler, Is There No Other Way? The Search for a Nonviolent Future, 192

17) Michael Toms, A Time for Choices: Deep Dialogues for Deep Democracy (Gabriola Island, BC, Canada: New Society Publishers, 2002), 173-7.

18) Frances Moore Lappé, and Anna Lappé, Hope's Edge: The next Diet for a Small Planet (New York: Jeremy P. Tarcher/Putnam, 2002), 132-3.

19) David S. Toolan, "In Defense of Gay Politics: Confessions of a Pastoralist," AMERICA, Sept 23, 1995, 21.

20) Karen Armstrong, The Great Transformation: The Beginning of Our Religious Traditions (New York: Knopf, 2006 (Kindle Edition)), xviii – xix

21) Juliet Schor, The Overspent American: Why We Want What We Don't Need (New York: HarperPerennial, 1999), 147-8.

22) Ben Lowe, Green Revolution: Coming Together to Care for Creation (Downers Grove, IL: IVP Books, 2009 (Kindle Edition)), location 269

23) Kornfield, A Path With Heart, 332-3.

24) Greg Boyle, Tattoos on the Heart: The Power of Boundless Compassion (New York, NY: Free Press, 2010 (Kindle Edition)), 71.

25) 1.) Ibid, 72.
2.) Laurel A. Dykstra, "Uncomfortable Words," Sojourners Magazine, June 2008, 48.

26) Francis, The Church of Mercy, location 351.

27) David Mikkelson, "The Story of Kyle," Snopes, 2014, accessed September 15, 2016, http://www.snopes.com/glurge/kyle.asp.

28) Jim Wallis, "A Test of Character," Sojourners Magazine, December 2010, 7

29) Patel, Sacred Ground, 71.

30) Jensen, Moral Ground: Ethical Action for a Planet in Peril, 62.

31) McLaren, The Secret Message of Jesus: Uncovering the Truth that Could Change Everything, location 2472.

AUGUST

1) Carter-Scott, If Life is a Game, These are the Rules, 46.

2) Fromm, To Have or To Be?, xxix.

3) Schor, The Overspent American, 100.

4) Sam Keen, Inward Bound: Exploring the Geography of Your Emotions (New York: Bantam Books, 1992), 77.

5) Lerner, The Politics of Meaning, 89.
6) David C. Korten, When Corporations Rule the World (West Hartford, CT: Kumarian Press, 1995 (Kindle Edition)), 261-2.
7) Mumford, Technics and Civilization, 426.
8) Needleman, Money and the Meaning of Life, 115.
9) Susan Howrath, Mystical Paths: A Novel (New York: Knopf, 1992), 224
10) Rohr, The Naked Now, 132.
11) Susan Howrath, Ultimate Prizes (New York: Knopf, 1989), 93.
12) Hendricks, The Corporate Mystic, 58-9.
13) 1.) McLennan, Transformational Thought, location 99.
    2.) Gernot Wagner, But Will the Planet Notice?: How Smart Economics Can save the World (New York: Hill and Wang, 2011 (Kindle Edition)), 216
14) Chuck Collins, "Taxes and the Common Good," Sojourners Magazine, April 2011, 30.
15) 1.) Father Leo Booth Quote.
    2.) J. Krishnamurti Quote.
16) Ford, Why Good People Do Bad Things, 202.
17) 1.) "DailyGuru.com," DailyGurucom RSS, Meditations from Conscious One Daily Guru, accessed January 27, 2007, http://www.dailyguru.com/.
    2.) Joseph F. Newton Quote.
    3.) Thomas Moore Quote.
18) Schor, The Overspent American, 21.
19) Lerner, The Politics of Meaning, 16-7.
20) David Howenstein, "Dependence on Nature" (My Writings – ESSAYS, 2015)
21) Michael J. Cohen, Reconnecting With Nature: Finding wellness through restoring your bond with the Earth (Corvallis, Oregon: Ecopress, 1997), 133-4.
22) Thomas Lewis, Fari Amini, and Richard Lannon, A General Theory of Love (New York: Random House, 2000), 198-199.
23) Lerner, The Politics of Meaning, 145.
24) Schor, The Overspent American, 96-7.
25) Don Shaffer, "Special CEO Report: Adjusting to a New Normal," RSF Quarterly, Spring 2012, 2.
26) Wheatley, Walk Out Walk On, 178.
27) ODE Magazine, May/June 2012, 64.
28) Stephen J. Gould Quote.
29) Borysenko, Guilt is the Teacher, Love is the Lesson, 7.
30) Williamson, A Return to Love, 61-2.
31) Patel, Sacred Ground, 148.

SEPTEMBER

1) David T. Suzuki, and Holly Jewell Dressel, Good News for a Change: How Everyday People Are Helping the Planet (Vancouver, B.C.: Greystone Books, 2002), 205-206.
2) Berry, The Dream of the Earth, 11.
3) Matthew Kelly, A Call to Joy: Living in the Presence of God (San Francisco, CA: HarperSanFrancisco, 1997), 185.
4) Anthony De Mello, The Heart of the Enlightened: A Book of Story Meditations (New York: Doubleday, 1989), 153.
5) Thomas Berry Quote.
6) Mumford, Technics and Civilization, 344.
7) Louv, The Nature Principle, 24.
8) Mello, Taking Flight: A Book of Story Meditations, 35-6.
9) Cohen, Reconnecting with Nature, 157.
10) Peter Tompkins, and Christopher Bird, The Secret Life of Plants (New York: Harper & Row, 1973), 270.
11) 1.) Ibid, 76.
    2.) Scott Atran, Anthropologist Quote.
12) Nancy Kress, Crossfire (New York: Tor, 2003), 177.
13) Wayne Teasdale, A Monk in the World: Cultivating a Spiritual Life (Novato, CA: New World Library, 2002 (Kindle Edition)), 8.
14) Cohen, Reconnecting with Nature, 82.
15) Delio, Compassion: Living in the Spirit of St. Francis, 106-7.
16) Winifred Bird, "Japan's Creeping Natural Disaster | The Japan Times," Japan Times RSS, accessed September 17, 2016, http://www.japantimes.co.jp/life/2009/08/23/general/japans-creeping-natural-disaster/#.V93XaGXwx8c.
17) Richard Louv, "The Future Will Belong to the Nature Smart," RSF Quarterly, Winter 2013, 4.
18) Richard Louv, "The Future Will Belong to the Nature Smart," RSF Quarterly, Winter 2013, 4.
19) Joseph C. Jenkins, Balance Point: Searching for a Spiritual Missing Link (Grove City, PA: Jenkins Pub., 2000), 272.
20) Thomas Berry Quote.
21) 1.) Marianne Williamson Quote.
    2.) Debbie Ford, The 21 Day Consciousness Cleanse: A Breakthrough Program for Connecting with Your Soul's Deepest Purpose (New York: HarperOne, 2009 (Kindle Edition)), 92.
22) Wayne W. Dyer, There's a Spiritual Solution to Every Problem (New York: HarperCollins, 2001), 244.

23) 1.) Margaret Young Quote.
    2.) "DailyGuru.com," DailyGurucom RSS, Meditations from Conscious One Daily Guru, accessed January 21, 2007, http://www.dailyguru.com/.
24) 1.) Denis Waitley Quote.
    2.) "DailyGuru.com," DailyGurucom RSS, Meditations from Conscious One Daily Guru accessed August 2, 2007, http://www.dailyguru.com/.
    3.) Marshall Goldsmith Quote.
25) Dalai Lama Quote.
26) Kornfield, A Path With Heart, 322.
27) Williamson, A Return to Love, 239.
28) Carter-Scott, If Life is a Game, These are the Rules, 42-3.
29) 1.) Thomas Szasz Quote.
    2.) Arthur Schopenhauer Quote.
    3.) Kurtz, The Spirituality of Imperfection, 223-4.
    4.) Baal Shem Tov Quote.
30) Ford, Why Good People Do Bad Things, 214-5.

OCTOBER

1) 1.) Williamson, A Return to Love, 58.
   2.) Vivian Greene Quote.
2) 1.) Marcel Proust Quote.
   2.) Henri Bergson Quote.
   3.) Henri Bergson Quote.
3) Ray, The Cultural Creatives, 341.
4) Sallie McFague, The Body of God: An Ecological Theology (Minneapolis: Fortress Press, 1993), 16-7.
5) Riane Tennenhaus Eisler, The Power of Partnership: Seven Relationships That Will Change Your Life (Novato, CA: New World Library, 2002), 169.
6) Berry, The Dream of the Earth, 21.
7) Tag By "A Quote by Inscription on a Church Wall in Sussex England C. 1730," Goodreads., accessed September 18, 2016, http://www.goodreads.com/quotes/784358-a-vision-without-a-task-is-but-a-dream-a.
8) 1.) Albom, Tuesdays with Morrie, 156.
   2.) John Wood, Leaving Microsoft to Change the World: An Entrepreneur's Odyssey to Educate the World's Children (New York: Collins, 2006 (Kindle Edition)), 96.
9) Abdennour Bidar (French Muslim philosopher) Quote.

10) 1.) Buckminster Fuller Quote.
    2.) Covey, The 3rd Alternative, 66.

11) Kumar, You Are Therefore I Am, location 1260-70.

12) Michael Tobias, and Georgianne Cowan, The Soul of Nature: Celebrating the Spirit of the Earth (New York: Plume, 1996), 152.

13) Jared Rosen, and David H. Rippe, The Flip: Turn Your World around (Charlottesville, VA: Hampton Roads Pub., 2006), 208.

14) Miriam Horn, Bio, published: May 8, 2008, "Algae: A Promising Source of Fuel?" Climate 411, 2013, accessed September 18, 2016, http://blogs.edf.org/climate411/2008/05/08/algae_biodiesel/.

15) Krister Wilberg, "The Ecocity: Post-oil Age," World Watch, Vol 23, No. 2. March/April 2010, 12, 14.

16) Susan Freinkel, "In Each Shell a Story," Environmental Health, Science, and Policy, accessed September 19, 2016, http://archive.onearth.org/print/20846.

17) Hayden, Sharing the Work, Sparing the Planet, 43.

18) Cohen, Reconnecting with Nature, 174.

19) Ed Ayres, "Why Are We Not Astonished?" World Watch, May/June, 1999, 27-9.

20) Ruben Alvez, "Hope" quoted in Michael Tobias, and Georgianne Cowan, The Soul of Nature: Celebrating the Spirit of the Earth (New York: Plume, 1996), 247-8.

21) 1.) James W. Fowler, Stages of Faith: The Psychology of Human Development and the Quest for Meaning (San Francisco: Harper, 1995), 31.
    2.) Plato Quote.

22) Nagler, Is There No Other Way, 27.

23) Clinebell, Ecotherapy, 73.

24) Vaclav Havel (President of Czech) Quote.

25) Daniel Quinn, Beyond Civilization: Humanity's next Great Adventure (New York: Harmony Books, 1999), 86.

26) Lerner, The Politics of Meaning, 186.

27) Mello, Awareness, 89.

28) David W. Orr, Earth in Mind: On Education, Environment, and the Human Prospect (Washington, DC: Island Press, 2004), 208-10.

29) Harari, Sapiens: A Brief History of Humankind, 307-8.

30) Naomi Klein, This Changes Everything: Capitalism vs. the Climate, 2014 (Kindle Edition), location 8417.

31) Eric Rutkow, American Canopy: Trees, Forests, and the Making of a Nation (New York: Scribner, 2012), 33.

NOVEMBER

1) 1.) Lerner, Is There No Other Way?, 85.
   2.) Edmund Burke Quote.

2) 1.) Joan Baez Quote.
   2.) Edward Abbey Quote.
   3.) Ivan Illich, (www.popfizzdesign.com), Perspectives On Education, "Ivan Illich." – On Education and Schooling, accessed September 19, 2016, http:/education.irshaad.net/Ivan_Illich_On_Education_and_Schooling.html.

3) Randy Cunningham, @canislatrans, "Green and Blue," Earth Island Institute, accessed September 19, 2016, http://www.earthisland.org/journal/index.php/eij/article/green_and_blue/.

4) 1.) Soren Kierkegaard Quote.
   2.) Parker Palmer Quote.

5) Rohr, The Naked Now, 88.

6) 1.) Quinn, Beyond Civilization, 189.
   2.) C. S. Lewis, The Great Divorce (New York: Macmillan Company, 1946 (2015 Kindle Edition)), 136.

7) 1.) Sean Covey, The 7 Habits of Highly Effective Teens Workbook (Salt Lake City, UT: Franklin Covey, 1999), 48-9.
   2.) Ibid, 63.

8) Ibid, 36.

9) Daniel Goleman, Emotional Intelligence (New York: Bantam Books, 1995), 83

10) WorldWatch Magazine, July/August 1999, 18.

11) Harriet Beecher Stowe, Uncle Tom's Cabin (Mineola, NY: Dover Publications, 2005 (Kindle Edition)), 130.

12) Fromm, To Have or To Be, 138.

13) Nagler, Is There No Other Way?, 35.

14) Rudolph Steiner Foundation Quarterly, June 2004, 6-7.

15) 1.) McLaren, The Secret Message of Jesus, location 1665.
    2.) Wood, Leaving Microsoft to Change the World, 133.

16) 1.) David Bernstein and Susan Davis, Social Entrepreneurship: What Everyone Needs to Know (New York: Oxford University Press, 2010 (Kindle Edition), 24.
    2.) Klein, This Changes Everything, 405.

17) Albert Schweitzer, Reverence for Life (New York: Irvington Publishers, 1993 (Second Irvington Printing)), 81.

18) Kottler, Change, location 4472.

19) "Resurgence & Ecologist (Ecologist, Vol 22 No 4 – Jul/Aug 1992)," Resurgence & Ecologist (Ecologist, Vol 22 No 4 – Jul/Aug 1992), accessed September 20, 2016, http://exacteditions.theecologist.org/read/resurgence/ecologist-vol-22-no-4-jul-aug-1992-5345/77/3.

20) The Free Library. S.v. "Positive Notes," Earth Island Journal (December 22, 2001), accessed Sep 20 2016 from http://www.thefreelibrary.com/Positive+Notes.-a079128404.

21) Harvey, The Hope, 58-9.

22) Terry Dobson, "Aikido Surprise," On Train Ride (Abridged), accessed September 20, 2016, http://www.wanttoknow.info/inspiration/aikido_surprise.

23) Covey, The 3rd Alternative, 400-1.

24) "Reimagining the World," Earth Island Institute, @canislatrans, accessed September 20, 2016, http://www.earthisland.org/journal/index.php/eij/article/reimagining_the_world.

25) Nhât Hanh, and Arnold Kotler, Being Peace (Berkeley, CA: Parallax Press, 1987), 88.

26) Robert Conklin, How to Get People to Do Things (Chicago: Contemporary Books, 1979), 206-12.

27) Marco Visscher / Ode, "Deepak Chopra: 'Everybody Can Be a Great Leader'," Alternet, accessed September 20, 2011. http://www.alternet.org/story/151321/deepak_chopra:_'everybody_can_be_a_great_leader'.

28) Daniel D. Chiras, Lessons from Nature: Learning to Live Sustainably on the Earth (Washington, D.C.: Island Press, 1992), 179.

29) Ibid,179.

30) Korten, When Corporations Rule the World, 149.

DECEMBER

1) 1.) Mike Wickett Quote.
   2.) Deepak Chopra, and Gotham Chopra, The Seven Spiritual Laws of Superheroes: Harnessing Our Power to Change the World (New York: HarperOne, 2011 (Kindle Edition)), 40.

2) 1.) Alan Weisman, Gaviotas: A Village to Reinvent the World (White River Junction, VT: Chelsea Green Pub., 1998), 33.
   2.) Judy Wicks, Good Morning, Beautiful Business: The Unexpected Journey of an Activist Entrepreneur and Local Economy Pioneer (White River Junction, VT: Chelsea Green Publishing, 2013 (Kindle Edition)), location 4331.

3) 1.) Helen Keller Quote.
   2.) Source Unknown.

4) Milbrath, Envisioning a Sustainable Society, 258.

5) Marjorie Hope, and James Young, Voices of Hope in the Struggle to save the Planet (New York: Apex Press, 2000), 150.

6) Korten, When Corporations Rule the World, 262.

7) Ibid, 277.

8) Adam Kahane, Power and Love: A Theory and Practice of Social Change (San Francisco, CA: Berrett-Koehler Publishers, 2010), 8.

9) Mumford, Technics and Civilization, 303-5.

10) 1.) Harari, Sapiens: A Brief History of Humankind, 414 & location 6479.
    2.) David Loy, "The Nonduality of Good and Evil," David Loy: Buddhism, accessed September 20, 2016, https://www.csudh.edu/dearhabermas/loy01.htm.

11) 1.) Jurriaan Kamp, The Intelligent Optimist's Guide to Life: How to Find Health and Success in a World That's a Better Place than You Think (San Francisco: Berrett-Koehler Publishers, 2014), 40.
    2.) Elaine Fox (author of Rainy Brain, Sunny Brain), quoted in Juriaan Kamp, The Intelligent Optimist's Guide to Life: How to Find Health and Success in a World That's a Better Place than You Think (San Francisco: Berrett-Koehler Publishers, 2014), 40.

12) Jurriaan Kamp, "When Monks Rule," The Intelligent Optimist, Jan-Feb 2013, 44-47.

13) Charlie Badenhop, "Looking for a Better Life?" Do You Feel Disabled? Accessed September 21, 2016, http://www.trans4mind.com/counterpoint/index-authors/badenhop36.shtml.

14) ODE Magazine, Spring 2011, 29.

15) Jonathan Kozol, Illiterate America (Garden City, NY: Anchor Press/Doubleday, 1985), 76.

16) 1.) Canfield, The Success Principles, 432.
    2.) Forbes, accessed September 21, 2016, http://www.forbes.com/sites kevinkruse/2012/11/28/zig-ziglar-10-quotes-that-can-change-your-life/#1ea183896456.

17) Gay Hendricks, and Kathlyn Hendricks, Lasting Love: The 5 Secrets of Growing a Vital, Conscious Relationship (Emmaus, PA: Rodale, 2004), 94.

18) Marilyn Ferguson, and John Naisbitt, The Aquarian Conspiracy: Personal and Social Transformation in the 1980s (NY, NY: J.P. Tarcher/Putnam, 1987), 131.

19) Hendricks, Lasting Love, 82.

20) 1.) George Bernard Shaw Quote.
    2.) Carl Gustav Jung Quote.

21) K. Lauren De Boer Posted Feb 21, 2006, "New Cosmology: A Great Story-Our Common Story," YES! Magazine, accessed September 21, 2016, http://www.yesmagazine.org/issues/10-most-hopeful-trends/new-cosmology-a-great-story-our-common-story.

22) 1.) Howard Thurman Quote.
    2.) Ralph Waldo Emerson Quote.

23) Mello, The Heart of the Enlightened, 35-6.

24) 1.) "DailyGuru.com." DailyGurucom RSS. Meditations from Conscious One Daily Guru, accessed November 7, 2005, http://www.dailyguru.com/.
    2.) Franz Kafka Quote.

25) Robinson, Out of Our Minds, 81.

26) Walsch, Tomorrow's God, 339.

27) Wann, Simple Prosperity, 244.

28) Chopra, The Seven Spiritual Laws of Superheroes, 112-3.

29) 1.) Mahatma Gandhi Quote.
    2.) Thomas Berry, The Great Work: Our Way into the Future (New York: Bell Tower, 1999 (Kindle Edition)), 159.

30) David Howenstein, "Real Progress!" Jambo International, December 2013, http://jambointernational.org/en/2013/12/10/4036/.

31) 1.) John Anster Quote.
    2.) Abraham Lincoln Quote.

Bibliography

Abbey, Edward.

Albom, Mitch. Tuesdays with Morrie: An Old Man, a Young Man, and Life's Greatest Lesson. New York: Doubleday, 1997.

Alexander, Thea. 2150 A.D. New York: Warner, 1976.

Alvez, Ruben. "Hope." quoted in Michael Tobias, and Georgianne Cowan. The Soul of Nature: Celebrating the Spirit of the Earth. New York: Plume, 1996.

Alywn Rhys qtd. in Brower, David R. Forward. Green Plans: Greenprint for Sustainability. By Huey D. Johnson. Lincoln: U of Nebraska, 1995. ix-x. Print.

Anster, John.

Ariely, Dan. Predictably Irrational. New York, NY: HarperCollins Publishers, 2010.

Armstrong, Karen. The Great Transformation: The Beginning of Our Religious Traditions. New York: Knopf, 2006 (Kindle Edition).

Armstrong, Karen. Twelve Steps to a Compassionate Life. New York: Alfred A. Knopf, 2011 (Kindle Edition)).

Atran, Scott (Anthropologist).

Austin, Valerie. Self-hypnosis: The Key to Success and Happiness. London: Thorsons, 1994.

Ausubel, Ken. Restoring the Earth: Visionary Solutions from the Bioneers. Tiburon, CA: H J Kramer, 1997.

Ayres, Ed. „Let Them Eat "Cakewalk."» World Watch. November 1, 2003. 4.

Ayres, Ed. "Why Are We Not Astonished?" World Watch. May/June, 1999: 25-29.

Badenhop, By Charlie. "Looking for a Better Life?" Do You Feel Disabled? Accessed September 21, 2016.
http://www.trans4mind.com/counterpoint/index-authors/badenhop36.shtml.

Baez, Joan.

Bergson, Henri.

Berry, Thomas.

Berry, Thomas. The Dream of the Earth. Berkeley, CA: Counterpoint, 1988.

Berry, Thomas. The Great Work: Our Way into the Future. New York: Bell Tower, 1999 (Kindle Edition).

Bidar, Abdennour (French Muslim philosopher).

Biko, Stephen.

Bird, Winifred. "Japan's Creeping Natural Disaster | The Japan Times." Japan Times RSS. Accessed September 17, 2016. http://www.japantimes.co.jp/life/2009/08/23/general/japans-creeping-natural-disaster/#.V93XaGXwx8c.

Boer, K. Lauren De. Posted Feb 21, 2006. "New Cosmology: A Great Story-Our Common Story." YES! Magazine. Accessed September 21, 2016. http://www.yesmagazine.org/issues/10-most-hopeful-trends/new-cosmology-a-great-story-our-common-story.

Booth, Father Leo.

Bornstein, David, and Susan Davis. Social Entrepreneurship: What Everyone Needs to Know. New York: Oxford University Press, 2010 (Kindle Edition).

Borysenko, Joan. Guilt Is the Teacher, Love Is the Lesson. New York, NY: Warner Books, 1990.

Boyle, Greg. Tattoos on the Heart: The Power of Boundless Compassion. New York, NY: Free Press, 2010 (Kindle Edition).

Braden, Gregg. The Isaiah Effect: Decoding the Lost Science of Prayer and Prophecy. New York: Harmony Books, 2000.

Branden, Nathaniel.

Bronson, Po. What Should I Do with My Life?: The True Story of People Who Answered the Ultimate Question. New York, NY: Ballantine Books, 2003.

Bunting, Madeleine. "Comment: Intolerant Liberalism." The Guardian. 2001. Accessed September 12, 2016. https://www.theguardian.com/world/2001/oct/08/afghanistan.politics1.

Burg, Bob. "Gratitude – Your Gateway to Success: A Special Report." burg.com. http://www.burg.com/wp-content/uploads/2009/12/BurgGratitude.pdf (Accessed September 4, 2015).

Burke, Edmund.

Buscaglia, Leo F., and Steven Short. Living, Loving & Learning. New York: Fawcett Columbine, 1983 (Reissue Edition).

Camara, Dam Helder.

Campbell, Joseph.

Canfield, Jack, and Janet Switzer. The Success Principles: How to Get from Where You Are to Where You Want to Be. New York: Harper Resource Book, 2005 (Kindle Edition).

Carter-Scott, Chérie. If Life Is a Game, These Are the Rules: Ten Rules for Being Human, as Introduced in Chicken Soup for the Soul. New York: Broadway Books, 1998 (Kindle Edition).

Carver, Courtney. "The Story of the Mexican Fisherman." Be More With Less. May 24, 2010. http://bemorewithless.com/the-story-of-the-mexican-fisherman/.

"Charter of Compassion." Accessed September 05, 2016. http://www.charterforcompassion.org/index.php/charter.

Chevat, Richie, and Michael Pollan. The Omnivore's Dilemma: The Secrets behind What You Eat. New York: Dial Books, 2009.

Chiras, Daniel D. Lessons from Nature: Learning to Live Sustainably on the Earth. Washington, D.C.: Island Press, 1992.

Choi, Jeannie, and Bernard Lafayette. "Freedom Fighter." Sojourners Magazine. May 2011.

Chopra, Deepak, and Gotham Chopra. The Seven Spiritual Laws of Superheroes: Harnessing Our Power to Change the World. New York: HarperOne, 2011 (Kindle Edition).

Clark, Dan. "Never Too Old To Live Your Dream." In Chicken Soup for the College Soul: Inspiring and Humorous Stories About College. Cos Cob, CT: Chicken Soup for the Soul Publishing LLC, 1999.

Clinebell, Howard John. Ecotherapy: Healing Ourselves, Healing the Earth. New York: Haworth Press, 1996.

Cohen, Michael J. Reconnecting With Nature: Finding wellness through restoring your bond with the Earth. Corvallis, Oregon: Ecopress, 1997.

Collins, Chuck. "Taxes and the Common Good." Sojourners Magazine. April 2011.

Colson, Chuck|Published: November 29, 1996, By Eric Metaxas, and By John Stonestreet. "Tough Love With A Vengeance." Tough Love With A Vengeance. Accessed September 13, 2016. http://www.breakpoint.org/bpcommentaries/entry/13/11919.

Conklin, Robert. How to Get People to Do Things. Chicago: Contemporary Books, 1979.

Corso, Donna. When the Wind Chimes Chime. Bloomington, IN: Xlibris Publishing, 2013 (Kindle Edition).

Costanza, Robert. "Sustainable Wellbeing." Resurgence & Ecologist (Digital Edition). No. 279. July/August 2013: 39-41.

A Course in Miracles. Tiburon, CA: Foundation for Inner Peace, 1985.

Covey, Sean. The 7 Habits of Highly Effective Teens Workbook. Salt Lake City, UT: Franklin Covey, 1999.

Covey, Stephen R., and Breck England. The 3rd Alternative: Solving Life's Most Difficult Problems. New York: Free Press, 2011 (Kindle Edition).

Cunningham, Randy. @canislatrans. "Green and Blue." Earth Island Institute. Accessed September 19, 2016. http://www.earthisland.org/journal/index.php/eij/article/green_and_blue/.

"DailyGuru.com." DailyGurucom RSS. Meditations from Conscious One Daily Guru. Accessed March 5, 2004. http://www.dailyguru.com/.

"DailyGuru.com." DailyGurucom RSS. Meditations from Conscious One Daily Guru. Accessed April 29, 2005. http://www.dailyguru.com/.

"DailyGuru.com." DailyGurucom RSS. Meditations from Conscious One Daily Guru. Accessed March 5, 2005. http://www.dailyguru.com/.

"DailyGuru.com." DailyGurucom RSS. Meditations from Conscious One Daily Guru. Accessed June 27, 2005. http://www.dailyguru.com/.

"DailyGuru.com." DailyGurucom RSS. Meditations from Conscious One Daily Guru. Accessed November 7, 2005. http://www.dailyguru.com/.

"DailyGuru.com." DailyGurucom RSS. Meditations from Conscious One Daily Guru. Accessed April 24, 2006. http://www.dailyguru.com/.

"DailyGuru.com." DailyGurucom RSS. Meditations from Conscious One Daily Guru. Accessed January 21, 2007. http://www.dailyguru.com/.

"DailyGuru.com." DailyGurucom RSS. Meditations from Conscious One Daily Guru. Accessed January 27, 2007. http://www.dailyguru.com/.

"DailyGuru.com." DailyGurucom RSS. Meditations from Conscious One Daily Guru. Accessed August 2, 2007. http://www.dailyguru.com/.

"DailyGuru.com." DailyGurucom RSS. Meditations from Conscious One Daily Guru. Accessed June 9, 2014. http://www.dailyguru.com/.

Dalai Lama.

Dalai Lama (Bstan-'dzin-rgya-mtsho, and Jeffrey Hopkins. How to See Yourself as You Really Are. New York: Atria Books, 2006.

Delio, Ilia. Compassion: Living in the Spirit of St. Francis. Cincinnati, OH: St. Anthony Messenger Press, 2011.

Dobson, Terry. "Aikido Surprise." On Train Ride. Accessed September 20, 2016. http://www.wanttoknow.info/inspiration/aikido_surprise.

Dunlap, Thomas R. Faith in Nature: Environmentalism as Religious Quest. Seattle: University of Washington Press, 2004.

Dyer, Wayne.

Dyer, Wayne W. There's a Spiritual Solution to Every Problem. New York: HarperCollins, 2001.

Dykstra, Laurel A. "Uncomfortable Words." Sojourners Magazine. June 2008.

Einstein, Albert.

Eisenstein, Charles. The More Beautiful World Our Hearts Know Is Possible. Berkeley, CA: North Atlantic Books, 2013 (Kindle Edition).

Eisenstein, Charles. Sacred Economics: Money, Gift, & Society in the Age of Transition. Berkeley, CA: Evolver Editions, 2011 (Kindle Edition).

Eisler, Riane Tennenhaus. The Power of Partnership: Seven Relationships That Will Change Your Life. Novato, CA: New World Library, 2002.

Elgin, Duane. Voluntary Simplicity. New York: HarperCollins, 1981.

Emerson, Ralph Waldo.

Eppsteiner, Fred. The Path of Compassion: Writing on Socially Engaged Buddhism. Berkeley, CA: Parallax Press, 1988.

„EVANGELII GAUDIUM – Page 46." EVANGELII GAUDIUM. Accessed September 13, 2016. http://www.vatican.va/evangelii-gaudium/en/files/assets/basic-html/page46.html.

Ferguson, Marilyn, and John Naisbitt. The Aquarian Conspiracy: Personal and Social Transformation in the 1980s. NY, NY: J.P. Tarcher/Putnam, 1987.

Ferrini, Paul.

Forbes. Accessed September 21, 2016. http://www.forbes.com/sites/kevinkruse/2012/11/28/zig-ziglar-10-quotes-that-can-change-your-life/#1ea183896456.

Ford, Debbie. The 21 Day Consciousness Cleanse: A Breakthrough Program for Connecting with Your Soul's Deepest Purpose. New York: HarperOne, 2009 (Kindle Edition).

Ford, Debbie. Why Good People Do Bad Things: How to Stop Being Your Own Worst Enemy. New York: HarperOne, 2008.

Fowler, James W. Stages of Faith: The Psychology of Human Development and the Quest for Meaning. San Francisco: Harper, 1995.

Fox, Elaine (author of Rainy Brain, Sunny Brain). Quoted in Juriaan Kamp. The Intelligent Optimist's Guide to Life: How to Find Health and Success in a World That's a Better Place than You Think. San Francisco: Berrett-Koehler Publishers, 2014.

Francis. Church of Mercy. Chicago, IL: Loyola Press . a Jesuit Ministry, 2014 (Kindle Edition).

The Free Library. S.v. "Positive Notes.." Earth Island Journal. December 22, 2001. Accessed Sep 20 2016 from http://www.thefreelibrary.com/Positive+Notes.-a079128404.

Freinkel, Susan. „In Each Shell a Story." Environmental Health, Science, and Policy. Accessed September 19, 2016. http://archive.onearth.org/print/20846.

Freud, Sigmund.

Friedman, Thomas L. "Who We Really Are." In Moral Ground: Ethical Action for a Planet in Peril, ed. Kathleen Moore and Michael Nelson, 189-93. San Antonio, TX: Trinity University Press, 2010 (Kindle Edition)

Fromm, Erich, and Ruth Nanda. Anshen. The Art of Loving. New York: Harper & Row, 1956.

Fromm, Erich. To Have or to Be? New York: Harper & Row, 1976.

Fromm, Erich. The Heart of Man: Its Genius for Good and Evil. New York: Harper & Row, 1964.

Fuller, Buckminster.

Gandhi, and Louis Fischer. The Essential Gandhi: His Life, Work, and Ideas: An Anthology. New York: Vintage Books, 1983.

Gandhi, Mahatma.

Gardner, Gary. "The Virtue of Restraint." World Watch 1 Mar. 2001: 14-18. Print.

Gelder, Sarah Van. Sustainable Happiness: Live Simply, Live Well, Make a Difference. Oakland, CA: Berrett-Koehler Publishers, 2015 (Kindle Edition)

Goldsmith, Marshall.

Goleman, Daniel. Emotional Intelligence. New York: Bantam Books, 1995.

Gould, Stephen J.

Greene, Vivian

Hanh, Nhât, and Arnold Kotler. Being Peace. Berkeley, CA: Parallax Press, 1987.

Harari, Yuval Noah. Sapiens: A Brief History of Humankind. New York, NY: HarperCollins Publishers, 2015 (Kindle Edition).

Harris, Elizabeth. Violence and Disruption in Society: A Study of the Early Buddhist Texts. Sri Lanka: Buddhist Publication Society, 1994.

Harris, Sydney J.

Harvey, Andrew. The Hope: A Guide to Sacred Activism. Carlsbad, CA: Hay House, 2009 (Kindle Edition).

Havel , Vaclav (President of Czech).

Hayden, Anders. Sharing the Work, Sparing the Planet. London: Zed Books, 1999.

Hayden, Tom. The Lost Gospel of the Earth: A Call for Renewing Nature, Spirit and Politics. San Francisco: Sierra Club Books, 1996.

"Help Us Remember." beliefnet.com. Accessed September 04, 2016. http://www.beliefnet.com/prayers/protestant/compassion/help-us-remember.aspx.

Hendricks, Gay, and Kate Ludeman. The Corporate Mystic: A Guidebook for Visionaries with Their Feet on the Ground. New York: Bantam Books, 1996.

Hendricks, Gay, and Kathlyn Hendricks. Lasting Love: The 5 Secrets of Growing a Vital, Conscious Relationship. Emmaus, PA: Rodale, 2004.

Heschel, Abraham Joshua. Between God and Man; an Interpretation of Judaism, from the Writings of Abraham J. Heschel. New York: Harper, 1959.

Hesse, Hermann.

Hope, Marjorie, and James Young. Voices of Hope in the Struggle to save the Planet. New York: Apex Press, 2000.

Horn, Miriam | Bio | Published: May 8, 2008. "Algae: A Promising Source of Fuel?" Climate 411. 2013. Accessed September 18, 2016. http://blogs.edf.org/climate411/2008/05/08/algae_biodiesel/.

Howenstein, David. "Bicycle Benefits." My Writings – ESSAYS. 2015.

Howenstein, David. "Dependence on Nature." My Writings – ESSAYS. 2015.

Howenstein, David. "Our Greatest Challenge." Jambo International. June, 2010. http://jambointernational.org/en/2010/06/10/899/.

Howenstein, David. "Grow the Love." Jambo International. August, 2010. http://jambointernational.org/en/2010/08/11/1057/.

Howenstein, David. "The Importance of Having Fun." Jambo International. October, 2013. http://jambointernational.org/en/2013/10/08/3919/.

Howenstein, David. "Jambo Message Activities." Jambo International. August 2010. http://jambointernational.com.

Howenstein, David. "Real Progress!" Jambo International. December 2013. http://jambointernational.org/en/2013/12/10/4036/.

Howenstein, David. "Seeing the Miracles." Jambo International. April, 2013. http://jambointernational.org/en/2013/04/10/3593/.

Howenstein, David. "Volunteering your Way to JOY." Jambo International. June 2011. http://jambointernational.org/en/2011/06/20/1911/.

Howenstein, David. "A World Without JAMBO?" Jambo International. April, 2015. http://jambointernational.org/en/category/writing/page/3/.

Howatch, Susan. Mystical Paths: A Novel. New York: Knopf, 1992.

Howatch, Susan. Scandalous Risks: A Novel. New York: Knopf, 1990.

Howatch, Susan. Ultimate Prizes. New York: Knopf, 1989.

Hunter, Joel C. "Civility is Only a Beginning." Sojourners Magazine. March 2011.

Huntington, Samuel P. The Clash of Civilizations: And the Remaking of World Order. London: Simon & Schuster, 2002.

Illich, Ivan. (www.popfizzdesign.com), Perspectives On Education. "Ivan Illich." – On Education and Schooling. Accessed September 19, 2016. http://education.irshaad.net/Ivan_Illich_On_Education_and_Schooling.html.

Jenkins, Joseph C. Balance Point: Searching for a Spiritual Missing Link. Grove City, PA: Jenkins Pub., 2000.

Jensen, Derrick. "You Choose," Moral Ground: Ethical Action for a Planet in Peril. Ed. Kathleen Dean Moore and Michael P. Nelson. San Antonio, TX: Trinity University Press, 2010.

Jung, Carl Gustav.

Kafka, Franz.

Kahane, Adam. Power and Love: A Theory and Practice of Social Change. San Francisco, CA: Berrett-Koehler Publishers, 2010.

Kamp, Jurriaan. "The Honeymoon Effect." ODE Magazine. May-June 2012: 40. Print.

Kamp, Jurriaan. The Intelligent Optimist's Guide to Life: How to Find Health and Success in a World That's a Better Place than You Think. San Francisco: Berrett-Koehler Publishers, 2014.

Kamp, Jurriaan. "When Monks Rule." The Intelligent Optimist. Jan-Feb 2013: 44-48.

Keen, Sam. Inward Bound: Exploring the Geography of Your Emotions. New York: Bantam Books, 1992.

Keen, Sam. The Passionate Life: Stages of Loving. San Francisco: Harper & Row, 1983.

Keller, Helen.

Kelly, Matthew. A Call to Joy: Living in the Presence of God. San Francisco, CA: HarperSanFrancisco, 1997.

Kelly, Matthew. Rediscover Catholicism: A Spiritual Guide to Living with Passion & Purpose. Place of Publication Not Identified: Beacon Pub., 2010.

Khan, Maulana Wahiduddin (a great Muslim thinker).

Kierkegaard, Soren.

King, Martin Luther.

Klein, Naomi. This Changes Everything: Capitalism vs. the Climate. 2014 (Kindle Edition).

Kornfield, Jack. A Path With Heart: A Guide Through the Perils and Promises of Spiritual Life. New York, NY: Bantam Books, 1993.

Korten, David C. When Corporations Rule the World. West Hartford, CT: Kumarian Press, 1995 (Kindle Edition).

Kottler, Jeffrey A. Change: What Really Leads to Lasting Personal Transformation. 2013 (Kindle Edition).

Kozol, Jonathan. Illiterate America. Garden City, NY: Anchor Press/Doubleday, 1985.

Kress, Nancy. Crossfire. New York: Tor, 2003.

Krishnamurti, J.

Krishnamurti, J. Think on These Things. New York, NY: HarperOne, 1989.

Kumar, Satish. You Are Therefore I Am. Foxhole, Dartington: Green Books Ltd, 2010 (Kindle Edition).

Kurtz, Ernest, and Katherine Ketcham. The Spirituality of Imperfection: Storytelling and the Journey to Wholeness. New York: Bantam, 1994.

Lappé, Frances Moore. EcoMind: Changing the Way We Think, to Create the World We Want. New York: Nation Books, 2011.

Lappé, Frances Moore., and Anna Lappé. Hope's Edge: The next Diet for a Small Planet. New York: Jeremy P. Tarcher/Putnam, 2002.

Lappé, Frances Moore. Rediscovering America's Values. New York: Ballantine Books, 1989.

Lerner, Michael. The Politics of Meaning: Restoring Hope and Possibility in an Age of Cynicism. Reading, MA: Addison-Wesley, 1996.

Lewis, C. S. The Great Divorce. New York: Macmillan Company, 1946 (2015 Kindle Edition).

Lewis, Thomas, Fari Amini, and Richard Lannon. A General Theory of Love. New York: Random House, 2000.

Lickona, Thomas. Educating for Character: How Our Schools Can Teach Respect and Responsibility. New York, NY: Bantam, 1991.

Lincoln, Abraham.

Louv, Richard. "The Future Will Belong to the Nature Smart." RSF Quarterly. Winter 2013.

Louv, Richard. The Nature Principle: Reconnecting with Life in a Virtual Age. Chapel Hill, NC: Algonquin Books of Chapel Hill, 2012 (Kindle Edition).

Lowe, Ben. Green Revolution: Coming Together to Care for Creation. Downers Grove, IL: IVP Books, 2009 (Kindle Edition).

Loy, David. "The Nonduality of Good and Evil." David Loy: Buddhism. Accessed September 20, 2016. https://www.csudh.edu/dearhabermas/loy01.htm.

Mackay, Harvey.

Mackenzie, Don, Ted Falcon, and Jamal Rahman. Getting to the Heart of Interfaith: The Eye-opening, Hope-filled Friendship of a Pastor, a Rabbi & a Sheikh. Woodstock, VT: SkyLight Paths Pub., 2009 (Kindle Edition).

Mackler, Carolyn. 250 Ways to Make America Better. New York: Villard, 1999.

Mandela, Nelson.

McCarthy, Mary.

McCready, By Amy. "Can I Borrow $25? – Positive Parenting Solutions." Positive Parenting Solutions. Accessed September 04, 2016. http://www.positiveparentingsolutions.com/parenting/can-i-borrow-25.

McFague, Sallie. The Body of God: An Ecological Theology. Minneapolis: Fortress Press, 1993.

McLaren, Brian D. The Secret Message of Jesus: Uncovering the Truth That Could Change Everything. Nashville: W Pub., 2006 (Kindle Edition).

McLaughlin, Corinne, and Gordon Davidson. Spiritual Politics: Changing the World from the inside out. New York: Ballantine Books, 1994.

McLennan, Jason F. Transformational Thought. Portland, OR: Ecotone Pub., 2012 (Kindle Edition).

Mello, Anthony De, and J. Francis. Stroud. Awareness: A De Mello Spirituality Conference in His Own Words. New York: Image Books/Doubleday, 1992 (Reprint Edition).

Mello, Anthony De. The Heart of the Enlightened: A Book of Story Meditations. New York: Doubleday, 1989.

Mello, Anthony De. Taking Flight: A Book of Story Meditations. New York: Doubleday, 1988.

Merton, Thomas.

Merton, Thomas. New Seeds of Contemplation. New York, NY: New Directions, 1972.

Mikkelson, David. "The Story of Kyle." Snopes. 2014. Accessed September 15, 2016. http://www.snopes.com/glurge/kyle.asp.

Milbrath, Lester W. Envisioning a Sustainable Society: Learning Our Way out. Albany: State University of New York Press, 1989.

Mipham, Sakyong. Ruling Your World: Ancient Strategies for Modern Life. New York: Morgan Road Books, 2005.

Moore, Thomas.

Moore, Thomas. The Soul of Sex: Cultivating Life as an Act of Love. New York: HarperCollins, 1998.

Mumford, Lewis. Technics and Civilization. New York: Harcourt, Brace and, 1934.

Nagler, Michael N. Is There No Other Way?: The Search for a Nonviolent Future. Berkeley, CA: Berkeley Hills Books, 2001.

"Nails In The Fence." Inspiration Peak. Accessed September 03, 2016. http://www.inspirationpeak.com/cgi-bin/stories.cgi?record=50.

Naydler, Jeremy. "Perennial Wisdom – Making time to reconnect with our spiritual roots." Resurgence & Ecologist (Digital Edition), No. 279. July/August 2013: 46-7.

Needleman, Jacob. The American Soul: Rediscovering the Wisdom of the Founders. New York: J.P. Tarcher/Putnam, 2002.

Needleman, Jacob. Money and the Meaning of Life. New York: Doubleday/Currency, 1991.

Neill, Alexander Sutherland, Albert Lamb, and Alexander Sutherland Neill. Summerhill School: A New View of Childhood. New York: St. Martin's Press, 1993.

Newton, Joseph F.

"Nonviolent Communication." NVC Extracts From Marshall Rosenberg Books. Accessed September 04, 2016. http://www.ayahuasca-wasi.com/english/articles/NVC.pdf.

ODE Magazine. Spring 2011.

ODE Magazine. May/June 2012.

Orr, David W. Earth in Mind: On Education, Environment, and the Human Prospect. Washington, DC: Island Press, 2004.

Palmer, Harry. Living Deliberately: The Discovery and Development of Avatar. Altamonte Springs, FL: Star's Edge International, 1994.

Palmer, Parker.

Palmer, Parker J. Healing the Heart of Democracy: The Courage to Create a Politics Worthy of the Human Spirit. San Francisco, CA: Jossey-Bass, 2011.

Patel, Eboo. Sacred Ground: Pluralism, Prejudice, and the Promise of America. Boston: Beacon Press, 2012 (Kindle Edition).

Peck, M. Scott. Further along the Road Less Travelled: Wisdom for the Journey towards Spiritual Growth. London: Pocket, 2010.

Plato.

Proust, Marcel.

Quinn, Daniel. Beyond Civilization: Humanity's next Great Adventure. New York: Harmony Books, 1999.

Ray, Paul H., and Sherry Ruth Anderson. The Cultural Creatives: How 50 Million People Are Changing the World. New York: Harmony Books, 2000.

"Reimagining the World." Earth Island Institute. @canislatrans. Accessed September 20, 2016. http://www.earthisland.org/journal/index.php/eij/article/reimagining_the_world.

Renard, Gary R. The Disappearance of the Universe: Straight Talk about Illusions, past Lives, Religion, Sex, Politics, and the Miracles of Forgiveness. Carlsbad, CA: Hay House, 2004.

"Resurgence & Ecologist (Ecologist, Vol 22 No 4 – Jul/Aug 1992)." Resurgence & Ecologist (Ecologist, Vol 22 No 4 – Jul/Aug 1992). Accessed September 20, 2016. http://exacteditions.theecologist.org/read/resurgence/ecologist-vol-22-no-4-jul-aug-1992-5345/77/3.

Ridley, Matt. The Origins of Virtue: Human Instincts and the Evolution of Cooperation. New York: Viking, 1997.

Robinson, Ken. Out of Our Minds: Learning to Be Creative. Oxford: Capstone, 2011 (Kindle Edition).

Rohn, Jim.

Rohr, Richard. The Naked Now: Learning to See as the Mystics See. New York: Crossroad Pub., 2009.

Rosen, Jared, and David H. Rippe. The Flip: Turn Your World around. Charlottesville, VA: Hampton Roads Pub., 2006.

Rosenberg, Larry, and David Guy. Breath by Breath: The Liberating Practice of Insight Liberation. Boston, MA: Shambhala, 1998.

Rudolph Steiner Foundation. RSF Quarterly. June 2004.

Rutkow, Eric. American Canopy: Trees, Forests, and the Making of a Nation. New York: Scribner, 2012.

Rybicki, Leszek. "Enjoy Life." Jambo International. March, 2011. http://jambointernational.org/en/2011/03/09/1643/.

Schneider, Andrew.

Schopenhauer, Arthur.

Schor, Juliet. The Overspent American: Why We Want What We Don't Need. New York: HarperPerennial, 1999.

Schumacher, E. F. Small Is Beautiful; Economics as If People Mattered. New York: Harper & Row, 1973.

Schweitzer, Albert. Reverence for Life. New York: Irvington Publishers, 1993 (Second Irvington Printing).

Shaffer, Don. "Special CEO Report: Adjusting to a New Normal." RSF Quarterly. Spring 2012: 2-4.

Shantideva (Buddhist mystic).

Shaw, George Bernard.

Shenk, Joshua Wolf. Lincoln's Melancholy. Boston: Houghton Mifflin, 2005 (Kindle Edition).

Simons, Nina. "Learning Love Through Limbic Liaisons." Nina Simon's Blog, September 26, 2013. http://www.ninasimons.com/#!Learning-Love-Through-Limbic-Liaisons/cd23/D6E07CC1-85AA-4532-945B-68E8E9BE90A0.

"The Seven Wonders of the World." Reconnections. Accessed August 19, 2016. http://www.reconnections.net/seven_wonders.htm

Smith, Alexander

Speth, James Gustave. Red Sky at Morning: America and the Crisis of the Global Environment. New Haven: Yale University Press, 2004.

Solnit, Rebecca. A Paradise Built in Hell: The Extraordinary Communities That Arise in Disasters. New York: Viking, 2009 (Kindle Edition).

Spretnak, Charlene. States of Grace: The Recovery of Meaning in the Postmodern Age. San Francisco: HarperSanFrancisco, 1991.

Stearns, Richard. The Hole in Our Gospel. Nashville, TN: Thomas Nelson, 2009.

Stone, Douglas, Bruce Patton, and Sheila Heen. Difficult Conversations: How to Discuss What Matters Most. New York, NY: Viking, 1999 (Ebook 2010).

Storey Alan. "For the Healing of the Nation." Sojourners (May 2011): 30.

Stowe, Harriet Beecher. Uncle Tom's Cabin. Mineola, NY: Dover Publications, 2005 (Kindle Edition).

Suzuki, David T., and Holly Jewell Dressel. Good News for a Change: How Everyday People Are Helping the Planet. Vancouver, B.C.: Greystone Books, 2002.

Szasz, Thomas.

Tag, By. "A Quote by Inscription on a Church Wall in Sussex England C. 1730." Goodreads. Accessed September 18, 2016. http://www.goodreads.com/quotes/784358-a-vision-without-a-task-is-but-a-dream-a.

Tasch, Woody. Slow Money. White River Junction, VT: Chelsea Green Publishing Company, 2010 (Kindle Edition).

Teasdale, Wayne. A Monk in the World: Cultivating a Spiritual Life. Novato, CA: New World Library, 2002 (Kindle Edition).

Thoreau, Henry David.

Thurman, Howard.

Thurman, Robert (Professor/Author) in Mackler, Carolyn. 250 Ways to Make America Better. Ed Carolyn Mackler. New York: Villard, 1999.

Tobias, Michael, and Georgianne Cowan. The Soul of Nature: Celebrating the Spirit of the Earth. New York: Plume, 1996.

Tolle, Eckhart. A New Earth: Awakening to Your Life's Purpose. New York: Plume, 2006.

Tolstoy, Leo.

Tompkins, Peter, and Christopher Bird. The Secret Life of Plants. New York: Harper & Row, 1973.

Toms, Michael. A Time for Choices: Deep Dialogues for Deep Democracy. Gabriola Island, BC, Canada: New Society Publishers, 2002.

Toolan, David S. "In Defense of Gay Politics: Confessions of a Pastoralist." AMERICA. Sept 23, 1995.

Toy, Baal Shem.

"Two Wolves." Virtues for Life. Accessed September 12, 2016. http://www.virtuesforlife.com/two-wolves/.

Turkovich, Marilyn. "The Charter for Compassion." Charter for Compassion. Accessed September 09, 2016. http://www.charterforcompassion.org/index.php/charter.

Tytler, Alexander Fraser. The Decline and Fall of the Athenian Republic, quoted in John and Janice Corson, "The Rise And Fall Of Great Civilizations: From Apathy to Dependence to Slavery." Sociological Issues. September 1, 2009. Accessed August 08, 2016. http://www.corson.org/archives/sociological/S27_090109.htm.

Valles, Carlos G. Unencumbered by Baggage: Father Anthony De Mello, a Prophet of Our times. Gujarat, India: Gujarat Sahitya Prakash, 2003.

Visscher, Marco / Ode. "Deepak Chopra: 'Everybody Can Be a Great Leader'" Alternet. Accessed September 20, 2016. http://www.alternet.org/story/151321/deepak_chopra:_'everybody_can_be_a_great_leader'.

Wagner, Gernot. But Will the Planet Notice?: How Smart Economics Can save the World. New York: Hill and Wang, 2011 (Kindle Edition).

Waitley, Denis.

Wallis, Jim. "A Global Call for a New Social Covenant." Sojourners Vol. 42, No. 5 (May, 2013): 7.

Wallis, Jim. "A Test of Character." Sojourners. December 2010.

Walsh, Neale Donald. Conversations with God Bulletin. Print. December 1998.

Walsch, Neale Donald. "Happy New Year." Conversations with God Bulletin. Print. December 31, 2005.

Walsch, Neale Donald. "The Killing of Osama Bin Laden." Conversations with God Bulletin, Print. May 6, 2011.

Walsch, Neale Donald. Tomorrow's God: Our Greatest Spiritual Challenge. New York: Atria Books, 2004.

Wann, David. Simple Prosperity: Finding Real Wealth in a Sustainable Lifestyle. New York: St. Martin's Griffin, 2007.

Washburn, Nicole. "A Challenge to the letters on Population." From Readers, Letter to the Editor. WorldWatch, JANUARY/FEBRUARY 2004.

Weisman, Alan. Gaviotas: A Village to Reinvent the World. White River Junction, VT: Chelsea Green Pub., 1998.

Weiss, Brian L. Messages from the Masters: Tapping into the Power of Love. New York: Warner Books, 2000.

Well, H.G.

Wheatley, Margaret J., and Deborah Frieze. Walk Out, Walk On: A Learning Journey into Communities Daring to Live the Future Now. San Francisco: Berrett-Koehler, 2011.

"When We Dead Awaken: Writing as Re-Vision", by Adrienne Rich." Cest La Vie. 2011. Accessed September 06, 2016. https://emeire.wordpress.com/2011/01/28/when-we-dead-awaken-writing-as-re-vision-by-adrienne-rich/.

Wicks, Judy. Good Morning, Beautiful Business: The Unexpected Journey of an Activist Entrepreneur and Local Economy Pioneer. White River Junction, VT: Chelsea Green Publishing, 2013 (Kindle Edition).

Wickett, Mike

Wilber, Ken. No Boundary: Eastern and Western Approaches to Personal Growth. Boulder, CO: Shambhala, 1981.

Wilberg, Krister. "The Ecocity: Post-oil Age." World Watch. Vol 23, No. 2. March/April 2010: 11-17.

Williamson, Marianne.

Williamson, Marianne. "Our Greatest Fear." Our Greatest Fear Marianne Williamson. Accessed September 12, 2016. http://explorersfoundation.org/glyphery/122.html.

Williamson, Marianne. A Return to Love: Reflections on the Principles of a Course in Miracles. New York, NY: HarperCollins, 1992.

Williamson, Marianne. Everyday Grace: Having Hope, Finding Forgiveness, and Making Miracles. New York: Riverhead Books, 2002.

Wilson, Colin. Mysteries. New York: Putnam, 1978.

Wood, John. Leaving Microsoft to Change the World: An Entrepreneur's Odyssey to Educate the World's Children. New York: Collins, 2006 (Kindle Edition).

WorldWatch Magazine. July/August 1999.

Yeats, William Butler.

Young, Margaret.

About Jambo

Jambo International Japan

JAMBO International Center is a grassroots organization that began in Tokyo, Japan in January, 1996. The name "JAMBO" was chosen since it is the Swahili greeting (with the organization originally focusing on support of groups in Eastern and Southern Africa) and sounds similar to "Jumbo," meaning big (hearted).

"Having Fun Doing Good" is the motto that guides every activity at JAMBO.

JAMBO's Goals are

1) To provide enjoyable activities, especially those that give people more exposure to and appreciation for the natural environment

2) To raise funds for reliable organizations that are working for natural preservation/restoration and human development

3) To raise funds or to volunteer for environmental (and/or human) betterment

4) To serve as a liaison between the do-good organizations JAMBO supports and local residents, providing opportunities for them to meet and get more involved with each other

To meet these goals, JAMBO holds a variety of programs regularly which can be seen on the JAMBO website (see link below). In 2012, the JAMBO Network was founded, integrating JAMBO International with Jambo School (providing English education and outdoor opportunities for students) and Jambo Volunteers (providing volunteer opportunities, mainly with environmental restoration work). And in 2015, JAMBO INTERNATIONAL INC was officially established as a charitable organization in the United States.

Jambo International Inc (USA)

JAMBO INTERNATIONAL INC is a tax-deductible 501(c)3 charitable organization in the United States with the stated purpose to raise funds for environmental protection groups and human development organizations. Ideally, funds go to groups that are doing these activities simultaneously.

JAMBO's mission is "to assist in the development of groups which get people actively involved in nature/social activities to support worthy environmental/human development organisations," using JAMBO Japan as a model.

The JAMBO idea challenges the practice of individually addressing social, environmental (nature), and spiritual issues in its attempt to harmonize these issues. It is hoped that his book will provide a boost to the spiritual dimension of this dynamic trio.

LINKS:

Jambo Facebook - https://www.facebook.com/JAMBO.int

Jambo International Japan - https://jambointernational.org/en/

Jambo International Inc (US) - https://www.jambo.ngo

For more information on other parts of the JAMBO Network or general questions about JAMBO, contact David Howenstein at david@jambointernational.org.

Book Proceeds

50% of all profits made from the sales of this book will be donated to JAMBO International, with the purpose of weaving these ideas into its programs and moving towards a more integrated implementation of these soulscapes into a strong community of like-minded, dedicated, fun-loving folk.

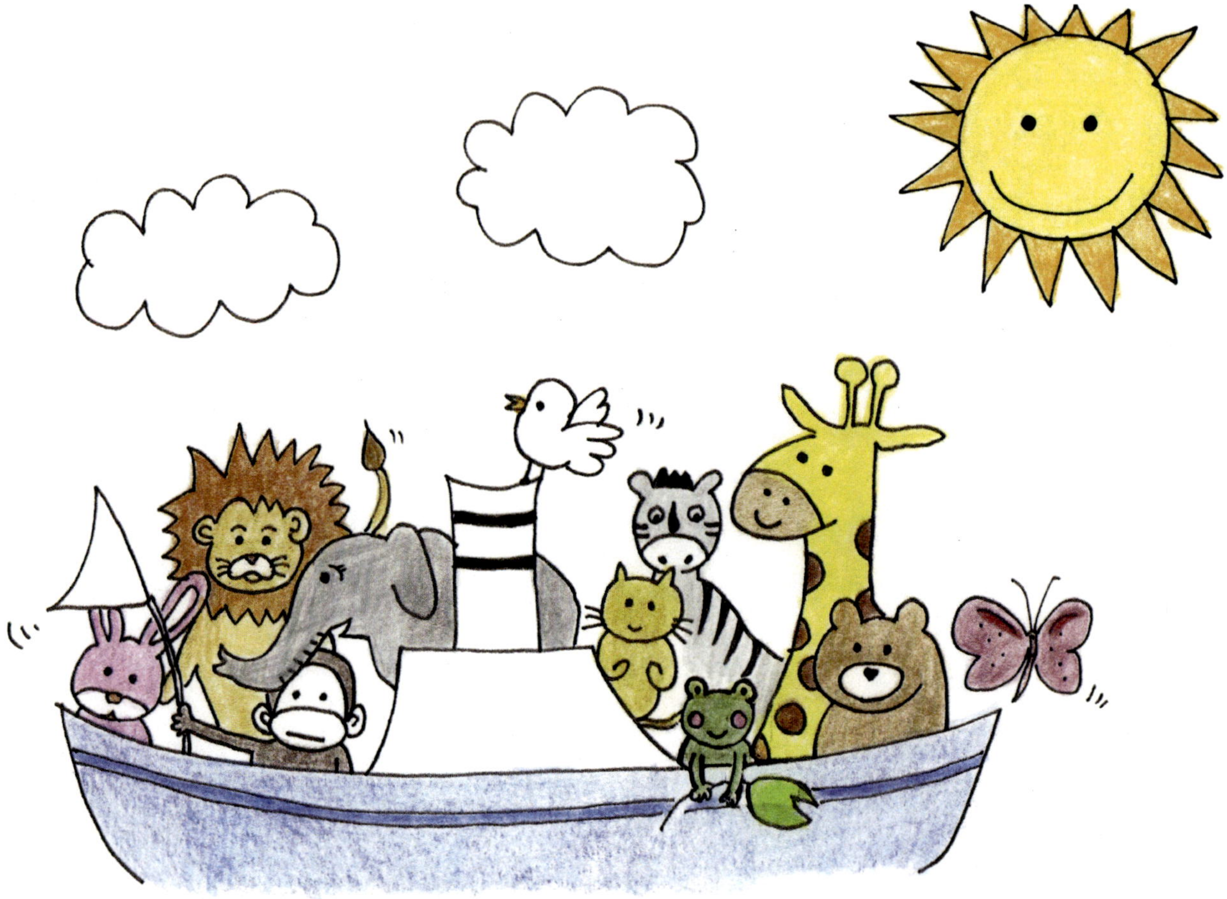

About The Author

David Howenstein was born in St. Louis, MO (USA) in 1960 and grew up there until the age of 18. After some "quality floundering time," he went on to major in Peace Studies, English, and Philosophy at Wilmington College, a small Quaker school in southwestern Ohio. His interests in spirituality and service work come largely from his Roman Catholic upbringing and the Quaker influence during his college years.

He then went to Nagasaki, Japan to work as an English teacher at the YMCA for a few years before traveling around the world to find out what he wanted to do when he "grew up," only to discover that it's a never-ending process. After a two-year stint at Ohio University, completing his MBA and MAIA (International Affairs) programs, he returned to Japan (Tokyo) for five years as a teacher.

His passion for nature and seeking ways to empower the disadvantaged moved him to take a two-year "sabbatical" traveling between Japan, the US and Eastern/Southern Africa, visiting over 100 organizations working with development and environmental issues. In the process, he came to realize his longing to return to Japan and set up an organization that brings people into contact with nature while supporting organizations, especially in Africa (where the need seemed greatest), which are working to improve the poor's living conditions at the same time as preserving/restoring the natural environment.

This desire led him to found Jambo International in Tokyo in January, 1996. As of this writing, he continues his teaching while serving as the Director of JAMBO. Please see "*About Jambo*" for an explanation of the entire network.

David hopes that this book will be the beginning of developing close connections with others who also envision the embodiment of the reflections herein and the "Having Fun Doing Good" concept that lies at the heart of JAMBO.

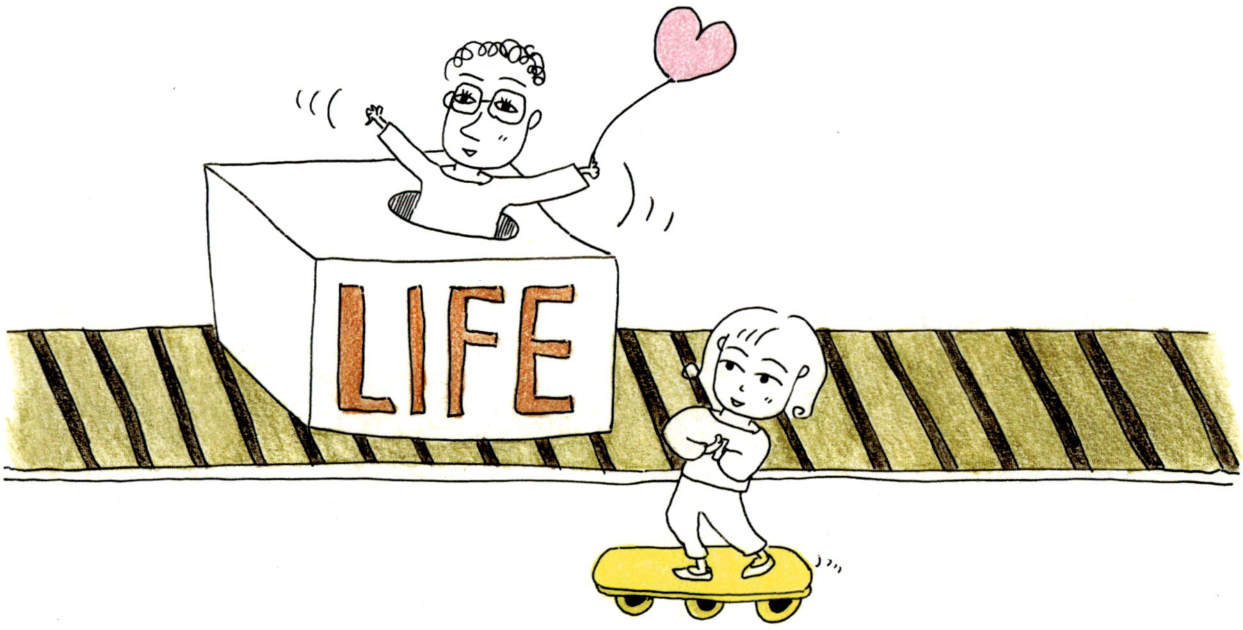
LIFE